THE THING ABOUT
Prague...

THE THING ABOUT
Prague...

How I gave it all up
for a new life in Europe's
most eccentric city

RACHAEL WEISS

ALLEN&UNWIN
SYDNEY · MELBOURNE · AUCKLAND · LONDON

Allen & Unwin
83 Alexander Street
Crows Nest NSW 2065
Australia
Phone: (61 2) 8425 0100
Email: info@allenandunwin.com
Web: www.allenandunwin.com

Cataloguing-in-Publication details are available
from the National Library of Australia
www.trove.nla.gov.au

ISBN 978 1 76011 102 1

Set in 13/17pt Garamond Pro by Post Pre-press Group, Australia
Printed and bound in Australia by Griffin Press

9 8 7 6 5 4 3 2 1

The paper in this book is FSC® certified.
FSC® promotes environmentally responsible,
socially beneficial and economically viable
management of the world's forests.

For my mother, Angela Karpin
and my grandmother, Suzanne McLeod

Prague never lets you go . . .
this dear little mother has sharp claws.
                              —Franz Kafka

1

In 2005, I took a year out of my life to live in romantic Prague and write a novel of literary genius. I returned to Sydney after my year was up with a manila folder full of scribbled notes and half-formed ideas, no nearer to joining Kafka in the literary canon, but at least having produced a light travelogue about my year abroad. I resumed my ordinary life, fully expecting to simply pick up where I had left off. Life did return to its normal rhythm but something was not sitting right—I was restless. I was forty-one, still unmarried and childless. I made my living as a mid-level administrator—I had a nice boss and engaging work managing a team of personal assistants. It's not a bad life, being an administrator, but it's not the most exciting life either.

It was a visit to my doctor that decided me. I was there for my annual check-up.

'Are you exercising?' she asked, her eyes on the blood pressure valve.

'Yes,' I replied.

'What do you do?'

'Yoga twice a week and I walk to work.' I felt like I used to at school when I'd done my homework—proud, and relieved that I could give the right answer.

'That's good,' she said, still gazing at the valve and twitching her hand on the pump. 'A regular exercise routine is important in middle age. Sets you up for a good old age.'

There was a stunned silence. At least, I was stunned. The doctor seemed to think nothing had happened. Did she just call me 'middle-aged'? Did she just say *old age*?! So I'm middle-aged, with old age just around the corner?

In the office bathroom the next day, somewhat hungover, I noticed in the mirror that my eyelashes were holding up my eyelids. I put a thumb under my eyebrows and lifted. The lids lifted too. I slowly let the pressure off. The lids dropped back, exhausted, onto my lashes.

Up to then I had thought my year's stay in Prague had been the same as my years anywhere else, just surrounded by castles. But as I poked fruitlessly at my eyebrows, thinking, *aging is just one daily indignity after another, isn't it?* it occurred to me that if I had to cope with varicose veins, with crease lines from my pillow staying on my cheek until mid-morning, with mysteriously swelling feet (I don't even want to think what that's all about), with, in fact, middle age, I'd rather do it somewhere with romantic cobbled streets, midnight-blue evenings, snowflakes and cheap beer. Not in a dreary office block in Sydney. I felt that if I stayed here I might just as well choose a plot at Rookwood Cemetery and get it over with.

I'd like to say that my decision to move to Prague permanently was based on something grand and noble—a desire to trace my roots, a sense of adventure, my literary heart yearning to burst into flower in the sweet soil of Old Europe—but I can't. The truth is that I had nothing better to do. If anyone asked me why I was going (and everyone did), I said airily, 'Oh, you know, to cast my bread upon the waters and see what happens—do something different.' Giving them the impression that I was brave and adventurous beyond words when in fact I was simply rudderless beyond words and frightened of getting old.

The decision, once made, brought with it a raft of other decisions. What should I take? What would I do when I got there? Should I tell my mother, or wait until I landed and then give her a phone call? All of them too difficult to contemplate.

I looked around at my belongings. My sister, who had once spent a year in London, had had a garage sale—'I made a thousand dollars, just like that!' A thousand dollars would come in handy. Mind you, my sister had had a house full of interesting artefacts from Africa, top quality china, vases, silver spoons and children's toys. I had a few bookshelves made of particle board held together with the red paint I'd used on them fifteen years ago when I picked them up off the street, plus some aluminium pots and pans, an unused Mixmaster I'd won in a trivia quiz, a couple of pot plants and a cat.

I'd picked up Thelma along with the bookshelves and what to do with her was quite a problem. I loved that little cat. She and I had been together for most of my adult life and all of hers. She'd been a tiny scrap no bigger than the palm of my hand when I found her and had started purring the instant I stroked her little ears.

Thelma had been abandoned, poor little mite, so I took her in and loved her. I read somewhere that feral animals become domestic after five generations of being bred as domestic. My little Thelma took one. She was a cat who loved to snuggle up by the fireside, snooze through Saturday morning on my bed, and eat. A lap only had to form in the house and Thelma was on it.

She had a special affection for men, the little minx. The only people she wouldn't sit on were people who adored cats and wanted nothing more than for Thelma to sit on them their entire stay.

What to do with Thelma was my first problem. I really didn't feel I could take her with me, as much as I wanted to. She was fifteen years old and I worried that the trip would kill her. Also, I didn't know where I was going to live when I got there and I didn't want her having to change locations too many times. We'd moved a lot when she was little but in her old age we'd stayed put, mainly because I noticed she was finding it harder and harder to orient herself when we moved. She'd stay at home for weeks before she ventured out and, even when she did, she didn't go very far.

I had vowed I wouldn't move her again. I could see her getting happier and happier as the months passed and she made the territory her own. What would she do in an entirely new country? And what about the snow? Thelma thought the heater should go on as soon as she saw a cloud in the sky.

If she was like that in Sydney, how would she cope in a Czech winter? No, Thelma would have to stay.

She had boarded at her Aunt Cynthia's place when I went to Prague the first time. Thelma's Aunt Cynthia had two other cats, both of whom lived like kings. They had their own baskets with a special electric warming pad each, and Cynthia, who worked from home, spent her days moving their baskets around the verandah, the cats sitting superbly within, following the sun.

I told myself that sending Thelma to live there was like putting her in a luxury retirement home. I took her over, put her in her special basket, stayed and chatted for a bit, then stood up to leave.

Never will I forget that moment. I opened the front door and walked out. Thelma came pounding up the hall and Cynthia quickly shut the screen door. Thelma scrabbled at the mesh frantically, panic stricken. As she saw me move away, saying goodbye, not coming back to rescue her, she stayed at the door, her front paws pressed against the mesh, her eyes huge and glued to me—betrayed.

For the first time it occurred to me that the decision 'I will move countries' had unforeseen consequences. To this day I'm haunted by that look on Thelma's face. She'd never panicked like that when I left her with her Aunt Cynthia for holidays. I don't know how she knew that we wouldn't be living together again, but she did. My heart still stops with missing her.

As for my possessions, I decided to set them free. I contemplated selling them on eBay but my brother-in-law pointed out that they were worthless. I thought you could sell anything on eBay, but apparently that's just propaganda.

The neighbourhood Thelma and I had washed up in was a down-at-heel, inner-city suburb, full of drug addicts and council houses and single mothers with screaming kids. It was also full of first-time immigrants, scraping together money from laundry and corner-store businesses to send their kids to university so that the kids would not have to live in this suburb as adults.

My block of flats was a mini-Vietnam. Most of the displaced elderly inhabitants, relying solely on their neighbours and daughters for community, had fussed over Thelma, so I had a special affection for them. In my last day in the flat, I knocked on my neighbour's door and told her, in sign language, that I was leaving, that she could come and raid my place for anything she wanted and could she please tell the other Vietnamese. A flood of Vietnamese mixed-goods merchants' mothers descended and swept the place clean.

My fridge, which had originally been given to me by a friend who got a pay rise and decided to upgrade her white-goods, went to a young couple who were living with the single mum upstairs and who were unable to afford even knives and forks. He had no teeth and she was covered in tatts. As he took the fridge off my hands (and the hideous white-plastic-handled cutlery I'd been loathing for the last decade) he said, 'We're really grateful. We've just found a place to live. I'm really going to try this time. I know hitting her's wrong.'

I almost took the fridge back, but then she came in and asked if she could take a bookshelf—'we don't have one'—and she seemed so nice. Why make judgement calls about her choice of man? That was her business.

My own parents had done as the Vietnamese were doing—made sacrifices so I could get a proper education and rise from the bottom of the heap. I and the woman across the hall, who was the same age as me and single as well, were nevertheless still living on the bottom of the heap. In a city as expensive and fast-paced as Sydney, if you were single and only earning a moderate wage, your accommodation options were quite limited.

The Vietnamese were first-time immigrants, but their children would live in a better suburb. The rest, however—the single mums and the terminally unemployed—were stuck there from birth to death, and their kids would be too. For them, living on an even grimmer wage than my own, life was horrifyingly precarious. How much lower could any of us go? A caravan? The street?

The only things I couldn't part with were my books. Like everything else I owned I'd been carting those books around for twenty years. But, unlike everything else (except Thelma), they had real value for me—they were like old friends. I contemplated setting them free but after the trauma of parting with Thelma I was more careful to ask myself how much I actually cared.

The question of moving my books caused a terrible family commotion. I investigated moving companies. The first one offered to move them for six thousand dollars. After I'd come to, I called others, thinking I must have struck pirates. But no, apparently it was going to cost me at least five thousand dollars to move my books from Sydney to Prague and the company who gave me that quote was so dodgy that I finally settled on one that would do it for five thousand five hundred, but who wasn't proposing to ship them via Kazakhstan to keep costs down.

I only needed a minute to ask myself if it was worth it. Of course it was. I'd lost Thelma, I couldn't lose my books as well. They were all I had. But then, in an unthinking moment, I revealed these plans to my father.

'Why are you taking your books?'

'Because I love them.'

'But they will take up so much space.'

'I don't love space, I love my books.'

'How are you going to get them there?'

'A moving company.'

'A moving company?! How much is that going to cost you?'

'. . . Um . . .' *Curses! Why didn't I see that coming? Quick, lie!*

'How much?'

'. . . Um . . .' *Dammit, lie better than that!*

'A lot? It's a lot, isn't it? How much?'

'Well it's. . . well it's. . . okay, it's about five thousand dollars. But I can't live without them.'

'Five thousand dollars!!'

Sigh. This was not going to go away quickly. Dad enumerated for me the many, many ways in which five thousand dollars could be better spent. I tried not to disagree too much, finally putting an end to this agonising conversation by saying, 'Yes, well, I'll think about it.' The coward's response.

Naturally, it became the subject of scandalised horror for my family. When I called my father a few days later, my stepmother answered the phone.

'Hello, darlink,' she said, very lovingly, because we do get on well, my stepmother and I. 'How are you?'

'I'm fi—'

'*WHY ARE YOU TAKING YOUR BOOKS TO PRAGUE?*'

'Well, you know how it is, I just . . .' But she wasn't listening. Her feelings were running too high.

'I took all my books from Russia, and what do they do? They just sit there on the shelves! Gathering dust! I had read them all. All! I never picked them up again. You have read your books! Why must you take them with you?'

And so on. No point arguing. I just went ahead and shipped them, and the hot topic in the family gossip circle became my stubbornness in the face of reason.

I visited Thelma again every week before I left. Cynthia and I wanted her to know that she had two mums now, not that she'd lost one. We were as deluded as any parent who's abandoned their children in divorce. ('Mummy and Daddy love you just as much, and here's a new bike to prove it.') Thelma knew she didn't have two mothers.

She punished me mightily at first. On my next visit, she sat with her back pointed towards me and pretended to be absorbed in something outside in the garden. I stroked her ear and she bit me. Who can blame her? She had right on her side. On my second visit, she thawed a little, enough to let me tickle her chin for a few minutes—before biting me. After that, things got easier. She never really forgave me but she did eventually pad up to me and demand some lap time.

I think Thelma had done her calculations. She'd looked around—at the electric heating pad, at the aunt who was home all day and who fed her roast chicken for lunch if she was looking like she needed cheering up, at the two cat companions, both of whom she'd managed to boss into submission—and she'd asked herself if she was doing badly on this deal. I think she realised that in fact her life had improved although, like me, she was living without the special bond we had. But she was bonding with Cynthia. When it was time for me to leave for good, Thelma, to my relief, was talking to me again and had settled in to her new home.

2

I arrived in Prague in March. I love a new beginning. I could
see my life in Prague spreading before me, glowing and new.
*I'll get up at dawn, meditate, do my yoga, then have a healthy
breakfast, followed by a day of writing my new novel. And when
I need a break from writing, I'll go to the gym, or study my Czech
or write amusing columns to sell to the* New Yorker. I calculated
that at the end of a year I would be thin, calm, flexible, and
have a world-famous, really cool blog and a three-book deal.
Yes, beginnings are fun for me, mainly because I really believe
my life is going to be just as I am imagining it, forgetting the
little matter of the self-discipline I so manifestly lack and the
forty or so years of modest failures to prove it.

Actually, for the first two months I really did have a great
time. Having already lived there a year, I knew enough of
Prague and the language to feel at home. When I emerged

from the baggage claim area into the Arrivals hall, wheeling the suitcase that contained my world, I strode past the bored taxi drivers holding cardboard signs—I didn't need anyone to pick me up!—straight to the Information Desk. Not to ask how one gets to the centre, in apologetic English, as the polite but panicked American man in front of me was, but to buy a monthly pass, in the Czech language I'd been practising on the plane.

'*Dobrý den. Ráda bych měsíční jízdenku, prosím.*' Hello. I would like a monthly travel pass, please.

The woman behind the glass looked astonished, as well she might, and then she lit up. At last! Someone had bothered to learn Czech!

'*Žžřtňčéčdřtňžéčrdžž!ĎáččňóušřřřřžáážýŽďťéušžř!TŽďáňč óřúřřďť!*'

Ah.

She saw the blank look on my face and smiled indulgently. 'Your Czech is very good,' she said, in perfect English.

'I must practise more,' I replied, also in English but still feeling buoyant, and took the pass from her. What a nice woman, and how much she must have been impressed by me, a tourist who knew her way around the airport and transport system and even a bit of non-pidgin Czech. I wheeled the bag to the 119 bus queue, thrilled I could remember exactly where it was. Thrilled, in fact, with everything about the first few minutes of my new life.

I made my way by bus and metro to my father's flat, a communist-built concrete block (*panelák* in Czech) in a light industrial district where I was going to stay until I found a place of my own. His flat was kept there for him and any of our Czech family to stay in when they came to Prague. It was clean and light, floors and surfaces as uncluttered as a hotel room, cosy enough but lacking the personality of a lived-in flat. That suited me exactly. I wanted a space that was unmarked, somewhere to simply be while I gradually invented my new existence. I parked my bag on the bare wood floor, removed my toothbrush and pyjamas, and hung up my few clothes in the wardrobe, which was empty apart from my father's winter coat.

My inner clock had stopped owing to jetlag but I could see that the late winter dark was closing in. I remembered the pub around the corner; a quiet, cosy place full of locals, which served cheap and hearty Czech meals—dumplings, pork and the truly amazing, unbeatably world-class Czech beer. When I got there the tables were mostly empty, it being only about 5.30. My favourite spot—up the back where I could watch the crowd and not feel too exposed myself—was free and I sank into it.

A waiter, whose face I remembered and who seemed to remember me by the smile he gave me as he plonked down the cutlery jar, took my order, which I delivered to my immense personal satisfaction in Czech. Although, to be honest, 'Beer and schnitzel, please' is hardly Shakespeare. Nevertheless, it was Czech, and it was understood. I felt talented and strong. I felt home.

That first night in the pub, in the jetlag dreamworld that is like being in a space pod, I splashed down the beer like a local and ordered a second, while I read my Czech grammar book. Looking back on that night, I'd recommend selling every-thing you own, leaving all your friends and your family and moving to the other side of the world if only to experience the feeling I had of actual, real, unalloyed, joyful, baggage-free freedom.

I began my new life full of starry-eyed resolutions. The next morning I woke up at 5.30, radiant and energetic, the pre-dawn light just brushing the room in a way that made me feel at one with the burgeoning, pearl-grey day. I got up and put a cushion on the floor to sit on, then one for my back, two for my knees, a final one for my right ankle, which always gives me trouble when I sit cross-legged, and meditated. At least I did what I think is meditating, as commanded by my *How to Meditate* book.

For me, meditating is trying not to think of anything but sitting . . . and then daydreaming relentlessly. Every few minutes I'd realise I wasn't meditating—I'd pull myself back (like pulling a cow back onto the path, says my book), count backwards from 100 and try to concentrate on every number. 100 . . . 99 . . . So far, so good. *Gosh I'm hungry—can I remember where to buy eggs? I think I'll need eggs for breakfast. Fried? Mmm.* I love fried eggs, and I'm quite good at them, getting a soft yolk and slightly crispy white. *Do they sell bread in the corner store or only* rohlíky? *Hmm. I think I'll have ro*—D'oh! Start again. For some reason, the book commands you to start again if (if!) you lose count.

100 . . . 99 . . . *Good, good . . . 98 . . . You can do it . . . 9*—*Ha ha, how cute is the cartoon at the end of the Czech news? Off to bed now kids, look—the little kid on TV is going to bed, time for you to bugger off too so Mummy and Daddy can get stuck into the slivovice. Can't think why every country doesn't do it . . . D'oh!* 100 . . . 99 . . . And so on.

Astoundingly, I meditated every morning for the first week. But then it started to eat into my day, because I was getting up at 9 am. So by the time I'd put out the cushions, got comfortable, done the initial relaxation exercises— a deathly dull routine of breathing in one nostril and out the other, which only served to significantly increase my tension levels—it was 10.30 and half the morning was gone.

I made feeble resolutions to get up at 5 o'clock again, but they came to nought. I wasn't very good at meditating to start with and I didn't seem to be getting any better. I never really relaxed and my knees hurt. I tried lying down but then I just fell asleep.

The trouble with beginnings is they quickly turn into middles, where it's all about avoiding the daily grind and lying around cursing myself for my laziness and watching my fantasies evaporate. Although I tried to maintain a sense of wonder and joy in my bright new life, within a couple of weeks mundanities began to press in on my dreamworld ever so slightly and as more weeks passed they pressed more urgently. I needed a job and I needed a flat, I needed some kind of internet connection and I needed a phone service. I barely spoke any Czech—just enough to say, 'I'll have a beer and schnitzel, please'—and that one phrase, as helpful as it was, wasn't going to solve any of these problems for me.

Job hunting in those first three months proved increasingly depressing. I wasn't sure what I wanted to do, but I knew I didn't want to teach English like every other expat, although my father was pushing me to. 'Look, darling, get yourself a certificate and you can teach at the university,' he'd said.

He was obsessed with the idea of my being a teacher at 'the university', meaning Charles University in Prague, one of the oldest in Europe.

'It's not that easy, Dad.'

'Of course it is! They need English speakers!'

'No they don't.'

'How do you know? Have you been there?'

Well, no, I hadn't been there, but Dad had this strange idea that I'd just be able to walk into Charles University speaking English and everyone would reel back in amazement and offer me a job as a professor of English. The Czechs are some of the best educated people in the world. Everyone goes to university. Charles University didn't need me.

'Well, no I haven't been there but . . .'

'Why must you be so stubborn!?' It was the usual ending to our conversations.

I suppose I could have got a teaching certificate and joined the hordes of Brits and Americans working for horrible cowboy outfits for a pittance, but two things stopped me.

First, I don't have what it takes to work for a horrible cowboy outfit. There are plenty of them in Prague. 'Schools' set up by glassy-eyed bandits, mainly from Russia and America—men who'd arrived in Prague like rats off a cargo ship that'd washed up on a tropical paradise filled with vulnerable foreigners who had no other way of earning a living, and natives desperate to learn the language of the internet. Living was cheap, wages were low and labour was plentiful.

I heard tale after tale of teachers working for minimal rates a few hours a week, having to travel three hours for every one they worked and not getting paid for their travel time, being

16

done out of their pay, being promised visas that never materialised. I kept hearing of jobs lost with no notice and ghastly bosses. I'm no good at screaming at people just to get paid. I did have to do it once, when I worked for a cowboy outfit in Sydney that had taught computer skills to the unemployed. I know myself; I can't stand that sort of stress.

Second, I didn't want to teach English because that was the job that all the expats did, and I didn't want to be in the expat crowd. I didn't want to work with a whole lot of Americans and Brits, where I'd have to talk endlessly about the food and television we'd left at home. I wanted a job, any job, one that was more like an ordinary job. Somewhere where I might actually get to talk to some Czechs in Czech. I wanted to make a life here, a permanent life. I wanted to be Czech.

Unfortunately, with no Czech language the jobs I could apply for were limited. In fact, there weren't any. None. There were jobs for people who couldn't speak Czech but they were for people who had other useful languages, like Norwegian and Dutch. These were call centre jobs—not the most glamorous work, but I'd have done it if I'd had just one other European language. The horrible fact was that everyone in Europe could speak English. That's why I was so sure Charles University wouldn't be impressed by my English if I went there. They'd only be astonished by my inability to speak so much as a single other international language. Not many people in Europe can boast such a handicap.

No, non-Czech speakers were useful only if they could also speak another European language. The call centres were set up in cheap Prague to service more expensive European locations—Scandinavia and Holland, for instance. Not Australia or America.

Day after day I trawled the internet looking for a job I could actually do, anything, anything at all. I spent my first month in Prague searching on www.expats.cz, then my second searching on www.expats.cz and biting my fingernails. By the third month, feeling sicker and sicker with anxiety, I was looking at courses in Teaching English as a Second Language, 'just in case'.

3

While I was looking for a job I looked for a place to live. Getting a place of my own had even more urgency about it than getting a job because getting my own place was about putting down roots, about making a home. I had left nothing—literally nothing, except Thelma—back in Australia.

As of March I had been completely without roots. Everything I owned was on the high seas, no doubt shortly to be plundered by Romanian Customs, and I had no more than a passport, some clothes and a dawning realisation that complete freedom's not all it's cracked up to be. It's dislocating. At first it's marvellous but after a while you begin to crave boundaries, for something that ties you to the ground. For the first couple of weeks I lay back and revelled in the feeling that no-one and nothing ruled my life. Then as the blurry, unstructured days passed, I began to long for people to make

19

demands of me, to make me get out of bed, do something, do anything.

No, I needed a house and a job. The house-hunting was important, not least because it gave me something productive to do while I waited for a job to provide me with deadlines. I was determined to buy a flat in Prague. Before I had looked at house prices I'd taken a walk along the river and decided that what I'd really like would be a lovely flat in the top of a building overlooking the river—a converted nineteenth-century palace, preferably with a statue of a couple of naked Greek men over the portico. Then I looked at house prices. The glassy-eyed Americans and Russians already owned those flats. They were as expensive as New York warehouse loft conversions.

So I fished around and came up with the area I thought would suit me. Like any city, there are different areas for different sections of the community. The industrial area on the river bend in an area called Holešovice had a certain amount of investment appeal. It was slowly, slowly being transformed from industrial dump to exclusive residential paradise, but not fast enough for my liking. You'd have to wait twenty years before it became really desirable and—what with my middle age, the foot swelling and the dropping eyelids—I didn't think I had twenty years to hang about. I needed somewhere I could love now, not somewhere I'd love in a decade when I'd quadrupled my money but when I might very well be dead from some medieval fluid-retention disease.

The inner city of Prague, the bits with all the thirteenth-century stone houses, was out of the question. It was too expensive for a start, but also thronged with tourists. You'd have to fight like a salmon struggling upstream just to get to your front door. The outer suburbs were unappealing—I was already living in one and the strain was beginning to tell. I needed to live somewhere where I could stay out drinking all night and be able to stagger home without having to wait for night trams for forty minutes.

I know that sounds like my life was ordered around alcohol consumption but I was single, middle-aged and rootless. Quite frankly, I would've been insane not to be factoring in alcohol consumption. Besides, if I was going to live in a romantic city, I wanted to live in the bits that had cobbled streets and high ceilings. I finally settled on Žižkov.

Žižkov was a poor area so I could afford to buy property there, and it was also an interesting area. Gypsies lived there, artists lived there. Revolutionaries had gathered there in Prague's history to fight off the Austrians and the communists. It had a seedy, down-at-heel, comfortable feeling about it—a bit tatty around the edges, but gradually being burnished up. The streets were cobbled, or being cobbled. The houses were old, apart from a few patches of crumbling housing-estate blocks built by the communists. I made a mental note to avoid those streets. I wandered around getting a feel for the place and every time I did I was more and more convinced Žižkov was the place for me. And it was in Prague 3, a perfectly acceptable postal code.

'You know they are selling a flat in my block?' said my father, who was apparently completely serious. My father's flat, although lovely on the inside, was in a dreadful communist-built apartment block in Prague 9, the last word in concrete-cancer and scratched aluminium—grey and decrepit.

I wouldn't live there if Daniel Craig . . . Oh no, wait, yes I would. I'd live anywhere I might be near Daniel Craig. Okay, well I wouldn't live there unless Daniel Craig lived there too.

'Uh-huh. Um, no I don't think I want to live there.'

'What is wrong with it?' cried Dad, his voice rising, preparing to be offended.

'Uhh . . . I need to be more in the centre.'

'Centre! What is more central that Prague 9? You have the metro and the tram—in fifteen minutes you are in the Old Town. What are you talking about, not central? In Sydney, fifteen minutes from The Rocks is central.'

He did have a point, but to get to most places from Prague 9 I had to take two trams. I had already decided that I needed to live on the Tram 9 route, because Tram 9 comes every three minutes. It really makes a difference to your life, waiting three minutes or waiting twenty for a tram, if you rely on them. In Sydney, I'd had to drive everywhere, and that was the thing I was most grateful to be free of—the damn car. I'd started to really loathe having to drive, no matter where I wanted to go. In Prague, I could walk or take the tram. Prague's compact. The trams are electric and easy. This aspect of life, the ease of getting around, I really wanted to take advantage of.

'Yes, yes, it's close,' I said, soothingly.

'Look, darling, you have to be sensible. You can have a new flat—big, right on the metro line. What more do you want?'

It was useless to tell him that what I wanted was romance. My father's answer would have been 'Can you afford romance?' Well, no, of course I couldn't. But I was still going to buy it.

Finding the real estate wasn't so hard because there was a real-estate boom in Prague and crates of real-estate magazines jammed every doorway. There were three of these mags, and I took to picking them up every week. At first, everything being in Czech, it took me a little while to work out what I was looking at. A couple of times I saw something unbelievably cheap right in the centre, like in a thirteenth-century building at the foot of the Castle, and—forgetting that something that's too good to be true usually is—I'd get all excited. Then I'd discover, after half an hour with the dictionary, that what they were offering was an option to make a bid at a later date. That gave me a clue as to the likely final price: astronomically out of my league.

I told myself I didn't want to live with all those tourists anyway, which was true, but I couldn't guarantee that if I'd had the money I wouldn't have bought a thirteenth-century palace right at the Charles Bridge.

The looking in the magazines was easy. There were lots of flats and lots of agents. It was making the phone calls that was hard. At the high end of the market, exclusive agents with glossy ads pitched to the glassy-eyed cowboys or the American expats who had jobs with Accenture and who were looking to buy in Prague 1. These agents all spoke English. In frayed and grimy Prague 3, only Czechs were looking to buy. While Czechs, like all Europeans, have two or three languages at their command, the three they mostly have are Czech, German and Russian, their communist heritage still being played out in their schoolrooms where these languages are the standard. English has yet to become common linguistic currency. So, I had to call agents and in my halting Czech ask about the flats I'd seen in the magazines.

I learned the words and numbers I needed before every phone call—'Flat', 'Reference Number 31490', 'Can I see it tomorrow?' Invariably, and I mean every single time, a long, long string of Czech, as long and complex and incomprehensible as a blackboard full of quantum theory, came pouring out of the phone at me.

'I am. Sorry,' I would say, my Czech being at the stage where I had to translate every word in my head before saying it, 'I do not. Speak. Much Czech. Please. Could you. Speak. Slowly.'

Which would be followed by another long and incomprehensible stream. I could, however, pick out a few words. Usually what it sounded like to me was this:

'*Žzyšúkzsáříňřňčů*Tuesday*ščzžýěšuíáéíásáíéšířájscibiuaéí áěýh.*'

'Please. I can. See it. On. Tuesday?'

'*Žzyšúk*Yes*říňřňčů*Tuesday*ščzžýěšuíáéíásáíéšířájscibiuaéí áěýh.*'

Intensely relieved that I'd managed to guess right, it was on to the next thing:

'Please. What. Time?'

'*Éáéétgýgnqpoiwputáéíáuščůlkafn*Ten*ěéíášýčžžéqíáýč.*'

'Please. Ten am?'

'Yes, yes,' and then more Czech. This time I could tell from the tone that 10 am was what they had said and they were getting ticked off with this conversation with someone who, while foreign, was also obviously a halfwit.

To a people-pleaser like me, the agony was excruciating. I said 'please' a lot because I knew that, in business, the Czechs are very, very polite and formal people. When speaking to a stranger, particularly in a business context, they weigh down their sentences with elaborate flourishes. What they were saying to me was something like 'If it would be a matter of convenience to you, Mrs Weiss, we may possibly be able to visit the flat on the morning of the 14th, if it should also happen to be an appropriate time for Dr Engineer Svoboda, the owner of the property. If you are agreeable, I will call Dr Engineer Svoboda and endeavour to make arrangements with him that will be of convenience to all parties.' When all I could cope with, especially over the phone, was 'Flat free. Tuesday. 4 pm. Yes.'

Now multiply this experience by one thousand. I made five phone calls a day and every one required a preliminary pep talk from my sensible, brave self to my cowardly, whimpering self. Every single one was a nightmare of Czech. On the occasions when I did manage to make an appointment, two out of every five times the agent simply didn't turn up. The market was so booming and the Czechs so frankly unattuned to basic business concepts like 'selling' after fifty years of communism, that agents would turn up only if they didn't have something better to do.

Staggeringly, when they did turn up, most times the places they showed me were unspeakable—smelling of mould and dead cat, the walls falling in, a room full of yellowing patches of plaster and exposed wires where a bathroom should be. For a Sydneysider accustomed to the business of real estate—where you paint your house and scatter IKEA cushions around to make it look like it is always in that glossy, *Better-Homes-and-Gardens* state, hoping to add an extra grand or two to the price—the idea that you might put a doss house on the market at the going rate (they sold by the square metre in Prague) was extraordinary to me.

The real estate agents didn't even look apologetic, or refer to the 'investment opportunity'. Mostly they stared out the window, smoked a cig and waited for me to finish looking around. Truly, Czechs had a long way to go in the business of consumption.

4

The whole focus of my life in those first few months was putting down roots and establishing myself in my new city; casting on, as it were, so I could knit myself into the life and soul of Prague. In addition to a job and a home, a social life was imperative.

Having already been an expat was a major bonus, because I could at least start by tapping into the networks I'd found the first time around. One of these was the Lazy Vinohradians, a weekly social group started years ago and carried on religiously by a lanky, laconic Englishman, Mike. Vinohrady was a rather cool area of Prague, the place where you lived if you were earning a Western wage but still wanted to live among real Czechs rather than in the tourist areas. Apartments there were large and light, beautifully renovated in sculpted buildings. There was a decent shopping mall, a famous wine cellar and tea rooms. The idea was that Vinohrady had loads of good places to eat and plenty of people to dine with, so there was no reason for Lazy Vinohradians to leave the area except to go to work. Every Thursday a different restaurant was nominated, sometimes one of the established favourites and sometimes an experiment.

On the first Thursday of my return to Prague I checked the expats.cz site and saw that the LV dinner was being held at one of the old standbys, U Tří Prasátek, At the Sign of the Three Pigs. Turning up was one of those times when the world is perfect and fresh. There they were—Mike and two of my old hiking friends, Irish Pam and Mathematics Neil. There I was, free of all baggage and newly arrived in my new life, which was now delightfully sprinkled with familiar old friends who were surprised and delighted to see me again (I'd not advertised my return). I slotted into the long dining bench like I'd just been there yesterday. During the year I'd previously spent in Prague this group had provided me with many friends and casual acquaintances—people to go to the movies with, go hiking, swap information.

Almost immediately, though, the trouble with expat life became obvious. Nearly all of the people I had hiked and chatted with were gone. Mike, Pam and Neil were long-term expats, the kind that I wanted to be—they had ordinary jobs and Czech friends; they came to expat events to keep their social lives interesting. Mike was in IT, Neil taught maths at one of the universities and Pam did something that sounded like money for jam with a telecommunications company. She *said* she was a project manager, but she didn't seem to do any actual work.

'Are you here to stay now?' she asked.

'I'm here for good—or at least for ten years.'

'Have you got your *živno* yet?' This was Mike.

'My what?'

'Oh, you don't know about this.' He and Neil exchanged a grin. 'The Czechs are joining the Schengen zone, so all you non-EU folks need to get a visa.'

'The Americans are going crazy,' said Neil. He and Mike were both English.

'What's the Schengen zone?'

'It's the European borderless zone. The Czechs want to join it but for you that means they'll tighten up visa restrictions to comply with the EU regs, so you can't just hop over to Dresden to renew your three-month visa. You have to have a real visa. Most people get a *živno*.'

A vague unease stirred within me. If there's one thing I really loathe in life it's paperwork. Forms, regulations, sentences like 'In order to get your PX53 you first need to complete your IF1X5495(b), but only if you are a non-contributor. If you are a contributor, you need to get a D26 permit and only then can you apply for a 99(c)3PO.' And so on. You'd think this aversion would be a handicap to an administrator but in fact it's not. In my administrative life I was the person in charge of the people who could talk that language all day, every day. I had immense respect for them. I did the strategy and they made the paperwork fit. My job was way easier, in my view.

What I'd previously liked about Prague was the laxity of their visa regulations. In my year in Prague I'd just hopped over to Dresden every three months, put a foot over the border, had my passport stamped in the train and, *voilà*, I was legal.

This, this Schengen and *živno* . . . this sounded complicated. The smug look on Neil and Mike's faces told me I was right to feel unease.

Pam saved me with a change of subject. 'Can we go hiking? I haven't been since you were here last.'

I promised to start the hiking group again. Mike said he'd hike when hell froze over, but I could help him run the LV if I liked.

———·———

Pam wanted to go hiking because it's a great way to meet new people, especially other expats, but I needed something more stable than expat company. I needed something real, something embedded in Czech society, to form my true social grounding. Hiking and LV meet-ups were all very well but they were only going to meet my peripheral needs, they weren't going to be the foundation of my life. One day, sitting in my father's flat, perusing the *Prague Post* for jobs, flats, anything really, I came across a small ad: 'English service. Spanish Synagogue. Rabbi Morton Narrowe.' *Yes! The Jewish community. That'd be fun. I'll go along there and offer to volunteer. Maybe a Purim play needs writing, perhaps they need an alto in their choir.*

The next Friday, I went in search of Rabbi Narrowe and the Spanish Synagogue. According to the map, it was not far off the Old Town Square—Staroměstské náměstí—a fabulously ornate, cobblestoned square bounded by buildings of Austro-Hungarian magnificence. It's a miracle of wealth and privilege in the heart of Prague, servicing tourists, expats and ambassadors. At its edge the buildings house EU ambassadors and an art gallery or two. Shaded cafés fringe the feet of these buildings, offering 'Authentic Czech Food' and beer to the tourist trade. Swarowski crystal and traditional Czech handicrafts shops nestle together next to ATMs in the narrow streets leading off the square.

To get to the Jewish quarter you have to go down Pařížská, one of the streets off the square and the most expensive street in all of Prague. An Yves Saint Laurent shop—the word 'shop' seems wildly inappropriate, so let's say 'salon'—is on the corner of Pařížská and the Old Town Square. I have never set foot in this place where terrifically slim, smooth women glide on thick carpet and young men in dark uniforms are poised to spring forward and open the door. In my casual jeans and tatty bag, I never had the social courage to enter.

Off Pařížská is Široká and down Široká should have been, according to Google Maps, the Spanish Synagogue. I walked all the way down, then all the way back, then down again and back. It wasn't there. I was looking for something ornate, Moroccan, cupola-ed. I walked past the grey concrete façade that my map assured me was the site of the Spanish Synagogue several times, puzzled, and then I reached the coffee shop the map told me came after the synagogue. It was only when I saw a security guard appear at some wooden double doors set in the middle of the nondescript grey wall that I realised that here—looking more like a communist warehouse than a thousand-year-old breathtaking edifice—must indeed be it.

'*Je to tady služby?*' I asked the guard. Is the service here?

He nodded, not smiling and not offering anything more to the nice, friendly, inoffensive person in front of him. If there is one thing the Czechs like to do, it is to be rude to people who need their services. Small shops are a nightmare of sullen aggression.

I pinched my nose and reminded myself that I had brought this adventure on myself and that, if I'd wanted life to be easy, I could have stayed in the office in Sydney and built up my pension.

'*Ted*?' Now?

He shook his head and held up six fingers. '*Osmnáct hodin*.' Whatever he'd said didn't sound like 'six' to me, which was '*šest*', but I took his meaning. The service started at six, and it wasn't six. Come back later.

When I got back at just before six, there was a queue outside the Spanish Synagogue, and disappointed tourists were being firmly turned away by three security guards. The Jewish quarter is a must-see on every tourist's tick list. It was not bombed during the war, in common with so much of Prague, which was occupied early and thus spared aerial destruction—so it is beautiful. It is steeped in mystic history: golems, thousand-year-old graveyards and dark, low-lintelled stone synagogues from a time when no-one stood taller than five foot three. It has an air of the deeply tragic overlying the mythical—an ancient world, well beyond the understanding of this one, mixed with centuries of pogroms and oppression.

Tourism in the Jewish quarter is tightly regulated. You cannot just go and see one synagogue, you have to buy a ticket that will give you access to all six of them. There is no choice about this. The Jewish Museum dictates that it shall be so, and every synagogue has this regulation posted prominently on a tin sign at its main door—you have to buy the one-and-only type of ticket at the one-and-only outlet, and it's not cheap. It's six synagogues' worth, whether you like it or not.

I had some sympathy with non-Jewish tourists who tried to pretend they were worshippers so they could avoid the fee and see an ancient temple in action, but they had no hope. Even I could tell who was an ordinary tourist and who a Jewish tourist taking time out from their holiday to come and pray at a Friday night service. The non-Jewish tourists craned their necks to see through the doors as they opened to let each person in, hoping to get a glance of the interior. They bounced back and forth, chittering in excitement and antici- pation. Jewish tourist worshippers looked disconsolate and complained about the service starting at six. They thought it was supposed to be seven—when had it changed to six? They might have missed it—the website really shouldn't be so vague. It was only because they knew, from people in the States who'd just got back from Prague and had told them that, no, it was still six and it wouldn't change to seven until later in the year. They kept their faces impassive and serious for the guards, submitting to an inspection with the grudg- ingly proud feeling of doing their duty to the community. The non-Jewish tourists looked surprised to be asked to do this. No, it wasn't hard for the guards to pick them out and tell them they couldn't come in.

It was something of a secret thrill to be let in after hours, one of the genuine punters, in a part of town that was given over to tourists for the other 166 hours in the week. It gave me the feeling I was craving—that I belonged, that I had a right to be where I was, a person with business to do in this thousand- year-old building in Prague. When my turn came at the door,

I submitted to the guards with a studiously expressionless face, making eye contact only to nod that I understood the drill. They dug through my bag and ran the metal detector around my coat.

Already, after my previous year in Prague, I'd picked up a peculiar fact about Europe: anti-Semitism remained spookily strong. You grew up in Australia and you didn't realise that hatred of Jews was this thing that was soaked into the soil of Europe—a throbbing vein. I hardly know how to explain it, except that you could feel it. You could feel it in their literature, all around you. National Guard skinheads hated Jews. I was used to a Hating Right that hated black people or Asians. But Jews? It seemed so eighteenth century, so *Oliver Twist* and *Ivanhoe*.

My father had a cousin who was given over to the Nazis by a man in his village. *In his village.* They're only small, those villages. Everyone knows everyone else from babyhood. This man, who'd known my father's cousin from boyhood, told the Nazis he was a Jew and got him sent off to camp. My cousin did not survive but, when his mother got out, she went back to her village, sought out the denouncer, marched up to him and socked him one. My father says the women in his family were hefty, sturdy types who could get a crack in when they chose.

The three security guards at the Spanish Synagogue presented a formidable force. In Sydney, on a Friday night, kids and parents mill about outside the synagogue, moving like a tide in and out of its doors. Was there even a security guard? Not that I could recall. And that was for a couple of hundred people. Here there were three—for a congregation of about twenty.

And at last I was inside and sitting in a pew, waiting to pray. The Spanish Synagogue might have been blank concrete on the outside, but it was pure Moroccan baroque on the inside. It had been designed in the Moorish style: graceful, embossed arches supported a mezzanine along the walls. Every surface on the walls and ceiling was decorated with intricate, tessellated art nouveau designs brightly picked out in reds and greens and shining gold. On each side, glass-topped cabinets displayed ancient torahs and letters, silk kippahs from previous centuries and silver cups and medallions. The floor was smooth and cool, wet-grey granite slabs. Two small sets of darkly golden pews took up the centre, with a wooden pulpit at the front. I sat in the pews and rested my eyes on its magnificence, filled with joy and love.

That first Friday night the shul was hushed—there was just the shuffling and clicking of reverent feet, the quiet whispers and rustles of a handful of people settling in its cavernous space. We exchanged brief smiles of hello if we happened to be in the same pew, but we largely ignored each other, all of us concentrating on the business of preparing for communion with God.

At the stroke of six, just as the service was about to start, the inner doors burst open and a fantastically noisy horde of teenagers barrelled through, laughing and poking at each other, yammering at the tops of their voices. From their conversation I gathered they were Israeli teenagers on a youth-group tour. Their noise was extraordinary.

After ten minutes, the kids were relatively settled in their seats but still shrieking. Then a rabbi appeared at the podium and held up a commanding hand, saying, 'Guys, guys, a little shush.' They only abated a fraction but the rabbi—a young, blond man with a distinctly American twang to his accent, clearly well accustomed to Israeli youth groups—started anyway, giving an introduction in English, to my relief, and then launching into the Kabbalat Shabbat.

The service wasn't the same as the one I was used to. All the songs were different, except for one or two. There was a lot less singing and a lot more talking, and some of the spoken service was in Czech. I kept up as best I could. There's a section of the service in which we all fall silent, the quiet in the room allowing each person to commune with God. During this bit you are supposed to read pages and pages of a prayer called the Amidah.

When I first started going to shul in Sydney I used to read this section devoutly, bowing in all the places where the Sydney prayer book helpfully added 'Bow Here'. After a few months I began to skip the boring passages and then I ditched the lot—I simply turned the pages at regular intervals, timed to look like I was reading it, and bowed when my neighbours bowed. After a while I pulled myself together and stopped pretending for the rest of the congregation. By that time I'd realised that most people were as unconscientious about the Amidah as I was.

At the Spanish Synagogue, however, I was more exposed. I felt I was among real worshippers here, people who kept Judaism alive in the face of pogroms and ghettos—real commitment, of a kind that's hard to find in sunny, lucky Sydney. The Czechs had omitted the words 'Bow Here' in their prayer book and I was embarrassed to find I didn't remember where the bows were supposed to occur—had I really been paying so little attention during the central plank of the service? I kept a furtive eye on my Israeli neighbour, nervously wondering if she noticed I didn't really know what I was doing, and gave a hasty bow whenever she took a graceful knee-bend, doubling over like a swan taking a curtain call.

Afterwards I hung around and made myself talk to strangers. A life away from home does you good in one outstanding respect—you get good at meeting people. I launched myself at anyone who was standing around looking uncomfortable or just alone. The teenagers were taking up the time of the rabbi, so I gave up on meeting him this visit and concentrated instead on other congregants. There was an elderly couple from the States who were making a trip to Prague and Budapest, taking the Vltava-Danube cruise from one to the other. They seemed nice and we exchanged items of interest about our respective countries for a while before they left, Friday night observances made.

I met a slightly strange woman who lived in Prague but had a muddled story about how she came to be there, which seemed to involve a previous life as a diplomat that was somewhat at odds with her bedraggled hair and long dirty nails. I was as nice as I could be for quite some time, nodding and smiling and saying, 'Gosh, really! How exciting! It must have been amazing!' and so on. But at the point where the poor woman suggested we have coffee and exchange phone numbers I began to look around wildly for an exit strategy.

A thin woman was turning away from her neighbour just as I was straining away from mine and trying to wish her a good—but distant—Friday night with a hearty 'Shabbat Shalom' farewell. The thin woman caught the look on my face, saw the yellow nails reaching for my sleeve and inter-vened smoothly.

'Shabbat shalom! You are a visitor?'

She had a very slight clip to her accent. Not a native English speaker, but the words came out as if she were. She grabbed my arm and bore me off, inexorably, leaving the poor mad woman to close her grip on the warm air where my body had been. My heart felt the cruelty of it but I have only so much time I can give to the psychologically draining, and religious institutions are replete with the psychologically draining.

My new friend's name was Anna and she was Czech.

'I have just returned from Amsterdam.' She had been doing her PhD in linguistics there. 'It was interesting, but now I must get back to work.'

'Did you not want to be an academic?'

She didn't know. It was hard to get a job and anyway she missed home. She had been away for five years. 'Now I am a translator.'

'English to Czech?'

'Yes, English of course. And French . . .'

'Wow, you have both of those fluently?' I'm always impressed by the European ability to speak more than one language.

'. . . German, Russian, Slovak (but that's easy), Dutch of course. Those fluently. I can get by in Croatian and Italian.' She paused and thought. 'And I guess Latin.'

I counted on my fingers. 'That's ten.'

'Yes, yes, I think that's all.'

'You speak ten languages?

'Yes, that's about right. Ten? Yes, ten.'

'Seven of them fluently?'

'Well, I had an advantage. We all know Russian and German from school, and then I've lived in Amsterdam for five years, and my family used to holiday in Croatia.'

This seemed unduly modest. The woman could speak ten languages. Anna had a rapid delivery. She was short and slight, wore no makeup, had unruly hair and hands that didn't stop moving. She was in a long, black slim-line skirt that stopped just short of the ankles above clumpy shoes. Her beige top was understated and close-fitting and her earrings were small silver Stars of David. She had disarmingly crooked teeth and pale lashes and a way of talking that suggested unbounded enthusiasm for whatever subject she was on. I asked her about the synagogues in Prague—was this the only reform congregation?

'Yes, the Spanish Synagogue is the only one. At least, it used to be the only one. A few years ago, a section of the congregation became dissatisfied with the way the Friday night services were being conducted and began to argue for a more conservative flavour. Naturally, no-one was able to agree on precisely how the Kabbalat Shabbat should be observed to everyone's satisfaction, so the agitators left to start their own shul along more conservative lines. Now, instead of one very small reform community in Prague, there are two utterly minute—but slightly different in crucial respects invisible to the outsider—reform communities.'

Naturally. I began to feel more at home.

'Have you heard the one about the Jewish guy who gets stranded on a deserted island?' she asked.

'Uh-uh.' I didn't know this joke.

39

Anna's bright eyes twinkled and her hand waving became more animated. 'He's all alone after a shipwreck but he makes the best of it, building a house, growing food. Finally a ship turns up to rescue him and he's showing the crew around the island home he's made for himself. "This is my home, and here is my garden. This is the storehouse I built for myself and here's the synagogue I go to." The captain sees another building, "What's that house for?" he asks. "Huh!" snorts the castaway, scornfully, "That's the synagogue I don't go to!"'

Anna doubled over, slapping her thighs. 'Isn't that great?! That's the synagogue I don't go to! So true! So true!'

5

Back in Sydney I once had a flatmate who believed in God. My mother and stepfather had brought me up as a strict atheist and taught me that religious types were crazed lunatics too stupid to see through the sham crutch they clung to like so many spineless maddos. Or words to that effect. They were very strict about it and no religious discussion was tolerated in our house, so my flatmate was pretty much the first believer I'd had a chance to discuss it with in any depth.

Sandra told me that she felt, at every moment of the day, as though she were held tight in a giant, loving pair of arms. There was a brief silence after she said that while she looked inwards to the place that always felt secure and I, taking this in, looked inwards to the place that I was always frantic to run away from.

What about hell? She was unbothered by hell, she said. What did heaven or hell matter when God was right here?

She said she trusted her feelings and did whatever felt right to her in her life, knowing—*knowing*, mind you—that God would look after her. *Knowing*. It was that that gave me pause. I'd been assured by my parents that such 'knowing' was unpardonable arrogance on the part of people too closed off to understand the vagaries of life.

Listening to Sandra, my familiarity with the vagaries of life seemed suddenly not so much sophisticated as needlessly terrifying. Following the happy precepts of my childhood, I trusted that no matter what I did there was always some bastard out there ready to do me over. I'm sure my parents meant well in preparing me for a world in which I would be on my own until I got money, but the serene look on Sandra's face told me there was something more to religion and belief than just mindless fear.

So I set about believing in God. It's not easy manufacturing belief—in fact, as it turns out, it's impossible. I went along to synagogue relentlessly for ten years, every Friday. I converted (my father is Jewish, not my mother), I learned all the prayers, read Hebrew, performed good deeds, volunteered, joined the choir, attended all the major ceremonies and some of the minor ones, had a bash at being kosher (I lasted exactly a week—good Lord, is that a boring diet), sang at the Montefiore Home and talked and talked and talked to God.

God never answered back. After ten years, I gave it away. You can only keep trying for so long. I'm sure God is a lovely fellow, but he and I are never going to meet. My blood outed, and it was atheist through and through.

All, however, was not lost. It turned out that being deeply involved in a community—even one that is full of people bickering about the exact interpretation of rules of the service and leaving in a huff when a visiting rabbi brings his guitar to the bimah—is very good for your spirits.

I'd joined a rather cool synagogue with a young female rabbi called Jacki. Fed up with years of being single and having every congregant hovering over her—When is she going to get married already, a nice girl like her? What is she waiting for?—Jacki set up the Bitter Single Women's Club. We had a sexy American head rabbi, who used the bank of his considerable charm to put it to the community at Yom Kippur that we are all one in God's eyes so we should embrace Palestinians rather than shun them. That had caused gasps and heart palpitations, but his sexiness swept all mutiny into the corner, where it formed a breakaway group that fought for more conservative services for two years until it finally got the use of the smaller hall for separate services held half an hour earlier than the main services and lasting an hour longer, to prove how much more committed they were. And we had a gay choir master who bitched about the sopranos to me in whispered asides and had pictures on his desk of his boyfriend in leather chaps at Mardi Gras.

Cool people came to the synagogue—an incredibly rich property developer, a TV personality, a famous madam. At Purim we put on a play every year, written by Jacki and starring a crowd of university students who wanted to be comedians and who'd been going to Jewish youth camps together since they were tots. And me, ahem. We competed to see who could dress up in the most outrageous drag and sang ABBA songs. They welcomed me into their happy, creative, funny gang and I didn't mind in the end that God remained mute—I sang and danced and felt the hug of my community and that had been enough for me. Yes, I liked the Jewish religious community— the Spanish Synagogue would suit me very well.

———•———

What with the synagogue, the Lazy Vinohradians and the hiking I felt that I'd made a good start on getting a group around me. I did one more thing—I signed up to Czech classes. These had never given me much in the way of friends before, but they did give me a place to go twice a week, and work and deadlines while I waited for a job as well as the ever-optimistic hope that I might one day be fluent in this insanely difficult language. Leading a hiking group, though, became the lodestone of my week.

When I arrived, it was March and freezing but I didn't want to miss out on a single second of the European seasons. I wanted to feel the biting cold of early spring, the dry killing heat of high summer. I wanted to taste the cherries right off the trees in July and the pears in September. I wanted to see the leaves turn for autumn and drop for winter, by which time it'd be so cold I'd only be able to walk the trails if I wore two sets of thermals and kept moving.

Irish Pam became a constant hiking companion. I liked Pam. She was cheery and hearty and could get on with even the most socially obnoxious by simply chirping until the first opportunity she got to say, 'Well, it's been grand, must go!' But I'd been a bit hesitant about posting the hikes on the web.

'To be sure,' said Pam (and she really did talk like that), 'we'll meet loads of lovely people that way and we'll have great *craic*.'

So I advertised on expats.cz. On the very first trip we were joined by a couple of Valley Girls, aged twenty or so, who talked about themselves non-stop for four hours. I thought Pam was enjoying their company—she was laughing and talking merrily with them while I was silently calculating how to ditch them at the end of the train trip home—when I got a text from her (she'd written it surreptitiously) saying, 'Please, God, can we make sure we get rid of them at the station?'

Later, I said to her, 'But you seemed to like them so much!'

'Sure, and I can talk to anyone if I have to. I wish I had the courage to just stay quiet, but I worry that people won't be having a good time.'

See, now, that's something that never worries me. I'm only worried about whether *I'm* having a good time so I'd been mute the entire trip.

But we didn't give up and bit by bit we grew a small coterie of regular hikers: Mathematics Neil, Pam, me and travellers passing through—hearty, happy, fun people who walked through rain without complaining, who swam in the rivers, who brought along chocolate and suggested great places to go afterwards.

Like a champion, Pam turned up every Saturday. She always went on a binge on Thursday and Friday nights because she was Irish, and thus compelled by blood and birthright to go out on the *craic* (an Irish term for having fun and drinking enormous quantities of beer and mojitos) but she never failed to kick herself out of bed at 7 o'clock on a Saturday morning and get herself to the station. Sometimes she wasn't techni-cally awake until about 10, by which time we were one hour into the trail, but she never moaned about it—she was just unusually silent on those mornings.

6

The Friday after I first went to the Spanish Synagogue, I returned and apart from the fact that there was a different horde of noisy Israeli teenagers attending it was the same service. I decided to make it my home.

Anna was not there so at the end of the service I joined the line of people waiting to see the rabbi. The Friday night line is composed of the same people whether you're in Sydney or Prague: elderly single ladies with a crush on the rabbi bearing knitted socks, self-important, prosperous men who liked to be able to say to their friends, 'I was telling the rabbi the other day . . .' and visitors from out of town. When it was my turn to come into The Presence, I found myself face to face with a very charming man, maybe thirty-five, slender, blond, with the easy social graces of a natural extrovert, who asked where I was from and welcomed me to Prague with what seemed to be genuine, hearty goodwill. I liked him immediately. More and more I felt like making my home here.

The rabbi was a busy man, though, with two hundred foreign congregants to greet, so I didn't take up his time with idle chitchat—he was already looking past me to the next fluttering lady. I came straight to the point and told him that I was looking to become involved in the life of the shul. I said that I'd been in the choir at home—perhaps I could join their choir here? The rabbi's eyes stopped wandering and fixed on me. He took me by the elbow, suddenly, strangely, keenly interested.

'You sing?'

'Yes, I sing,' I said.

'And you know the service?'

'Well . . . yes,' said I. It was not a complete untruth. I knew most of the service we had back in Sydney.

'Good, good. That's very good. And you want to help out?' The rabbi was gripping my arm with both hands now.

'If there's anything I can do . . .'

'You can lead the service here.'

'Um . . . what?'

'We don't have a permanent rabbi or a cantor. We're too small. We're always looking for volunteers. You can lead the service next Friday.'

I tried to rescue myself and my arm. I was keen, but not that keen. 'Um, well, I really only know some of the songs. I don't know the whole service,' I said, tugging my elbow.

His grasp tightened. 'Whatever. Someone else can do the bits you don't know.'

'But the songs I know are different to yours!'

'Fine, fine! Always glad to do things differently.'

'But I don't think I can sing on my own!' I was straining to get away, the whites of my eyes beginning to roll wildly.

'You'll be fine.'

'No, I won't.'

'Yes, you will.'

'No, I won't.'

'Yes, you will.'

I tried another tack. 'Isn't there something else I can do?'

'No, leading the service will be wonderful. We're so grateful. So, that's settled then. Give me a call!' And he released my arm, patted me on the back and pushed me out of the line before I could protest any further.

It turned out he wasn't the rabbi at all, but the very overworked director of the synagogue, and only too happy to have someone else take on some of the load.

Initially I had decided to just not turn up on Friday, but two things made me change my mind. First, I really did want to go to a regular shul and I couldn't bear the thought of going through the pain of trying to find another one. And second, on reflection, it didn't seem such a bad idea to me. I'd been singing along with our chap-clad cantor in Sydney for five years and I knew his songs well. As long as someone else did the prayer bit, why couldn't I do the singing? My voice wasn't great, but I could hold a tune and I wasn't afraid of getting up in front of a crowd, thanks to a lifetime of amateur theatricals. So why not sing the Sydney service here in Prague? I liked the idea of my hometown shul's influence extending all the way into central Europe.

The blond man's name was Peter. According to Anna, he'd come to Prague ten years earlier, when a group of

American businessmen, fired up by the romance of the newly freed Prague, had raised a bucketload of money to restore the Spanish Synagogue to its former glory and establish an English-speaking service for the expat reform Jewish community. Peter had been a boy who'd gone to California from his village in Slovakia the second the Berlin Wall fell and had returned to central Europe with his hair long and windswept à la Fabio. Ten years at the helm of a tiny community—negotiating for money with a board in America, overseeing the split and then the next split, negotiating with the Jewish Museum, keeping up good relations with the rabbis and congregants of the conservative and orthodox Jewish communities—had seen the depletion of much of his hair although, astonishingly, not the end of his boundless energy. He had married and settled down. Luckily his wife was a banker because he didn't make much more money than he had made busking in the Californian sunshine.

He was a cheery, haphazard man. I called him and we set up a time to rehearse on the Monday, but he cancelled that and then he cancelled the rehearsal we had agreed to for Wednesday. Then a Thursday appointment and a Friday morning meeting were also cancelled. What with one thing and another it wasn't until late that Friday afternoon, only three hours before shul, that I arrived at the office and was met by a harried Peter. His secretary had just quit, so things were in a certain amount of chaos. He wended his way from his desk through a corridor of paper to get to me.

'I know where everything is, it's just getting to it.'

He couldn't find a copy of the current Kabbalat Shabbat (which was different for each shul) but he did have a superseded copy which he assured me was close enough. We began with Lecha Dodi.

'We sing this one,' I said, and gave him a few bars.

'Oh yes,' he nodded, 'that's a very traditional version. We sing this one.' He gave me a burst of an entirely unfamiliar song.

'I don't know that tune,' I said. Had there been a mis-understanding? We were going to sing the tunes I knew, weren't we?

'It's easy. Listen, it goes like this.' He sang me another snippet.

No, apparently we weren't. Nor, it turned out, would we be singing my versions of Mi Chamocha or Adon Olam. In fact, nothing was going to be the same as the Sydney service other than Mizmor Le David and V'Shamru.

'Ah yes. Very traditional,' Peter would say dismissively, whenever I bleated out our shul's version of anything at all.

When I realised that I was going to have to learn a whole new service, I suggested to Peter that perhaps this Friday, just to be on the safe side, we could sing a couple of songs together. Maybe just the ones that I knew, and we could work up to the point where I would sing alone in a few weeks' time. He seemed surprised that I might not be willing to sing an entire hour of unfamiliar songs in public with only a couple of hours' rehearsal, but he kindly agreed.

'Besides,' he added, 'at first some people might not like the idea of a woman leading the service, but they'll get used to it. Well, they're going to have to, aren't they?'

I blenched. 'People here don't like women to lead?' I'd forgotten all about this strange Jewish prejudice. I mentioned

Jacki to Peter and he was astonished to learn we had a female rabbi.

'Women have to be so much better than men, don't they?' he said.

I was stumped for an answer.

Leaving Peter to change his trousers and shirt, I went to the Spanish Synagogue. Getting there fifteen minutes early, I sat outside looking over the Kabbalat Shabbat. Despite my best efforts, I'd forgotten every new tune I'd learned only an hour before and I now perceived that I had another problem: laziness being my own special curse, I never studied hard enough in Hebrew class. Consequently, I always use the English transliteration during services, telling myself, 'I'll brush up my Hebrew for next Friday.' I now found myself bitterly regretting my laziness because, looking at the text, I saw that there was a transliteration, but it was into the Czech alphabet, which is quite different from the English one: '*c*' for instance is pronounced 'ts', '*j*' is pronounced 'y', '*mě*' is pronounced 'mnye'. And so it goes on. These are only three of many, many differences.

As I read through the Czech transliteration, trying to figure it out, my collar tightened around my neck. It was the beginning of a hot summer, but I was wearing a high-necked shirt and jacket in a feeble effort to simulate modest piety. As my predicament became clearer to me, my temperature rose and my clothes began to feel like a straitjacket. The sun beat down and I started to turn red; my pencil slipped in my fingers as I tried to mark out the syllables in the text. But before I could get too far into untangling Lecha Dodi, the doors opened and I and about eighty Israeli tourists—I was to discover that on Friday nights we either had six people and a sprinkling of Americans, or six people and a gigantic Israeli contingent on a Jewish history pilgrimage—filed in past the security guards. I tried to reassure myself that it was going to be easy: Peter would be singing too—what could go wrong?

I sat in the front row, so Peter could call me up for the one or two numbers we had agreed on. To my surprise, when I caught his eye, he motioned for me to go up straight away.

'Welcome everyone, this is Rachael and today she and I will be leading the service.' *What?? You mean I'm stuck up here?* Yes, that's precisely what he meant. We must have had a communication blip back at the office.

I tried to look as though I knew what I was doing. We opened with Mizmor L'David. It's a lucky thing I knew the tune because, as soon as I opened the book, I saw I had another problem to add to my growing list. While rehearsing with Peter, we had used, you will recall, a superseded version of the Kabbalat Shabbat, but he had blithely assured me the differences between that and the current version were minimal.

One hesitates to call a holy man a liar, but the version I now had in my hands was completely different to the one in his office, which had had only the Hebrew text and the Czech transliteration. This version had the Hebrew text and the Czech transliteration, plus a Czech text, all jammed in together. So, in order to identify the Czech transliteration, I had to first work out what was true Czech and what was Hebrew Czech. I stared at my book, horrified.

Fortunately, I know Mizmor L'David so well I could sing along while frantically trying to find my place. I found it just as we hit the last note, and to my relief I hadn't stumbled.

Peter glanced at me and gave me a little smile to say 'Phew!' and I felt encouraged. *Okay*, I thought, *this is going to be okay.* I started to relax. I looked out at the congregation, and the first thing I saw was one of the Israeli tourists, glaring at me. Glaring? For an instant I thought I must be dreaming, and then a terrible idea crossed my mind: *Is he glaring at me because I'm a woman?* I looked at him and his glare intensified. *Oh dear. Oh my. Oh, this isn't good.*

Lecha Dodi was next and once again I had to find the right bit of Czech in the muddle of Czech in front of me. This was also one of the new tunes I'd comprehensively forgotten, so the first couple of verses were a bit hesitant as I bleated out the words a mini-blip after Peter. We got through it, but I was starting to feel rather tense. The Israeli was still glaring at me. I'd stumbled over some of the Lecha Dodi, I'd forgotten all the tunes I'd learnt that afternoon and, to add to it all, it was getting hotter and hotter. My collar and jacket were gripping me uncomfortably and I could feel beads of perspiration on my back. My shirt was sticking to me and my mind became occupied with a new threat—was I going to start smelling bad?

The very thought made my heart beat faster and the sweat beads increased and gathered into such a group they began to drip down my body. Small starter beads were joined by friends, until a slight but insistent stream was rolling down my legs. I glanced at the floor and to my appalled horror I saw a puddle—only two inches across, but a puddle nonetheless—forming at my feet. My worst primary-school nightmare was going to come true—it was going to look as though I'd wet myself. By now I was having trouble breathing.

It was at this moment that Peter turned to me and said, 'You can do Mizmor Shir.'

Well, you know, the key to good singing is relaxation. If you're not relaxed you won't be at your best. I cleared my throat and launched into Mizmor Shir.

'*Miz mor SHIR Le'om ha Shabbat . . .*' I sounded like an elderly mongoose yelling at her kids.

'*. . . TOV le'hodot, L'Adonai . . .*' The elderly mongoose was becoming shriller. *Pull yourself together, girl!* But it was no good.

'*. . . Ulezamer le shimcha elyon . . .*' The mongoose became hoarse with outrage.

I made it through to the end but it wasn't pretty. Peter seemed not to have noticed but carried on with the next bit of the service. While Peter sang, I scrambled through the book trying to find my place, and remember the tune, and work out the Czech transliteration, while all the time surreptitiously trying to squeeze my legs together to blot the ever-thickening stream and keep my foot on the spreading puddle. When I forgot to avoid his eye, the irate Israeli in the front row glared at me, reminding me that a woman's place is behind, not in front. Yes, well, if I'd listened to his kind I wouldn't be in this nightmare, would I?

Just when the end must be in sight and my ordeal nearly over, Peter turned to me and said, 'You know this one, don't you? Why don't you sing Magen Avot?'

You'd have thought he'd have learned his lesson. I do know Magen Avot, in a manner of speaking. I'd been singing along for years in Sydney, but we hadn't rehearsed this one that afternoon, I'd just said I knew it. However, I'd come this far, why not just blast away? So I nodded to Peter with every appearance of confident delight in what was to come and launched into it.

I'm afraid to say that halfway through I lost my way in the transliteration and then lost my way altogether. In the past, when I'd been singing in the shul choir and lost my way in a song, I'd look up and there would be our leather-bound cantor, something of a musical genius, looking straight at me and bellowing my note. This time I faltered and stopped and there was silence. Where was my cantor? He was in Sydney, too far away to come to my rescue.

There is no more excruciating experience than singing atrociously in public and then so utterly stuffing up that you have to stop singing in the middle of it, in front of a full house, at least one of whom would be thrilled to see you fail. Here I was, confronted by a deathly and lengthening silence, an Israeli congregant with an I-told-you-so look on his face, with soaking wet tights and a suspicious puddle at my feet. The worst had happened.

It was at this point that a strange calming thought came over me—in my whole life I would never again suffer a worse embarrassment. I turned to Peter, resigned to my fate and at peace at last with my God, and said quietly, 'I'm sorry, I've lost it. Can you take it from here?'

The last song of the evening was Adon Olam and, luckily for me, none of the tourists knew the Spanish Synagogue version, but everyone knew the Sydney shul version, so I was able to sing away at the top of my voice. You know what they say: as long as you open well and close well, who remembers what happens in between?

Despite the appalling ordeal I'd been through, I agreed to do it again. It turned out that Anna was the only person who could conduct the whole service apart from Peter, so they were only too glad to have someone else shouldering the burden. Even, apparently, someone as crap as me.

7

I wasn't expecting to make friends in Czech class. I could never work out why but people didn't seem to want to extend their studies to the pub afterwards. Perhaps it was because people doing Czech classes generally had lives already filled with friends and community—they were men who'd married Czech women, or students from America whose friends were other twenty-somethings. I was doing a week-long intensive when I met Andy and what stuck out about him was that for once it was someone else saying, 'Does anyone want to get a drink?' I jumped at the chance—everyone else said a slightly awkward no and shuffled off to their lives.

Andy and I chose to call our drinking sessions 'study meetings'. We drank more than we studied and he later told me that we had nearly not become friends after something I said at that first pub outing. I had said that if it wasn't for humans eating pigs, there wouldn't be so many pigs, and so that worked to the pigs' advantage. I was reading Dawkins at the time, as was the whole world, and I was seeing things from a gene's eye view.

I've changed my mind since then—no pigs should live in misery. Nor should any animals. Population growth suits genes but not the gene carriers and it's the gene carriers we need to concern ourselves with.

Andy was a strict vegetarian. His wife, Barbara, was also a vegetarian and didn't like beer. They'd been living in Prague for seven years under those conditions. How they managed to survive in a country which regards bacon as a vegetable I did not know.

Andy and Barbara did eat fish, and trout was widely available on the menus, but that was it really—trout, fried cheese and *šopský salát* (which is a moderately tasty salad of cubed cucumber, tomato and the Czech version of feta cheese)— these were the only things that could reliably be said to be vegetarian on your standard Czech menu, a menu which mainly consisted of pork, pork, pork, duck, beef, pork or pork. Pig genes were flourishing in the Czech Republic.

Andy was one of those people through whom you would eventually meet everyone living in Prague. The expat community was tiny and claustrophobic. Everyone knew everyone else's business and scandals decades old were kept alive owing to the lack of critical mass that might keep new scandals developing and of the difficulty of finding anything in Prague to be genuinely scandalised by. We lived in a place where sex was unfettered by religion, where taking a lover was considered routine—nay, obligatory—and people agitated for beer to be classified as a health food. Under those conditions, it's hard to work up a sweat about anything much.

Andy was an American journalist working on the *Prague Post*, an English-language newspaper of moderate readability that mostly kept translators in employment and was reputed to be one of the worst workplaces in the city. Andy was the kind of person you picture when you picture a journalist— someone who can spend many hours a day chatting to anyone who happens to be sitting on the bench next to them, a lover of music and gigs, a drinker of beer who could go all night. He was genial and easy to be with, passionate about the Republicans (he hated them) and seemed to know everyone in Prague. He loved nothing more than sitting in beer gardens shooting the breeze.

Through Andy and one of his contacts, I got a list of the top one hundred companies in Prague and emailed each of them, offering my services as an editor. I had one ace in my hand and that was the fact that I had written a book on Prague that was due to be published the following year. I also had a degree in English literature from a sandstone university—the first time in my life that that degree had ever been relevant to an actual job. I wouldn't study anything else given my time over, but it has to be said that it was probably the university and not the degree that had got me my previous jobs.

With my forthcoming book and the degree, I already looked many cuts above your average travelling English speaker; a quick re-working of my CV, to make it appear as though I'd devoted my life to editing, and I hit the phones and emails.

The first bite I got was from a legal firm. They were

interested, and more professional than I was accustomed to in Prague. They wanted me to complete a test to prove I could edit legal documents. I said that would be no problem. They sent me the test. It was incomprehensible.

It turns out that legal terms can be quite specific. I called my mother. My parents are professionals, which is why they'd put me through university, even if I did waste it on a literature degree. My mother is a lawyer. I read out the test to her and she explained—in long and painful detail, all the way from Sydney—what the terms meant and what needed to be corrected.

Unfortunately, her specialty was criminal law and this seemed to be largely concerned with conveyancing and property, so she was vague about at least four of the terms. 'I don't know, dear, that could either mean the owner has the right to buy or the owner has the option to buy. It's an important distinction and one you would have to know. Do you know any lawyers there?'

No, I didn't. It was afternoon in Prague and four in the morning in Australia (my mother doesn't sleep much). I said I'd send off the test anyway and see how we got on. It had taken us two hours to get through it. If I'd known what I was doing, I'd have been able to get it completed in ten minutes.

'Well, darling, you can always call me and we can do it together if you get the job.'

Which was sweet of her. I was becoming desperate. The lawyers had contacted me after I had spent four solid weeks of writing emails and sending CVs and making phone calls and getting absolutely nowhere. I was so desperate that I almost believed I really could do the legal editing via telephone with my mother in the middle of her night if I got the job, just until I got the hang of it and learned the language.

But as desperate as I was for any straw to clutch, even I could see this was never going to work. Luckily for me, the lawyers put it out of my hands by declining to accept my services.

8

Being part of the Jewish community, for me, is about doing something in this world to make up for my grandfather's early demise in the Holocaust.

Survivors tend to fall into two categories—those who talk about it obsessively and those who never refer to it. My own father is in the latter group. I am grateful to him for this as I'm not much of a one for feeling horror and fear. My grandfather was sent to Terezín, the camp just outside Prague in what was then Czechoslovakia—that much I knew. In one conversation with Dad, he told me that he used to go to Terezín to slip food to the members of his family. 'I could go to the area because I was uncut. The Nazis stopped men and boys if they thought they were suspicious, and tell them to drop their pants. If they were circumcised, they were arrested.'

All of his family from their small village were sent to Terezín, and all of them went first to the flat in Prague where my father, a young boy, lived with his Catholic mother. That's the way it happened. They weren't carted off in trucks from the village, they were given their papers and orders and they quietly closed up their lives and made their way to the city, stopping off at my grandmother's place. There she would fill their empty suitcases with dried bread and they would say goodbye and get on the bus to the camp. I always wondered: why didn't Dad get sent off to camp? They were sending half-Jews off, so why not him? I never liked to ask him that. He's not the type to dwell on the past—'Why make yourself miserable, darlink? I don't want to think about it.' And, apart from pointedly not buying anything German, he doesn't think about it. But just before I left for Prague I asked him.

'Oh, I got my papers,' he said, casually, and I cooled a sudden degree. 'The day I got them, my mother opened the letter and then turned around and marched straight out of the flat to the German police station. I never knew what happened, she wouldn't tell me, but I never saw the papers again.'

My grandmother and father became communists after the war, as everyone did—it seemed like such a good idea after the Fascists. My grandmother stayed one her whole life. She lived in a flat, spied on by the concierge, walking the line. Under the Nazis, she'd gone to the police to save her son from being sent off to camp. I imagine she pointed out he was her only living relative, and without him she'd be alone. He quit Prague the moment the war was over, leaving her there alone. Her husband was dead, her only son had gone, her country was in the hands of criminals. She was tough, that woman.

Dad and I had this conversation once, and never again.

When my father went to Sydney after the war, he became a super Jew. He joined synagogues, talked about Jews, mentioned Jews in every breath, read Jewish writers when he studied for his university entrance exams and all through his degree. However, the extent of his actual religious activity was to turn up on the High Holy Days and to sit around in coffee shops with Hungarians and Czechs, talking about how much better it was in the old countries.

When I was a little girl he took me to the synagogue, proudly. I dimly remember a gold and blue kaleidoscope way above me, and tiny women with big jewels and big hair, saying, 'Ent who iz zis?' in spoilt little-girl voices—who was this girl who was taking this man's attention? Dad beamed.

It seemed to me that the least I could do for my grandfather and my father was to support the Jewish community in Prague, to be part of it. The Spanish Synagogue was crying out for volunteers. With only a handful of us there to do anything I became part of their tiny community of helpers. Gradually I learned the shul's set of songs and stood up with Peter to lead everyone in singing along. If Peter was away, as he often was—raising money and visiting other synagogues in the Czech Republic and Slovakia, drumming up support for his latest project—then Anna led the service.

Anna was converting. Like me, she had a Jewish father and a non-Jewish mother; conversion was necessary before she could be accepted by the Jewish community. Unlike me, Anna had not opted for the reform, Jewish-lite version, which takes two years and you don't have to profess to believe that God literally parted the Dead Sea or handed Moses the twin tablets on the Mount. She was going for the full-on, Orthodox conversion, which takes five years and requires you to believe the whole fairytale and, furthermore, to demonstrate that you maintain a kosher household and diet. I had done rather well in my final exams—did I tell you that yet? I got 100 per cent in one exam, the highest score ever achieved at the Sydney shul, with all the blessings written out in perfect Hebrew as well as English. I got 98 per cent in the other exam to which my father, acculturating me further in the Jewish faith, said, 'What happened to the other two per cent?'

I did those exams the way I'd got through school—dumping everything into my short-term memory a week before the exam then dumping it all straight out again a week later, my brain having reviewed the files and decided I'd not use any of that information again. Consequently, I have only the most rudimentary knowledge of Jewish holidays, customs and blessings. Not so Anna, who was studying assiduously.

'Why are you taking the long way around when you only need to convert to reform?' I asked her. 'This is a reform shul.'

Anna looked slightly shifty. 'I would like to be able to attend the orthodox services.'

'So why don't you?

'I can't attend unless I've converted.'

'But you're convert-*ing*. Isn't that enough?'

Anna shuffled her feet. 'No, they are very strict.'

'So, you're doing all this work to join a club that won't have you yet? When this one accepts you and everyone likes you—including, incidentally, me?'

Anna gave up being defensive and said, 'Yes, well, you know how it is—of course I want to belong to the best club!'

And it is true that an odd thing about converts is they want to be part of the elite, and the elite make you work for it. I could remember debates among classmates—were we *real* Jews when we were converting to reform? Did that really count?

I had been happy with lazy conversion. I found the fundamentalist strands of the faith insulting to women and to most of the principles I hold dear. You know, respect and love for all, science, equality—the usually leftie grab-bag, I suppose.

Peter was there to lead the service maybe half the time. For the other half he was out in the community, a bundle of energy drumming up support. He was always losing secretaries, mainly because the pay and hours were rubbish and he himself was the most chaotic individual.

It took a while to get to know him because he was stretched so thin. But I have experience of volunteering and I know it's hard for people to believe that you really mean it and that you will reliably turn up. It was a few weeks after I joined that I finally managed to talk properly to Peter. We were at dinner with a handful of the Friday night volunteers when we got around to why I was in Prague, what I wanted and so on.

'How long have you been in Prague?' was the inevitable starter question.

'About three months.'

'And are you staying for long?'

'Yes, as a matter of fact, I live here now.' Most people were just passing through for a gap year or a short adventure.

'Did you come here with your husband?' Peter asked me. Astoundingly, I was always being asked this question.

It's amazing the number of people whose first thought upon meeting a travelling woman is that she must have followed her husband.

'No, I'm here alone.'

Peter's brows flew up. 'Really? That's unusual for a woman.'

'There are quite a few of us here.'

'Really? I wouldn't have thought it.'

After ascertaining I hadn't followed a husband's career to Prague, he asked, 'So, you are dating? You are looking for a husband, yes?' and before I could even answer that one, 'Does he have to be Jewish?'

I took my chance to say that yes, indeedy, I was looking for a partner, so that Peter would keep a weather eye out for me. 'And he doesn't have to be Jewish, no.'

'Probably just as well. You're a convert, aren't you? Most Jewish men will want an orthodox wife. Kids?'

The Czechs are famously blunt, and I was rather enjoying the full blast I was getting from Peter.

'No kids, no.'

'Why not? There's still time.'

'There is time, yes, but only just, and actually I'm not the mothering kind.'

'But would you have them if he wanted them?'

'I'd need to think about it . . . No.'

'You might change your mind.'

'I might, but I doubt it.'

Peter pondered that for a moment. 'That will make it harder to find you a husband.' And then he brightened. 'Still, you are not young, so he won't be young either and probably he will already have children.'

We wandered through the maze of what I did and did not want out of life, and then we got on to my life as a writer and administrator and I said again, 'You know, I really am keen to help out here. Is there anything else I can do apart from lead the service?'

Peter looked thoughtful. 'You're a writer, huh? So I guess your English is pretty good?'

'It's impeccable.'

Peter laughed. 'You have a big ego.'

'Not without reason.'

He grinned at me. 'Okay then, yes, there is something I need. Can you help me to write grant applications?'

I said that I could and that I'd had some experience of writing them both when applying for grants for myself (never successful) and when I'd had a job at a university in the research office.

And so began our partnership. Every Friday I went to Peter's office to help him draft letters to wealthy funders asking for grants for new projects or for them to update existing funding.

There's an art to applying for charitable grants and Peter was very, very good at it. The synagogue had three outreach arts projects on the go: a concert series, an art project aimed at schools to engage kids and teachers in creating art based on Jewish themes, and a series of debates. Peter was unbelievable at getting important people to come along to, say, a children's art exhibition, and then spinning that event out in every report we wrote. The mayor of Prague turned up to one of the debates and we shoved that into every 'Outcome' section of every report we ever wrote. Peter got musicians from India to one concert and we trumpeted that as 'international reach'.

This is what you have to do when you're begging for
money. You have to take every tiny advance and make the
most of it in the language the funders understand: Outcomes,
Effectiveness, Goals, Outreach, Strategy, and so on. Peter
scrambled and scrambled, magnifying any advantage we got,
no matter how minute, and sailing over the upsets, no matter
how near-fatal. Concert series had to be cancelled because
volunteers never materialised, important debaters—on whom
whole advertising campaigns had been run—would pull out
at the last minute, venues would cancel. All these things Peter
had to pretend hadn't happened while we wrote the glowing
reports and the importuning letters.

His own salary was paid for by the board, based far away
in the USA—apart from two board members who lived in
luxury on Pařížská. One of them was a doctor who made a
mint servicing the expat community and who had a young,
blonde, minked-up Czech wife. He only ever came to the
High Holy Day services and he didn't bow or read during the
Amidah. The other was a real estate agent, also accessorised
with a young, blonde minked-up Czech wife. His fortune had
come from property speculation and he was forever at the
shul haranguing Peter about what Peter should or shouldn't
be doing (without ever volunteering to do it himself), loudly
informing us that no Arab had ever contributed anything to
the world ('Algebra?' I wanted to say, but didn't) and quib-
bling over a 50-crown drink (about 3 dollars) on a shared bill
when we went out for Friday night dinner.

For his tiny salary, Peter was obliged to indulge both these
men in whatever whim occurred to them, which is why I
kept my mouth shut about the Arab Golden Age. The grants

covered not only the projects we undertook but also a few hours of secretarial support and the rent on his office.

Peter not only kept all these balls in the air, personally organising all the projects and doing all the outreach, but as leader he was at the beck and call of all the congregants. He sat through many cups of coffee with distraught people who didn't know whether they could continue on in the faith, with the desperately lonely, the religiously obsessed and the momentarily enthused. He would nod patiently, keeping his true feelings to himself. Throughout it all he continued on with his unstoppable energy.

Of course, his life had its advantages. He could wear what he liked to the office (more than once he'd be shouting outcomes to me from the next room, where he was shucking off his shorts and donning his suit for Friday prayers). He generated all the projects we did, so they were always something he was interested in. And in the end, as much as he had to flatter and cajole, sympathise and console, he was his own boss, creator of his own life and master of his own time.

Most importantly, the work he did was actually meaningful. People found their roots and religion through his projects. They discovered family histories nearly obliterated by war and oppression. Jewish and non-Jewish communities came to understand each other better. He and the priest from the Catholic church next door did event after event together, constantly banging the drumbeat of love and togetherness and mutual respect. In a world in which Nazi groups wanted to kill the Jews, the bowing and prestidigitation we did seemed more than worth it.

He and I got on amazingly and the only complaint I ever had was the agony of translating his enthusiastically fired-out Slovak/English dictation into meaningful, grammatical sentences, and finding synonyms for 'extreme' and 'successful'.

'This extremely successful project has been extremely successful five ways. First off . . . Why are you writing? Just listen to me, I have to tell you everything first and then we can write it.'

It was our first session together and Peter wasn't used to having any help on these grants.

'But if you say it all first then I'll forget it. Honestly, it's a lot easier if I write everything down as you're telling me and then we can work on it.'

'I need to start from the beginning. I need to say how it all is, yes? And then we can write. Writing is for after.'

I sighed and acquiesced. At the end of an hour of enthusiastic hand-waving, table-thumping and cries of 'This is an amazing project! Nothing like it has ever been seen before in whole of Czech Republic!', I said, 'Right, so what are the projected outcomes?'

'Just what I have been telling you!! This is a concert series unlike any other in the history of the Czech Republic. And Slovakia! Slovakia too, and Hungary! It is an international project. An amazing project.'

I held up a hand before he could repeat the entire tirade. 'Look, Peter, the trouble is that I need to write a couple of sentences, and I don't know which part of what you've just told me is the salient bit. Do you see what I mean?'

Peter thought for a bit. 'I see. I see. Okay, how about we do it your way and see.'

So this time I typed furiously as Peter spoke and, when he had spent too long on the theme of 'the most amazing project', I would say, 'Yes, but what is the *outcome*? The outcome, Peter!'

Because he spoke so fast and I had to type at top speed, I would end up with three pages looking like this: This exteremembly amamxing pofject is best in all of Czech repbucli never pbefor has beesn seen 20 people from sifdifferenct cutlrues like czehc gypsiy soflove hunafatrian jewish non-juewish acome totbet erther to teach children art and through art to find jewish cultuter. Some people finds tht athy have discovered juewsihs roots they never suspect but have kept hem quiet ecause of comun ism.

Which I would then spend hours changing to something like: One outcome of this project was to bring together a group of twenty people from different ethnic backgrounds: Czech, Slovak, Hungarian, Romany, both Jewish and non-Jewish, to teach children Jewish culture and themes through art. An unexpected outcome was that people whose Jewish heritage had been suppressed by their families during the war and the communist era discovered their Jewish roots.

Eventually, Peter learned not to just spend hours shouting at me about extremely amazing projects but to let me type while he was shouting at me, and we spent many happy hours together scraping small amounts of cash out of thin air.

9

I did not take an active part in any of the amazing projects, apart from attending the concerts and debates and the auction they held in the synagogue for the kids' art to raise a little more money. I felt that my volunteering duties had well and truly been fulfilled on my Friday afternoons and evenings.

The auction of the children's art was one of the first social outings Anna and I had together. For all her buzzing friendliness, Anna was surprisingly hard to get to know. We met a few times at synagogue and went with the others in the group for dinner afterwards but it was a few months before I could move Anna—whom I found fascinating—onto the next level of friendship.

Making friends is like dating. In this instance I was the keener party. Well, I was pretty much always the keener party, except among expats, owing to my lack of friends.

However, at dinner one Friday the subject of the auction came up and Anna turned to me and suggested we go together. I glowed and said yes. Not too quickly, I hope. But probably too quickly.

On the night of the auction we met at the pub. It was there that Anna really started to thaw. She and I each knew the other was single; in fact, it was the first subject that came up, no matter who I met. But as she opened up Anna began to tell me about her desire to have children, her longing to find a partner and about an affair that had just ended with, or so it sounded to me, an entirely unsuitable man.

'He already had children?' I asked. 'He didn't want any more? Sounds like that was a waste of your time, then.'

'Yes, but I loved him, and I am thirty-six. If I do not start soon, I may miss out on children.'

The poor woman was deeply troubled by her age and her desire for children. In Prague, women are slim and good homemakers; they like sex and get married early. They have affairs, and this is taken for granted, but that is because they do not expect to be crazy in love with their partners forever. They are a practical people, the Czechs.

Anna's problem was the stupendous size of her brain and her cosmopolitan outlook. She had travelled and she could write incomprehensible lengthy papers on abstruse ideas about the use of the future tense in the English language. It is difficult to find someone to suit you when you are quite so talented.

'You see, if something happens in the future, can you really say that it is going to happen? Is there therefore truly any such thing as the future tense? Is it not just a fiction?'

'Perhaps it is just a placeholder for the concept of the future.' I had a stab at what I thought might be a solution to this problem.

'Yes, perhaps,' she replied, nodding. Momentarily I felt quite brainy but then she launched into a further analysis of the problem, and I felt more bored than brainy.

And she had lived overseas, something not many Czechs of her age had done. Czech men love living at home—they do not want to move anywhere. Anna wanted the option of a life free to roam if the opportunity arose. Add to all this that her husband must be Jewish and her options narrowed quite considerably. For a Czech woman to be thirty-six and unmarried carried a social ignominy not seen in the West since 1952. And yet she found the men she dated unacceptable within minutes.

As for me, my loneliness was becoming the focal point of my life. I found myself longing for a partner, consumed by my isolation, by the lack of touch and warmth and love and chat. Being alone in a foreign country had intensified my loneliness to an almost unbearable degree. I was desperate to share the tiny events of the day with someone—anyone. I could find people to go out with, but what I needed was someone to stay in with, someone who would be with me without having to make arrangements. Someone to love. I found myself gazing on any man I met as a potential boyfriend, no matter how unlikely.

The discussion of her situation and mine required several pints of Staropramen, so by the time we were ready to leave for the auction we were moderately tanked. Although Czech, and therefore accustomed to beer, Anna was only slight and we'd had enough so that even she was weaving merrily as we found our place in the pews. I was staggering and glad of a seat.

We were both in tremendously good spirits. Anna and I had had one of those moments where you know you've found a soul mate. We'd talked easily and long about our most pressing and intimate problems. We'd shared her roll-your-own cigs, and discussed men, age, Jewishness, academic life, travelling, being a single woman and our desire for, and lack of, kids. We knew that, after this meeting, we would be in each other's lives for a long, long time. As we sat down we were full of love for all and fellow feeling.

The auction started and there was a short silence, so Anna put up her hand, wanting to get the thing going. Unfortunately, no-one else bid so within a minute she was the owner of a very pretty plate, painted by Jana Marková, aged six. Well and truly bottled, she started the bidding for the next one too, but luckily she'd broken the ice and she wasn't stuck with another plate.

Her joy in the occasion was infectious. Although I had no money at all, and certainly none to waste on items I didn't need, I stuck up my hand next and was fortunately outbid for a hand-embroidered yarmulke. Then we just went crazy and started bidding on everything, trying to earn the synagogue as much money as possible.

Bidding got quite heated over Item 27, a plate by Petra Evanová, aged 9, and suddenly I found that at 225 crowns the plate was going to be mine. Going once! Going twice! Sighing, I reached for my purse. But I was saved at the last second by someone prepared to pay 250 crowns for it, probably Petra's mother. Thank god!

'Did you want that plate?' cried Anna, her hand shooting up.

'No! Put your hand down!'

'I have 275.' A round of applause for the woman with her head in her hands. Luckily for my bank account, Petra's mother was prepared to pay the record price of 300 crowns—about 17 dollars.

Then Anna decided she wanted a bead necklace. Unfortunately, she didn't have her glasses on so she couldn't quite see the screen. I lent her mine, just in time for her to realise she'd bought the wrong necklace. So I told her, 'Don't worry, I've got some cash on me, I'll bid for the one you wanted.'

Two items later, her necklace came up, so I stuck up my hand. '50.'

. . . '60.'

Curses. I put up my hand again. '70.'

Then Anna put up her hand. '80.'

'Anna, what the fuck are you doing?'

'I'm bidding.'

'*I'm* bidding, you idiot! You're bidding me up!'

We left before we could go completely broke and resumed a riotous evening together, Anna taking me to a hole-in-the-wall pub she knew, where we drank beer after beer, smoked more rollies, ate Czech finger food and discussed life, the universe and everything. Anna told me that Czechs LOVE Australia because they think we're exotic.

She said that, under communism, *Skippy* was the only series from the West the communists allowed on television, and she and her friends had loved it.

'They probably thought it was so harmless—how could it possibly corrupt young minds?'

Anna roared with laughter. 'Yes! Australia is harmless. That is what you are! Ha ha ha! How wonderful to be harmless!'

I later looked up the Czech version of *Skippy* on YouTube and it's a hoot. All the voices were dubbed and the theme tune had different words.

Anna and I gave it a rousing chorus in the pub at two in the morning while neighbouring tables joined in at the tops of their voices, thus proving the show's immense popularity with the Czechs.

It was truly incredible how much Anna could drink. By the end of the evening I had reached that appalling state where the slightest movement made me want to lie down and stay very, very still. Yet on the tram home Anna chatted happily, seemingly barely affected by the vat-load of booze she had consumed.

I could barely lift a head, let alone answer and I was never more grateful than when she got off at her stop with a cheery '*Čau!*' and nausea-inducing bear hug. I staggered on home and collapsed into a coma.

————

Not long after I joined the synagogue I was sitting in a pew waiting for the service to begin when a tall, young blond man sat himself beside me. Deliberately. Wanting to strike up my acquaintance.

'Hello.'

I was startled. At first I thought he must be another lunatic and quickly prepared my arsenal of get-out techniques.

'Hi.' I tried to look reserved.

He held out his hand. 'I am Stanislav. And you are?'

'I am Rachael.'

'It is a pleasure to meet you, Rachael. You are new here, but I have seen you a few times.'

It was unbelievable, but there was no doubt about it—this handsome young man, who didn't seem to be a lunatic, was being charming to me. We chatted for some time, before and after the service. I told him that I was looking for a place to buy and he gave me his card.

'I am in banking. Let me know if I can help you.'

Briefly, I was floored. Everything about this conversation seemed to suggest that Stani was flirting with me, but he was so staggeringly young. Could it be? I left it for a couple of weeks, not sure what to make of it, and then one day a real estate agent was trying to explain something complicated that had something to do with one apartment building's finances. I couldn't figure it out and I was moodily cursing Czech housing complexity when it occurred to me that the person who might know about finance was the banker, Stani. So I called him. Diffidently, I have to say.

'Hi, Stani, ah . . . this is Rachael.'

Had he given me his number as a way of getting a date? How was this conversation going to pan out?

'Do you remember me? I hope you don't mind my calling you but I need help.'

'I wouldn't have given you my number if I didn't mean it,' replied Stani, baldly. 'What is the problem?'

I immediately felt comforted. This was no date call, he was just a guy who liked to help out. I told him what the real estate agent had said, and Stani said, 'Oh yes, I know what this is,' and went on to give me an explanation barely more understandable than the one I already had. No matter, I may not have gained any clarity on financing buildings, but I had gained another Czech friend.

Stani and I began to hang out together. If he was twenty-three, he was a day. We spent our time going to the movies and drinking beers, chatting of this and that, making up competitions to amuse ourselves while we drank, like who could name the most presidents of the United States. Stani almost invariably won these games. I kept thinking I should make up a game I could win for a change, but beer and pubs rather lend themselves to trivia and I'm not so great on that.

I could have won if we'd been discussing the real meaning of feminism in the modern world, but we never were. We had a surface relationship that nevertheless ran deep. I didn't quite get why Stani was spending so much time with me, but sometimes I got an inkling of something not quite right.

Peter said, 'That Stani is strange, isn't he?'

Was he? He seemed fine to me. I wondered if there was something I wasn't picking up due to the language difference. There are things that come through immediately if you are both speaking a shared native language.

Stani was a very nascent banker, and one of the new breed of young Czechs. He had spent a year in America during his studies and loved the West and all it contained. He came from a village in the far south of the Republic, where his entire family still lived. He was the only one who had made it to Prague, let alone out of the country. His boyhood had been spent tramping the woods with his brothers and eating his mother's dumplings. He still went home every second weekend.

His views on women were slightly strange. He had an inexplicable—to me—focus on looks and class and health. There was the touch of brood mare about his search for a girlfriend. He was working twelve-hour days and more in a Western bank and he had reached the stage where he was looking for the proto-wife. It seemed a bit early to me, but that's what it's like in Prague. You find a suitable life partner, settle down and prepare to have affairs.

While he fell in love frequently, he just as frequently, and for the most obscure reasons, would ditch the objects of his affection.

'She did not answer my texts,' he explained to me on one such occasion.

'Perhaps she was busy?'

'If she cared she would answer.'

'You've only be going out for two weeks.'

'I would never not answer her text.'

'What did you text her about?' Some context might help me understand the crime.

'I was asking her how her day was going.'

I thought about that one. 'And did she say why she didn't answer?'

'It does not matter. She does not care enough to answer.'

His girlfriends—all of them tall and blonde and healthy, with good jobs as lawyers, or studying (although one was ditched because 'She is not studying hard enough; she is not serious')—came and went like the rising and setting of the sun. It was no concern of mine. The subtleties of Stani's life were mired behind the language barrier and the age and culture gap. I just enjoyed his company and the moments of drama his life brought me.

10

Meanwhile, the agony of looking at flats continued unabated. I never really got why agents didn't turn up. At first I assumed it was because they'd not understood the date or time, or I'd not understood them, or that something was going wrong with the flow of broken Czech one way and over-formalised Czech the other way.

I changed my tactics, really nailing down the date and time in the conversation, saying it several different ways and getting an *ano* (yes) to each:

'Next Wednesday?'

'*Ano.*'

'The 22nd?'

'*Ano.*'

'St Peter's Day?'

'*Ano.*'

'At noon?'

'*Ano.*'

'12 pm, then.'

'*Ano, ano! Příští středu! 22. února! Den svatého Petra, v poledne!*'

'What?'

But when that didn't work, I began to think that in fact it was just that they didn't really get the concept of selling, even twenty years after the fall of communism. It just didn't seem to matter to them whether they sold or not. And when they did turn up, it didn't appear as though their clients cared if they sold or not either. Time after time in these dreadful, manky places I found myself wondering why they'd not even gone to the trouble of scrubbing the stains off the wall, let alone putting a bulb in the empty lighting sockets.

Why did I put myself through this pain? I had a place to live—my father's *panelák*—but what I wanted was to really be *living* in Prague, with a place of my own in a pre-war apartment building with an iron balustrade on the central staircase and elaborate tiles in the foyer. I didn't want to be stuck in the communist wastelands; I wanted to be right in the heart of Austro-Hungarian Prague, Coffee-House Prague, Havel-and-Hus Prague, Arty-Revolutionary-European Prague. My father's flat was made of concrete panels in Hopeless, Despairing, Crushed-Under-Stalin's-Boot Prague. I was going to be in my new life for ten years at least and I needed to be right in the heart of it even if living that dream meant living the nightmare first.

Complicating the search for a flat was my burgeoning heart. Although job and flat and community were occupying my attention, the extraordinary loneliness of freedom was beginning to cut into my heart and rub at my senses. I had been single for a very, very long time. I had had affairs and fallen in love, but nothing seemed to stick. It had gone on for so long that my family had given up even calling me 'picky' and now accepted that I was going to be the only one in the family who failed to get married. I had become a single-aunt fixture. This did not make me any less lonely.

And now, running free in my new country, my heart seemed to have gone completely crazy. I was falling in love with every man I saw. The real estate agents all spoke Czech, but two of them spoke English—one was a man who wore the Canadian flag on his lapel and another was of Cuban parentage. The Cuban's father had been able to come to Prague because he was from a communist country; he'd married a Czech woman.

This half-Cuban realtor was young and cute. I wondered if he found me strangely attractive, in an older woman sort of a way. He showed me a flat I had no interest in and told me it was overpriced. He warned me against looking in the cheaper parts of Žižkov—'Gypsies live there', which sounded fun and cool to me but which to Czechs meant dangerous and violent. I wondered if he had a girlfriend.

The one with the little Canadian flag was a hockey fan and he told me, in English, that he was also a fan of mine. For a minute I thought he was making a move, but then I saw his eyes look uncertain. I'm fairly sure he didn't mean to say 'I'm a fan of yours.' He probably meant to say, 'I'm a fan of your country', as everyone here is a fan of Australia. But we were in a flat that was at least a possibility, even though it had no bathroom, and I was remembering that I'd seen a lot of movies where the husband was having an affair with a real estate agent. There you were together, alone in a bedroom—it seemed so right. I wondered if I'd ever get to have an affair with a real estate agent, but the ones I met seemed not to have seen the same films as me, and none of them made a move.

The places I was looking at got smaller and smaller. I thought I needed fifty square metres, but anything that big in my price range was unrenovated. I considered the renovation option. I'm sure any writer braver than I was would have bought some dump, done it up and then written the hilarious tale of their renovation adventures with Czech tradesmen. But I just couldn't summon up sufficient courage or energy. I wanted to write another book, but there was only so much I was prepared to do to get funny material.

The first apartment I found that I actually liked was in Biskupcova, a street right on Tram 9 near an old cinema that showed *Casablanca* and sync-ed New York Metropolitan Opera nights. It was a forty-two square metre flat in a Functionalist building from the 1940s; square, plain, brown, and none too clean. The main door was covered in graffiti and the foyer was a miracle of grime and broken tiles. But there was something about this place—it had a certain tenement charm. The tiles might have been broken but they were original 1940s. The banister on the stairs was iron with green paint peeling off it.

When I walked into the flat, I knew I'd found a home. It just felt right. The sun shone in, it had an adorable entrance hall and two large rooms—one a kitchen/dining room and one a bedroom. Off the bedroom was an en suite with a bath.

The toilet was off the hall and had a hideous brass plate on its door—a small boy taking a wiz into a pot.

The owner was a strange, soft-bodied man with missing bottom teeth and about four hundred cats, so many of them crawling on him that he appeared to be wearing a moving fur coat. I managed not to fall in love with him, despite the overwhelming relief of finding a place I actually liked. The pipes had all been re-done, the lift was new, the roof had been re-tiled. These were the sorts of repairs that were going on all over Prague as Czech housing was brought up to EU standards (standards which included justice for gypsies, women's rights, dual carriageway roads and a whole lot of other things the EU would get when hell froze over). While I chatted with the guy I mentally ripped up the orange carpet to reveal the parquetry underneath, pictured myself in the bath, took down the pissing boy. I calculated I could live with the kitchen, which was tatty and ugly but not unliveable, at least until I became a world-famous author and got some money for renovations. I left with the agent, thoughtful.

Outside, I made him an offer, Sydney style. They were asking 2.1 million crowns (about 123,000 Australian dollars at the time). I offered 1.9 million. I pointed out all the flat's flaws and said it wasn't really what I wanted but that I'd stretch a point if they'd come down on the price. The agent, actually quite a nice fellow, said he'd ask the owner and we parted.

About a week went by and I heard nothing. I started to get nervous and despite my Sydney training I blinked first and called him.

'So, what did the owner say about my offer?'

'He didn't like the price.'

87

Silence. Surely he was going to continue.

More silence. Perhaps not.

'Well, would he like to make me a counter-offer?' I asked at last. What was the matter with these people?

'I will ask.'

Another week went by. I called again.

'The owner says the price is the last price.'

Okay, but why the agent did not call me to tell me this was beyond me. I upped my offer but, naturally, not to his asking price.

Another week went by. Trained as I was in Australian-style negotiation, I resisted as long as I could before finally calling again.

'I'm sorry, Mrs Weiss, but the flat is sold.'

After hanging up the phone I started to cry uncontrollably. It seemed that in the Czech market you do not negotiate, at least not if you're a foreigner. I had lost the only flat I'd wanted in four hellish months and I was facing another round of appalling phone calls.

Peter was very comforting. For a man who had a million things to do he managed to find time to listen to my problems on the Fridays we worked together.

'It's hard, yes? But you would not do this if it was not hard,' he counselled me. 'I remember California. It was hard, but it was an adventure. What would you do? Stay home? No! But it is hard.'

Yes, it was hard. It was taking a lot of deep breathing just to get through my days without turning to drugs or alcohol.

'But you will find something, yes? It will happen.'

I nodded miserably.

After the loss of Biskupcova Street I stopped looking for a couple of weeks. Despite my dogged, daily searching I still had no job and the panic was beginning to seep into me. Had I done something rash, just leaving Australia like that? Nothing seemed to be coming together. I was trying, trying, trying and kept hitting brick walls. A deep depression and even thoughts of suicide came to live with me. Day after day during that next couple of weeks I woke up to an ocean of despair. I became so sick of myself, I was past bearing it.

According to Shakespeare, sleep knits up the ravelled sleeve of care. Not my sleep. It knitted me a woolly jumper of dread and misery. Why did I have to wake up every morning in that state? *Another forty years of this? I don't think I can stand it.* Every morning I caught that thought and tried to turn myself into a Buddhist. *Ah, yes, Grasshopper, the Nothingness that Is.* Until one morning I was sick of even that thought. Who wants the Nothingness that Is? I want the Everythingness that Isn't. Why can't I have that? It sounds so much more appealing.

On that day I said to myself, 'Okay, I give you one more year of this and then you have permission to kill yourself.' And then I got out of bed and started looking again, for a flat and a job.

11

On the last Thursday in June, five months after arriving in Prague, I was reading through the job advertisements on expats.cz, my head in my hands. I was scrolling listlessly past all the ads for IT specialists at DHL and Monster, past the ads saying 'Use Your Languages at Work!', past the ads for Management Trainees and Office Juniors, past the ads for Telesales Consultant (Telesales Consultant! I'd rather starve first).

I scrolled past the endless ads for TEFL Certificate training, although I did pause to read how much one of those courses would cost and how long it would take. But the very idea of teaching English was so depressing. Was that why I had moved countries? To hang out with a lot of expats doing expat work? No, no and no, again I say no. No, I can't do it. I have to hang tough. I have to hold out.

Past the ads for Automotive Account Managers and Senior Business Consultants, my jawbone crunched into the palm of my hand, my fingers drumming on my cheekbone, trying to stay motivated. Past the ad that read 'Wanted. Writer. To write website content. Leisure and Tourism.'

My head shot up. For a moment I couldn't breathe.

Wanted. Writer.

Someone wanted me!

The rest of the ad said that they wanted someone with excellent English. Me! They wanted someone who had a proven track record of writing. Me again! They didn't need me to have a visa, they'd provide one. Woo hoo! They wanted someone who lived permanently in Prague. I'm here—here I am! There was no mention of needing to speak fluent Czech. And best of all (and I know this shouldn't count but somehow it did, it really did), the hotel had the most romantic name: At the Sign of the Three Bells. More than anything in the whole world I wanted to be a writer at a hotel in Prague called At the Sign of the Three Bells.

I sent in my CV with a heartfelt covering letter. I was naked with them. I told them that I really wanted the job, that it was the first job I'd seen that I actually wanted and not just one I'd applied for because I could do it. I told them I was resident in Prague and that I was here for good. I mentioned my forthcoming book (oh come on, how much more of a writer could I be?). I talked about my extensive (and illusory) editing work. I told them I looked forward to hearing from them soon.

And then I didn't hear from them for a week. A week. A week in which I prayed fervently to the God I didn't believe in. I was a committed atheist and yet I begged God to give me this job. I apologised for not believing in Him. I told Him that I didn't believe and that I never would but could He please, please, please give me this job anyway?

God made me sweat but at the end of that week I received an email from someone called Melissa Anderson from The Three Bells. All it said was, 'Thank you for your application. Can you please confirm that you are a permanent resident in Prague? This is a full-time position, not a contract position.'

This seemed slightly strange to me—I thought I'd already laid that question to rest—but I wrote back immediately to address this concern. Yes, I was living permanently in Prague. I did not have a residency permit yet but I was applying for one. (A complete lie—I was avoiding the whole business until Schengen became a reality.) I'd moved everything here and I was in the process of buying a flat. I had no intention of going anywhere. I was looking for a permanent position, not contract work.

I sent it off and waited. Another week went by. I agreed with God that, in the absence of belief, He really had no obligation to answer my prayers. When I had pretty much given up on The Three Bells and was looking once again at the TEFL courses 'just in case'—the phone rang.

I almost didn't answer it. The phone was only either real estate agents talking to me in incomprehensible Czech or my father wanting a report on how successful I was being in my new life. Both were stressful calls and I was depressed. But I answered it.

'*Prosím?*' (Hello?) *Please don't answer me in Czech.*

In a rather posh English accent, Oxbridge educated, a man introduced himself as Leonard from The Three Bells. Was this Rachael?

'Yes! Hello.'

'I have your CV. It's very impressive.'

I'm not a writer for nothing, you know. All my CVs are impressive, even the ones claiming I can do jobs I've never actually had. 'Thanks,' I said, 'I am very interested in this job.'

'How long have you been in Prague?'

'Five months.'

'And why did you come here?'

'I just decided to move here. I needed a change of life.'

'And are you staying?'

They seemed to be strangely stuck on this idea that I might be going somewhere. I had that Red Queen feeling—no matter how much I tried to persuade them that I was in Prague for good they couldn't be convinced. Was it something about me? Maybe deep inside, unknown to me, I had some premonition that I wasn't going to stay and this was conveying itself to others. The scary fact of the matter was that I had no choice but to stay. Having moved, I could hardly move back.

'Yes. Definitely. This is my home now. I'm looking to buy a place.'

There was silence on the other end of the phone as though Leonard were weighing up the sincerity in my voice. Finally (reluctantly, I thought), he said, 'Can you come in for an interview tomorrow?'

'*YES!*' *Don't sound desperate.* 'Yes. Yes I can.'

The next day, Friday, I put on a black skirt, thus indicating serious, business-like efficiency, and a bright red clingy top with white piping, thus indicating artistic creativity. It also revealed a lot of cleavage, always a help when you're being interviewed by a man.

'Too much cleavage?' I asked Stani.

'Perfect amount,' he assured me.

The Sign of the Three Bells was in Malá Strana, the ancient, cobblestoned part of Prague that huddles around the foot of the Castle. Its streets wind into tiny, crooked squares where sandstone staircases with rickety iron railings connect one street to another. There are red roofs with attic windows that catch the sun as it spills down to the river and the Charles Bridge from the Castle walls.

As I walked up Nerudova Street I thought of the offices that I'd been to recently, miserably applying for filing work or office administration—grey blocks in outlying, *panelák*-infested suburbs, miles away by bus. I didn't want to work there when I lived in beautiful Prague. I wanted to work in Malá Strana. Bustling, noisy, mazed Malá Strana with its oak doors built for the dwarves of the thirteenth century, its marble statues of Greek goddesses trailing fruit, its palaces converted into embassies, its bars and hotels. *Please, God, let me have this job.*

The Sign of the Three Bells was indeed at the sign of three bells. A wooden shingle, cracked and faded, hung slightly askew from an iron arm. The building was one of the shortest and thinnest on the street. It was made of grey stone, squashed between two ex-palaces, one with the most enormous statues guarding each side of the door—two men in togas clutching a discus each as if preparing to hurl them onto the street below. The pedestals they were standing on came all the way up to my waist so that from street level all I could see were giant feet, twisted up onto their toes and straining calf muscles. Who built these things? They were incredible.

A couple of shop workers were leaning on the pedestal having a cig in the mid-morning sun. I buzzed the bell.

'*Prosím?*' Yes, what do you want?'

'*Dobrý den. Jmenuju se Rachael. Mám schůzku se Leonardem.*' Good morning. My name is Rachael. I have a meeting with Leonard. And look! I speak Czech! See how much you want to hire me?

There was silence at the other end. Then the door clicked open.

I found myself in a long hall with a white architraved ceiling, a tiled floor and on the walls a couple of battered mail boxes and some framed sepia prints with watercolours washed through. It was quiet and cool, the street sounds muffled. *Oh, please give me this job.*

At the end of the hall was a staircase. After I'd wound around it three times it brought me face to face with one of the most magnificent doors I'd ever seen in my life. It had to be from the fifteenth century, it had to be. It was hugely thick oak, carved into squares, each square with an iron diamond in the centre.

This door opened up onto another hall at the end of which I could see an office. A printed sign on a white A4 sheet announced 'The Three Bells'. The office had wide double doors that were standing open to the hall.

I walked in, playing the part of the confident woman, and stood just inside the entrance. At first glance the room seemed to be packed to the ceiling with people. I stood watching and saw that in reality it was just a rather small room with six people sitting at computers, all talking at once, on the phone or to each other. The heaving room ignored me.

A black man was looking over the shoulder of one of the computer users, listening to him talking. He glanced around at me and then away again. He didn't look happy. Another contender for the job? Maybe.

A girl in knee-high socks, her purple hair pinned on one side with a butterfly clip, appraised me while she was on the phone. Then she too looked away when she saw me looking at her.

A harassed-looking man, sitting on a couch in the middle of the room and talking to a thickset young man standing in front of him, said in the same clipped English accent I had heard on the phone, 'But I don't understand what the problem is. I say it over and over again until I'm blue in the face. I can't understand why it's not being done.'

'Because it doesn't make sense!' said the younger man, his voice rising. 'We've tried it and it doesn't work.'

'Look, I just don't care. I don't care. I just don't have the strength! Just do it, just stop arguing and do it.'

There was a silence as the young man thought about saying something, then changed his mind. 'Fine. Fine.' And he stalked away to one of the computers.

The harassed man watched him go then looked around and saw I was standing there. 'Oh right, you're the writer.'

'Yes, I am.' Firm, yet friendly. My god, these interviews are minefields, aren't they? Every damn word and look is important.

He looked distracted. 'Yes, yes, right.' He stared into the distance for a bit. I kept a poker face.

Finally he came back to earth. 'Okay.' He jumped up and looked around at the people in the room. Everyone ignored him. 'Okay.' He slung a bag over his shoulder. 'Let's go upstairs.'

So I assumed this was Leonard. He marched at enormous speed out of the room, and I had to totter as fast as I could on my high heels. ('Too high, Stani?' 'Perfect.') Leonard took the stairs two at a time as I studied his rear view. He was wearing very creased fawn-coloured trousers and his bottom pointed towards me every time he lifted a leg to his chest. His hair was a mat of wild ginger and his bag flapped against his side in his haste. At the top of another round of stairs he took me into a kitchen and we sat at a wooden table, Leonard sweating slightly, me trying to seem cool and calm yet enthusiastic.

'So.' Leonard looked at me. I looked at him. Under the ginger hair, his rather lovely brown eyes were amused. 'So you live here?'

'Yes.'

'How long have you been here?'

'Five months.'

'And are you planning on staying?'

Good. Lord. Not. This. Again.

I swallowed my irritation and decided to play it firm.

'You know, Leonard,' I said, putting on my ever-so-slightly-English accent, 'I've been asked this question several times by this company and I don't know what more I can say to convince you. I moved everything here, I have nothing left in Australia and I am buying a flat here.'

Leonard let out a laugh and his face lit up. 'It's just that we've had a lot of people leave. And it's usually women who come here with their boyfriends and then he's unfaithful to her and she gets fed up and moves back to the States.' He paused. I didn't bite. No-one gets near my personal life if I don't want them there. 'So I need to be sure that you're going to stay.'

I gave him a smile in return. A reassuring smile. 'I'm staying.'

'Right, right. Well anyway, we have this project. It's . . . Do you know what page rank is?'

'Yes.'

'What is it?' Leonard said this very much as though he was expecting to catch me out.

Better luck next time, Leonard. 'It's the rank given to individual web pages.'

'And do you know how it works?'

I thought about this. 'No.'

'Right. Well, page rank works through a combination of referrals and content. Google has a complicated algorithm but basically what happens is that the more sites there are that refer to yours, the higher your page rank. But the sites that refer to your site have to be high quality. You can't, for instance, just copy content. Google takes points away for referring sites that repeat content. Do you follow?'

'Yes.' Actually, this was kind of interesting. I had no idea this was how it worked. Leonard started drawing me diagrams and explaining the intricacies of the Google page-rank system and the Alexis ranking, which apparently was also important. I was pretty impressed. He seemed to have worked this out all on his own.

'So, what I want you to do is to create a whole lot of high-quality websites, sites that other people would refer to so as to get their page rank up, do you follow me? Because referring sites need to have a high page rank, and we'll have all those sites pointing to the Three Bells site. This is a long-term project, maybe six months before we get any results, but I'm committed to it. If it works we'll create a whole portal.'

I wasn't sure what the difference was between a portal and a website but I decided I'd probably work it out eventually.

'Now.' Leonard smiled at me suddenly. 'My problem is writers. There are a lot of writers in Prague. I've had a lot of writers apply for this job. What I need is someone who can just get the content right and isn't going to spend a lot of time on poetic imagery.' Leonard paused. We were getting on quite well, probably because I hadn't said anything but had only indicated that I understood what he was saying. He spoke fast but I'd managed to keep up with most of it and he only seemed to need nodding. Here, though, I thought I'd better indicate that I knew how to do the job.

'Yes, I see how that would be a problem. You need facts and figures, and helpful information for tourists, not a lot of fluff about the mystical night draping the Charles Bridge in shrouds of history.'

Leonard grinned. So I'd got that right then. I could just imagine the trouble he might have had with writers in Prague—many could barely compose a sentence without the weight of the cobblestones and old palaces pressing in on them, demanding a sense of artistry few of us have. It was almost as if they felt that if they weren't using words no-one else had ever heard, or images of almost incomprehensible complexity and depth, that they weren't being real artists. Hence the proliferation of foreign writers and the paucity of any actual writing. Since I am a writer of light travel memoirs, the burden of artistic expectation never troubled me.

Leonard shot out of his chair and charged down the steps, shouting to me, 'Come and do a test.'

O . . . kay.

Back in the office, Leonard sat me at a computer.

'Now, what I want you to do is write a website on the Charles Bridge. You've got twenty minutes.'

'Uh. I'm pretty sure I can't write an entire website in twenty minutes.'

'No, well, see how you go. John can explain it to you. John!' The thickset man came over. 'Tell Rachael what she has to do.'

'What?'

'I have to go. I'll be back in twenty minutes.' And he rushed out.

John looked at me and sighed. I've been in a lot of corporate workplaces and I recognised the look on his face. It was the look of someone with an impossible boss—of someone who had been asked, yet again, to lead a project when he had no idea of what the goals or purpose or even tasks of the project were. It was a disgruntled look—a look that was searching for someone to blame, and it was falling on me.

I decided to get John on side. I gave him a sympathetic smile, deep understanding lurking in my eyes. 'You don't have any idea what I'm supposed to do, do you?'

Reluctantly, he smiled back: 'No.'

'That's okay, don't worry about it. I'm sure I can work it out.'

His face chameleoned rapidly through light and shadow. He was free! Or was he? Should he really let me just get on with it? What if I messed it up? Yes, he was free—he could always blame me if I got it wrong and Leonard got upset.

'Okay,' he said. 'Let me know if you need anything.' And he turned away, relieved of at least one annoying task.

It was one of those situations where it's so unworkable you don't even have time to panic. Twenty minutes to write a website? And the people who worked there didn't know what I had to do either? And I desperately wanted this job? Yeah, I was screwed.

Being screwed, I just didn't worry about it. Cheating furiously, I logged onto every site about the Charles Bridge I could find, paraphrased what they said, flung it into a Word document and put squares where I thought pictures might go, using the first thing I thought of as a caption. It was a dog's breakfast.

Leonard came back in exactly twenty minutes. 'So let's see what you've done. Ooh, a spelling mistake.'

'Yes, I was just about to correct it,' I lied.

Leonard read through. 'Hmm . . . uh-huh . . . Yes, yes . . . Alright, alright. Alright . . . Are you sure that's right?'

'Um . . .' *Am I sure? I did this in twenty minutes. What, you think I fact-checked?*

'No, well, never mind . . .' He kept reading. 'I don't think I would have put it like that . . . alright . . . uh-huh. Why is there a picture of the Judith Tower there?'

Because I just put anything in. Anything! 'Because I refer to it in the text.'

'So you do, so you do.'

He kept reading. 'Oh, I wouldn't have put it like that . . .' *I am so not getting this job.* 'Good, so why don't you start on Monday?'

And just like that I was employed.

12

Having fallen in love with the flat on Biskupcova I became fixated on that one street. Nothing else would do. It was at least a relief to narrow down my search to that one postage stamp of an area. The flats around there were reasonably plentiful, although they remained as manky as ever. I managed to see about four a week—I was getting better at communicating with real estate agents—but all of them were a no on first sight.

On the day I met Leonard and he gave me the job at The Three Bells, I had two flats I wanted to see in the afternoon. The first one was promising. The second was too small for me, only forty square metres, but I was giving it a go since it was off Biskupcova and two minutes from the Tram 9 stop and it looked quite pretty.

The first one, though, was the one I thought I might buy. It was on Biskupcova, the golden street, fifty square metres, well priced and renovated. It was on the third floor, high enough up that it would be quiet and private and get good light. Yes, this was the one for me. But unfortunately it was also one which the real estate agent felt not the slightest need to sell—he failed to turn up for my appointment and didn't answer my phone call asking where the hell he was.

I was too happy about my new job to do much more than sigh and move on. *I'll go see this other one. It'll be no good, but then I'm done for the week and I can go get a beer.*

I was early for the appointment, as I always was. I like to wander around for a bit, checking out the feel of the place. Zelenky-Hajského was a tiny street, its pavement pleasingly cobblestoned. The apartment building itself was an acceptably romantic 1930s block, recently painted yellow and in good nick. I'd rejected some flats on first sight of the block; if it wasn't cared for then the co-op board wasn't doing its job properly. This one, I could see, was well looked after. There was a Vietnamese mixed-goods store on the corner (*just like in Sydney!*) and a chemist a block down. It was quiet and peaceful. The flat was too small, though, and I was only looking at it because . . . well, I wasn't sure why, but I thought I might as well.

The real estate agent was on time for a change. He told me his name was Štěpán. A nice man, fair-haired and built like someone who'd played rugby at school and still hadn't realised that all that muscle was slowly turning to fat. He was about thirty, cheery and pleasant. He didn't have much English but he had enough so that between us we could figure out what was being said.

'This is good street,' he said. 'No gypsies.'

When real estate agents said things like this it always took a few seconds for the words to float down from the edge of my consciousness and for me to grasp their meaning. I was so unused to dislike of a race of people being openly, cheerfully, acceptably expressed that I needed time to find a place for it in my brain.

Štěpán unlocked the front door and the first thing I noticed was the foyer tiles: a 1930s terracotta styling of a dog. The next thing was the lift. This was a true gem—an old clanking thing that had accordion doors in black metal. It rose through the centre of the building with the stairs looping around it.

'Will be changed,' said Štěpán, apparently thinking that this was a bonus. 'Will be new.'

'I like it the way it is.'

Štěpán smiled. 'EU rules. Must be changed.'

The stairs had the lovely styling on the rails that the one in Biskupcova had had. Nothing had changed in this building since it was first installed. I really loved that. We clanked up in the lift.

At the fourth floor we stepped out into a small hallway and walked around. I could see that the old flats had been chopped in two (by the communists, for sure). Some had the original double doors, with double handles and a name plate. The unluckier ones had plywood single doors. Miss Beerová's—*mine*—had a double door. I gave an inward fist pump.

Štěpán rang the bell and immediately a young woman flung open the door and said, 'Miss Weiss? It is very nice to meet you' in halting English and with a shy smile. She had smooth black hair over a glowing face. She was dressed in a shapely tartan skirt and sweater and looked every bit like a young secretary with artistic flair. Her English, apart from that one sentence, was pretty much non-existent.

It didn't matter. We shook hands and I stepped into a tiled foyer, which was tiny but filled with light. In front of me were two doors—one led into a kitchen/dining room and the other into a bedroom/living room. At the end of each room I could see huge windows with light pouring in and a glimpse of roof tiles beyond. There were two doors on either side of the foyer.

'Bathroom,' said Miss Beerová, opening the one on the right.

'*Hezký*!' Gorgeous. It was cute and tiny, done out in white tiles with matte red tiles in a line along the wall and cream paint above. A minute washing machine snuggled between bath and toilet.

Miss Beerová beamed. 'I did,' she said, pointing to herself and then looking uncertainly at Štěpán. 'Did?'

He nodded approvingly, 'I did it.'

'Yes, I did *it*.'

'*Je to krásné*.' It is lovely.

Across from the bathroom was a smaller door with a large clunky key in it that had obviously been there since 1931 when the apartments were built. This was the door to a cupboard. I wanted that key to be mine. It had been there since before the war. I wanted to live with it.

The kitchen/dining room had a small gas stove and sink with two benches with two wooden cupboards above and below. The other room, the living room, had a bed in one corner. Eva had decorated her flat in an eclectic 1950s style, with a round yellow plastic TV and white walls painted with giant blue dots. It was light and airy and free. And completely, utterly charming. I stepped into the living room, took one look and turned around to Štěpán.

'How much did you say it was?'

'1.3 million crowns.'

'I'll take it.'

'What?'

'I love it. I'll take it.'

'But you only have been here ten minutes.'

'Ten minutes is enough. I'll take it.' I turned to Miss Beerová. 'Don't sell it to anyone else!'

Miss Beerová beamed. 'I do that. I see, I like!'

Štěpán looked stunned. 'Okay. I never see anything like this. You do not want to think about it? Okay. Okay then. We will do the contract. Okay.'

I left on a cloud. In one day, in the space of four hours, I'd got a job *and* a flat, and both of them were magical. I was a writer (of websites, to be sure, but still a writer) with a divinely charming flat with double doors and a foyer, an eighty-year-old key and a view of rooftops in the cool area of Žižkov, with the postcode of Prague 3—not 1 or 2, but not as far away as 9—right next to the best tram line in Prague. I was down the road from a cinema that showed experimental flicks and ran simultaneous events with the New York Metropolitan Opera.

Finally, *finally*, I would have a foothold in real life in Prague and it was a glamorous real life, it was a romantic real life, it was exactly what I'd imagined my life might be. Stani and I celebrated my success over a beer, even though I knew the actual purchasing of the flat would be a long process, involving a lot of stamps and officials. 'You know, that's the bit I really dread,' I confided to him. 'I'm not that great with bureaucracy at the best of times, but in Czech . . . Oy.'

'I will help you with this.'

'Oh no, I couldn't possibly ask it of you.'

'I will help you. Why do you not think I would help you?'

'But, Stani, surely you have better things to do with your time?'

'I will help you.'

He almost seemed offended that I was refusing his offer. I wondered if there was something peculiarly Western about my reluctance to put him to so much trouble. It seemed so above and beyond, but Stani was insistent. Perhaps this was a Czech thing and I was coming across as a bit mean by refusing. I didn't know. I stopped protesting.

'Stani, I would be so grateful to you if you would. You can't know what it would mean to have you there, just making sure that everything was going as it should be.'

'Of course. I am your friend. Of course I will do this for you. I will be your interpreter.'

I gazed at him in wonder. What a good friend this man was.

I received a contract from the real estate agents. Štěpán had struck me as a decent and trustworthy chap. He just had an air of pleasantness, an open face; he had a general sense about him of a man who gets on and does his job and then goes home to his wife and young family and gets on with being a good father. He didn't seem like a shark. I sent the contract to Stani, just to be sure that it was in fact a contract I was proposing to sign and to check that there was nothing in it that would cost me extra.

'I have changed something to make it more beneficial to you,' said Stani.

'Gosh really, what did you change?'

'There was a statement there about the time in which you had to pay the deposit and I made it more favourable to you.'

That seemed strange. Wasn't the timing of the deposit a standard matter? And anyway I was paying cash, so it didn't matter to me when I paid the deposit. However, I was too grateful to him to really consider whether it was normal or not. 'Thank you, Stani! I don't know where I'd be without you.'

Sometime later, Stani rejected another term of the contract. 'I have made it more favourable to you.'

He seemed very serious about this, but this time I did wonder if more favourability was really necessary. I wanted to say, 'Listen, old chap, as long as I'm paying no more than I have to, I'm just fine with a standard contract.' But I didn't want to seem churlish or ungrateful, and indeed I was very grateful for his dedication to my wellbeing.

The next time Stani asked for a change, Štěpán's agency refused. 'Oh well,' I said. 'You've done amazingly, so we're okay if they don't change this one.'

Had he done amazingly? I had no idea. I was totally in the dark about what he'd been doing, but the flat was still going to be mine and no disaster had happened.

We signed the papers at the real estate agency, but during that meeting a peculiar thing happened that I never quite got to the bottom of.

I hadn't seen Miss Beerová during the negotiations for the contract and when I arrived at the office I gave her an excited hello. We didn't have time to do much more than greet each other before we were in the office—me, Stani, Miss Beerová, Štěpán and another guy, who was either her lawyer or the agency's. It mattered nought to me who he was because as far as I was concerned this was a happy, easy meeting to sign the papers and crack the champagne. It was all in Czech so I did little other than try to practise my comprehension by listening. I didn't understand much of what was said and didn't expect to.

I did understand, however, a tight face. And that is what Štěpán had. Stani was talking. And talking and talking. He was waving the contract about.

At one point, Stani turned to me and said, 'I am telling them we are not satisfied they would not make the changes we wanted.'

What?

'Ah, Stani, you know I—'

But Stani was back to his stern talking. I heard Štěpán say, 'No, we will not change that.'

Stani breathed through his nose and leaned back. 'They are being difficult.'

At that moment I caught Miss Beerová's eye. She had seemed to me a very sweet woman, Miss Beerová. She looked like the kind who sees the good in all. I saw in her eyes a certain amount of dismay. An inkling that I may not be being represented entirely as I would have liked began to penetrate.

'You know, Stani, you have done wonders already. Why don't we just concede this one?' Whatever the fuck it was.

'I don't like it.'

'Well, we can't win 'em all. And you have been magnificent. I really am just happy to sign.'

Stani looked at the contract, his jaw clenched as though I were a capricious client. 'Very well, if that is what you want.'

'You know, it is,' I said. 'It really is.'

'Very well.' Stani turned to Štěpán and conceded the point.

Štěpán didn't look gratified. He looked as though he was glad to be at the end of an annoying conversation. I smiled at Miss Beerová. She smiled back, relieved. I think she realised I had no idea what was happening. I still have no idea but I have a horrible feeling, looking back, that Stani had taken a perfectly standard exchange of a standard real estate contract and had turned it into a drama.

There was one last hurdle to leap, however, a problem that had arisen with the co-op board, known as the *družstvo*. Apparently, the fact that I was not a Czech citizen meant that I was not acceptable to the *družstvo* under their regulations.

'They are not legally entitled to say that under EU law,' fumed Stani.

No, I'm sure they weren't, but they were saying it and what was I going to do? Sue them in The Hague? No. I talked to Eva about it. We had quickly stopped being Miss Weiss and Miss Beerová, and were now Rachael and Eva. Our conversations took place in English and Czech, with heavy use of dictionaries.

'Mr Konečný is very . . .' she searched for a word, 'precise?' She meant he was a stickler for doing things exactly right. 'He is good chairman.'

You could see that from the state of the block. However, it probably meant that Mr Konečný was not going to bend any rules.

110

'We will demand the *družstvo* change the rules,' announced Stani.

'That might take a long time, mightn't it?'

'Years.'

In the end we bought the flat in my father's name. Eva came up with this solution and negotiated it with Mr Konečný. He agreed, although it took her a few meetings and required a vast amount of paperwork from me, including my father's National ID card, his birth certificate, his passport, statements of his status in the Czech Republic (pensioner), documents proving ownership of his other flat, his mother's birth certificate and his tax returns for the last three years— all of it officially notarised and stamped. Luckily it didn't have to be transcribed by an official translator, which would have necessitated that translator's official stamp, so the paperwork was only half of what it might have been.

The final thing needed before we could complete the sale was Mr Konečný's signature. Eva took me to meet him and his deputy in their attic office on a Saturday at 7 pm. I dressed neatly and conservatively, pretending I was entirely respectable and signalling my worthiness to belong to the community of Zelenky-Hajského 10. The deputy was another woman, a Mrs Kohoutková. Eva, possibly sensing a cultural bridge for me to gap, said, 'I will talk. Okay?'

I picked up the hint. No Western forthrightness to be displayed in this meeting.

I nodded. 'Okay.'

We climbed the stairs to the attic room. On the way up, I noticed the door to a small communal balcony that looked onto a wild inner garden. Someone's washing was on the line on the balcony. Instinctively I sensed that whose washing went out there and when was a matter of fine social distinction and I resolved never to take the liberty.

Eva and I entered a small, concrete-floored room with a wooden school desk at the far end. Behind it sat two people. Mr Konečný was about sixty, with short white hair and a shirt buttoned to the neck. Mrs Kohoutková was younger, in her late forties, I'd have guessed, also neatly coiffed and carefully dressed but looking a lot less stern than Mr Konečný. She rose as we entered and came up to me to do the meet and greet with Eva. Miss Beerová, so nice to see you. And you, Mrs Kohoutková. Mrs Kohoutková, may I present Miss Weiss. Miss Weiss, this is Mrs Kohoutková. A pleasure, Miss Weiss. A pleasure, Mrs Kohoutková. Miss Weiss, this is Mr Konečný. Mr Konečný, may I present Miss Weiss. A pleasure, Mr Konečný. A pleasure, Miss Weiss.

Once all the handshaking and bowing had finished, Mr Konečný sat down again—he had not come out from behind the desk—and Eva, Mrs Kohoutková and I sat down after him. I took the chair that was a little back while the two Czech women sat demurely on the edge of their seats, knees pressed together, ankles crossed, Mrs Kohoutková on one side of him and Eva opposite. They leaned in solicitously to Mr Konečný and explained the situation, a conversation that I tried to follow. Miss Beerová would like to sell her flat to Miss Weiss. Miss Weiss is very respectable and has a Czech father. Of course, she will live in the flat, but the father will be the owner.

Mr Konečný looked very serious and annoyed and furrowed his brow; apparently there was a very great problem.

A very, very great problem. Eva and Mrs Kohoutková exchanged glances and then swung smoothly into Czech female action. Between them they assured and pleaded and explained and soothed until finally, after half an hour of this, with Mr Konečný looking by turns mollified and disgruntled, he deigned to nod and smile and say alright then, what was all the fuss about, of course we would sign.

And they did. And just like that, I owned a flat.

13

On my first day at The Sign of the Three Bells I was introduced to Christian John. His name was John but as there were two Johns and this one was a devout Christian and the other one not so much, 'We call this one Christian John and the other one Atheist John. That way we can tell them apart,' Leonard explained.

Christian John smiled wanly. He was only about twenty and primed to be polite—he was both small-town American and Christian, so he didn't have much choice.

Atheist John, also an American, was more of an entrepreneurial, impatient New Yorker type of American. I recognised him as the man who'd been given the task of telling me what to do during my interview test. He pointedly kept his back turned, typing ever more furiously, when Leonard—slightly nervously, I thought—glanced at him and said, 'Isn't that right? You're Atheist John because you're an atheist, aren't you?'

'Mmm,' said Atheist John, not stopping his typing.

'They seem to get on alright, though,' continued Leonard. 'Even though Christian John is a real Christian.'

Later on, Leonard said, 'Don't mind Atheist John. He's got an attitude problem.'

The job seemed strangely fun. Christian John and I had to create tourist websites. The idea was that these websites would all link back to the Three Bells site, and in this way the page rank would keep going up.

'This is a long-term project,' explained Leonard again. 'I expect returns in six months.' That seemed reasonable. And I'm good at long-term projects. I can plug doggedly away at something and get nothing for years, sure that the result is going to happen. It's a gift. Christian John had the air of a patient man too.

Christian John took care of the technical side, and I took care of the text and pictures and links. It all suited me so very well—I can't stand the technical side of anything but I didn't have to touch it. I was in Prague, writing tourist websites on Prague. I was in heaven. And they were going to get my visa for me too. And I was being paid cash.

'We'll get you a contract, but you can just start for now. I'll have Dita sort it out when she gets back.'

That seemed reasonable too. Dita was the manager at The Three Bells.

'What we're going to do is have specialist sites. So we'll have one on getting around Prague, and one on restaurants in Prague, and one on day trips, and—ooh ooh . . . we'll have

115

one on getting ripped off in Prague—you know, what to look out for and how to avoid being robbed. And do one on the Castle—better do that one first. Well, that's enough to be going on with for now. I'll be back in a couple of days to see how you get on.'

So Christian John and I started. Our first site was Getting Around Prague. This was a relatively easy matter of taking information about Prague airport off the Prague airport site, slightly rearranging it and putting it on our own. Since it included a great deal of taxi and train information, finding text was pretty easy. Christian John put together a banner and chose a font, I found some pictures and between us we put together a very nice little site.

From there, we moved on to the other sites. We had a few going at a time, while I collected information and he played with designs. We did the sights of Prague, beer halls, a beer tour of the country, main tourist sites outside of Prague—one on Karlsbad, one on Marienbad.

Leonard took very little notice of us, except for asking, 'How's it going?' and looking over my shoulder and saying, 'You can't put that taxi company in there—we use Prague Taxis and they won't be pleased if they see us advertising ABC.'

'But ABC is the only one that's not corrupt! We can't leave them out—they're also the only ones at the airport.'

'Hmm. Yes, yes, I suppose so.'

'Besides, they won't know this is our site, will they?'

Leonard brightened. 'No, they won't, will they? Maybe you should leave Prague Taxis out—make them more dependent on us.'

Christian John looked sideways at Leonard. He sometimes had trouble with Leonard's moral compass.

After a week, Leonard beckoned me out of the room. 'I want to talk to you.'

He took me upstairs to the garden outside the Mozart Rooms. All Leonard's apartments were named for romantic people who had had something to do with Prague, or at least the Austro-Hungarian Empire—the Mozart Rooms, the Battenburg Suite, the Leopold Apartments. The Mozart Rooms was a two-room apartment overlooking the cobbled street below with its own garden. Despite the fact that it was June, the height of the tourist season and warm and sunny, the garden was very rarely used and was frequently free for feckless employees—the Ukrainian cleaners, the American phone operators, me—to go for a quick cig and respite from the hotel.

Leonard sat me down at the wooden table.

He glanced at me from under his floppy hair and gave me the buttoned-up smile my nephew gives me when he wants to share a joke he heard on the playground. I was beginning to seriously like Leonard.

'Now I've got something to put to you,' he said. 'And I don't want you to think it's too weird.'

'Okay.'

'You can't tell anyone else about this. This has to be strictly between us.'

'Okay.'

'It's not that there's anything shady, it's just that it's one of my other businesses and I don't like my employees knowing too much about my business dealings. It's none of their business. Okay?'

'Okay.'

'But there's nothing wrong.' Leonard searched my face. I kept it still.

'How would you like to work for me in another capacity?'

'Sure,' I said. And I did want to. I liked this Leonard. He was odd but he was fun and he was full of vitality, something I sorely needed in my life.

'The thing is it's a bit strange and you may not like it.' And he did things that were a bit strange. I liked that too.

'Try me,' I smiled at him.

He laughed. 'I have this business which I've had for quite a while. I write horoscopes for magazines, lots of magazines around the world. It's really rather good money. The thing is that I can't keep doing it on my own. You have to keep track of who's got theirs, some are weekly and some monthly, and you have to be careful not to write the same thing each month.' Leonard stopped talking and chewed his lip. 'It's really quite annoying. They get so precious about it too, if they happen to get one that's the same as the last time. And then you have to keep an eye on the invoices—it can be six months before they finally pay up. Anyway,'—he shook himself back to the present and away from these bitter reflections on magazine editors—'I want to hand it on to someone else. It's quite easy really.'

'Okay.'

'I've written a programme, quite a simple programme really. Here, I'll show you.' Leonard enthusiastically pulled a pad from his bag and swivelled around to sit next to me, drawing on the paper and talking at me. 'You see all you have to do is put your comments into categories. So—Romance,

Work, Family, Personality, see? And then I have some stock phrases: "You have been feeling misunderstood recently", "A strange coincidence has brought back an old memory", and so on.'

Leonard carried on with the enthusiasm of a genius scientist with Asperger's. He tended to spit as he talked, foam flecks forming and leaping, and I nudged out of their way as I saw them coming. His nylon shirts smelled faintly strange—a sour smell, not exactly sweat and not exactly not sweat. Not exactly pleasant. Definitely no wife watching his laundry habits. The flat shiny bottom on his nylon trousers was a frying pan of wrinkles, always.

I began to wonder if Leonard really was a genius. He was certainly very smart and very, very frenetic. He was forever rushing into the office, barking out his dissatisfaction and then rushing out, crying, 'I haven't got time for this!' I felt a faint stirring of attraction despite the odd smell and the spittle.

'Now the thing to remember,' Leonard was saying, 'is that people love to be flattered. Something like "You are being undervalued at work and at home. A break may be in order" always goes down well. You'll need to adjust it for the time, of course—monthly and weekly. Oh, we've got one daily as well. Now, you do need to know about the planets and what they mean.'

'Mean?'

'Yes, the planets all have meanings. Venus—that's love of course. Mars is war and conflict—use Mars for masculine things. Pluto is a good one—that's for things that are underground, and it usually means a foreboding or a portent.

So you have to be careful. You can't say "Pluto is rising in Cancer, so Cancerians can look forward to love"—that would be ridiculous.'

We caught each other's eye and exploded into laughter.

'No, no,' I said, wiping my eyes. 'You wouldn't want to say anything that didn't make sense.'

And so it came about that I became a horoscope writer. And a syndicated horoscope writer at that. My first syndication! Bizarrely, one of the papers he serviced was *The Geelong Advertiser*, so my sterling words were being published in Australia, all the way from Prague. All looked very rosy with the world indeed.

I really loved being a horoscope writer and for a few weeks I enjoyed saying, 'I write horoscopes' to people at parties when they asked me what I did. I had seriously underestimated the status that horoscopes hold in people's minds, and I'm just talking about the magazine horoscopes. At one party I told a guy about my horoscope job—a guy with a PhD.

'You do the charts?' he asked.

'No, I make it up.'

'But you need to know the charts, right?'

Pause.

'No. I make it up.'

'Seriously??'

There was a long, long pause while I tried to compute 'has PhD' plus 'thinks horoscopes are real' and failed to make these two things compatible.

'Seriously.'

'You know,' he said, 'I bet lots of those astrologers just make it up.'

In the end I had to stop telling people what I did for a living because it upset them too much when I told them it was all invented. I began to see that astrologers are like magicians—people don't want to know how it's done.

14

In those first months I kept a close eye on the expat social scene, looking for groups that were both interesting to me and filled with people who were long-term stayers, rather than short-term expats. I had noticed that there was a local group of Hash House Harriers—they're a running group who say they're drinkers with a running problem, which was quite amusing, but I ummed and ahhed about contacting them for a few weeks. I'd known of this group in Sydney too, where incredibly fit, lycra-clad young consultants would run from pub to pub, sculling a beer at every one. I hesitated about joining in Prague at the age of forty. I'd been up for it once but now, not so much.

A nice glass of wine in a comfy chair had become my speed. A very comfy chair. Preferably an armchair in someone's home. The ideal for me is a coterie of delightful, witty, lazy friends—people who like to hang out in their pyjamas, watching films and talking. Although I love hiking, and restaurants are fun, the criterion for me is ease—expending the least amount of effort in order to be with the like-minded. Running at full speed in gym gear from one pub to the next, getting progressively drunker then having to run drunk does not qualify as easy.

But when you're out to make friends you have to do things you don't want to do. I had to force myself to get out and mingle, even if it meant wearing lycra to do it. I emailed the local Hash leader and said I was more of a walker than a runner, and not terribly fit, and asked if that would be okay in his group. 'hello rachael, yes that will be fine! hardly anyone runs lol so you'll fit right in. J,' was his response.

This sounded more promising and some of my dread lifted. The runs took place all over Prague and the first one started at a train station, which would be easy.

On the designated afternoon I got to the station and looked around for the runners. There were some people hanging about looking like a group waiting to become a bigger group. Some of them had trainers on and one of them, a fattish man, had a clipboard. Could this really be them? The fattish man, spotting me coming towards them looking uncertain, raised his hand.

'Rachael?'

Yes, this was them. My dread disappeared altogether. A couple of young men were wearing the skin-tight crotch-grabbers and Nikes. The rest were middle-aged women and distinctly chubby middle-aged men, all in jeans. The leader of the Harriers, a younger, blond man, was cute and alone. I wondered if he was single. He introduced me to everyone (I forgot all their names instantly) and told me how it worked. The idea of the HHH is that a 'hare' lays a trail the day before, leaving clues in flour (that had been the job of the man with the clipboard). The rest of the runners find the trail, which must end in a pub.

The Czech version was a bit easier than the Sydney version—there was a pub stop in the middle where you did, indeed, have to scull a pint, but that was the only one before the end.

The bouncy young men (and one young woman) streaked off at the starter's whistle and the rest trailed behind. A woman in high heels chucked away her cig end and strolled in their wake. Now this I really admired. Here was I, fretting because I might not be sufficiently keen and fit, and here was she, smoking and in heels. You go, girl.

As it turned out, most of the group ambled along chatting amiably. Indeed, the pace was so slow that I, a brisk hiker, found myself restlessly walking ahead, thinking that if I went that slowly I'd probably fall over. The super-keen ones ran ahead, shouting 'On! On!' when they found a trail. They were running, and so left the walkers far behind. I, being one of the fast walkers, found myself getting to the flour signs first and having to interpret them. This I would do by saying something like 'I think we need to go left'.

I'd done that a couple of times when an American voice behind me said, 'I don't hear "On! On!", Rachael. That's what you have to say when you figure out a clue.'

I turned around to reply to her, a slight woman with greying chestnut hair and smiling blue eyes. 'I don't think I can say "On! On!" Can't I just say, "We go this way."?'

'Nope, 'fraid not. Gotta say "On! On!" And ya gotta say it like you mean it.'

At the next flour sign I gave a small yelp 'On! On!'

'Attagirl!'

Two hours after the start of the walk—and after only a mile or so—we congregated in a pub in the middle of a forest. I'd been waiting for the slow walkers to catch up at each of the flour signs so I wouldn't get separated from the group. I came into the clearing where the smiling woman, Marion, was standing with the high-heels wearer, who was lighting up another cig.

'Come sit with us,' said Marion. The smoker was Tanya.

They were lovely. Tanya sloshed back a full beer but Marion had water, thus letting me off the social hook. I can't walk and drink, it just gives me a headache.

At the time of this first run, I was still looking for a flat. I was soon to find Zelenky-Hajského, but I didn't know it then. I had just lost the first flat and was bemoaning the difficulties to Marion and Tanya.

'I have a real estate business,' said Marion.

'Really?'

'Really. We have lots of flats. I could see if I can find you one.'

I was flooded with relief. 'I'd love that!'

'Now, I think I have a card in here somewhere,' Marion rummaged about in her bag. 'Let's see . . . oh here, this is it.'

She gave me a glossy card. I glanced at it and laughed.

'That's okay. I know who you are, and you've got nothing I can afford.' It was the card for Svoboda & Williams, the classiest real estate agency in town. They had made their fortune on their reputation. In a town where customer service was a concept unknown before 1989 and only dimly recognised since, Svoboda & Williams had imported American customer-service values (thanks to Marion, the Williams in the picture, as I found out) and was sweeping the field clean. The field, that is, of wealthy, company-sponsored expats who could afford giant apartments in the centre of town with a view of the Castle and/or river. In my long search for a suitable flat, I had been stuck with the Czech real estate agencies. I had occasionally looked longingly at the Svoboda & Williams site, with their luxuriously purple web pages, but they hadn't been of any conceivable use to me—they never did have anything I could afford. Marion had started by renting out just one flat. She'd built up a fantastic business.

Tanya was a property developer. Both of them seemed deeply impressive. They had real jobs and real apartments in the middle of town.

Talking to them, I thought not only 'Yes, these are the real stayers' but also 'These are the women I want to be.' They were assured and successful, charming and friendly.

At the end of the walk, all the runners and walkers congregated at a bar, where we drank and sang Hash House Harrier songs. The HHH songs were of the bawdy kind, involving exaggerated winking references to Dick! and Cock! After the bawdy songs came the drinking games. The leader, instead of appearing cute, was now appearing tedious and I noticed he ran to fat. I did wait until the end, and joined in the drinking games, but I made one beer last rather than using one scull for each game. Increasingly I realised this was not going to be my scene.

At the end of the evening, I said goodbye to Marion and Tanya and walked away, a tiny bit dispirited. And then a voice shouted behind me, 'Rachael!' I turned to find Marion hurrying up to me.

'Say, do you play Scrabble?'

'Do I? You're looking at the 1996 fourth place in the New South Wales Scrabble Tournament. I have a trophy to prove it.'

'Ooh, a trophy—Tanya's going to love playing with you.'

And that's how my Scrabble group came together. It was exactly what I required in friends.

Tanya's apartment was the most fantastic thing I'd ever seen. It was in an ex-palace, now converted to gloriously high-ceilinged apartments. From both her balconies, Tanya enjoyed a picture-framed view of the Castle and looked down onto cobbled streets and red-tiled roofs. The apartment itself, which seemed to be endless, was filled with antiques she'd picked up for a song in the early days, when Czechs had embraced IKEA as a breath of fresh air from the West. In a frenzy of rejection of the old regimes that had so stifled them, they'd turfed out all their old furniture, which they'd had since the mid-nineteenth century, for the modern and new. Happy days for cashed-up Americans escaping from the capitalist regime that was so stifling them.

Marion and Tanya were single, rich and free; they were fulfilled in their jobs. Here were two really impressive women. Our first Scrabble game was succeeded by a second and a third.

A few weeks later, I stopped going to the Hash House Harriers. The seemingly unattached leader wasn't interesting enough to endure the drinking games and songs about Dick and Cock, and the walks were too sedate for me, although one or two did show me bits of Prague I'd never have seen otherwise. I might have stuck it out, but the ritual drinking afterwards—ritual and compulsory, as it turned out—and the ritual drinking songs that went with it, as well as the crushingly sexual nicknames we all had to be given, seemed all too much.

I did try sneaking off before the walk finished, with mixed results. The insult to the group was made clear in ways I can't quite put my finger on—perhaps it was the slightly brittle ribbing about it the next time I turned up. And there was the persistent, *in*sistent joshing. Refusing to wear a cup on my head and sing 'I have to go down on him' (or something of that ilk) was simply not an option.

I left before they could give me a nickname that I just knew was also going to be unpleasant to wear. The leader's spurned ex was in the group and not too happy about other unattached women joining. I gave the Harriers away, satisfied that I'd collected the best of the group—Marion and Tanya and Zsuzsa, their Hungarian embassy friend. ('Too many Zs, I know! Even for Hungarians it is too many Zs!')

The thing about this group of people was the quality of life they had. Zsuzsa was a career embassy employee. Not a diplomat, but a high-level functionary who had spent fifteen years living all over the world, courtesy of the Hungarian government. She'd been posted to the Middle East, Africa, Europe. Her house was filled with Namibian statues, Turkish carpets, broad-weave cushion covers from Morocco, a giant sofa from Germany, a round bed. ('Impossible to get sheets, darling, but so lovely.') Her apartment, which Marion had found for her, was in one of the streets in Vinohrady named after a country or great city—Americká, Římská (Rome), Italská, Belgická—and that denoted immense wealth. Well, reasonably immense wealth.

Through my Scrabblers I met others, mostly American, who lived in vast, carpet-hushed apartments on Pařížská. These people really were incredibly wealthy; all their money had been made during the first heady days when communism opened up to capitalism, when the Czechs had no idea how to go about entering the free-market world and needed lawyers to tell them what to do. Lawyers who now commanded a view of the Old Town Square from two floors of antique-filled ex-palace.

It was with Zsuzsa that I had an illuminating discussion. We were talking about corruption. 'It is unknown in Hungary,' she said. 'Not like it is here in Česko.' This was the local name we all used so we didn't have to keep saying 'The Czech Republic', which gets wearing after the first five times you say it, and unspeakable after the first one hundred. 'Here, you pay for everything, but in Hungary, corruption has been wiped out.'

'It's the same in Australia,' I said. 'We have the occasional bout of corruption, but then there's a royal commission and everything settles back down. It's not endemic like it is here. The idea of paying a policeman if you're stopped in your car— it'd be ridiculous.'

'You don't pay the police?' She sounded astonished.

'No. You do?'

'Of course we do.' Zsuzsa looked incredulous. What was I, an idiot? 'You always pay if you are stopped.'

'But you said corruption had been wiped out.'

'It has,' said Zsuzsa. 'We still pay the police, though.'

The Australian idea of a corruption-less state—the idea that you pay no-one and that public servants are paid to do a job and just do it—is still novel and astounding to the ex-communist countries. The idea that there's a police force that doesn't stop your car in order to be paid cash, which you will have conveniently in your glove box for just this occasion, is so outside Zsuzsa's world view that she can say 'Corruption has been wiped out' while reaching for the glove box, uniform-clad wrist at her window.

There were many times in Prague when I was proud to be Australian, and this was one of them. We may have occasional periods of police corruption and brutality but we're shocked by them. And when the inevitable official inquiry uncovers the bloody truth, our editors keep it on the front pages for month after month, every grim detail, until we've stamped it out.

———•———

I began regular Scrabble evenings with Tanya and Zsuzsa, who took turns hosting, providing insanely delightful food—delicacies bought from the most expensive shops in Prague, the only places where the food matched up to Western standards of quality and variety.

Zsuzsa was brilliant at cooking. She'd once had a catering business on the side, and had thought of leaving the diplomatic service and going out on her own. 'But catering, it's so dull really. I love to cook, but I don't want to be bothered with all that. The bar mitzvahs, the weddings. It's too much stress.'

But her time with us did have an end date. After three years she would have to move again. It was a condition of her job that she couldn't stay in the one place. It had been hard on her in some respects. She was now forty-five.

'And I notice the difference. When I was twenty, plenty of people wanted to be friends with me. When I got to forty, not so many. It's harder to socialise, to make friends in new places. You're not so attractive after forty.'

There had been one or two lovers, but when she had moved they had stayed. That sort of life really only worked if you started out with a husband and he was prepared to come with you everywhere you went. Otherwise you were alone, and getting older.

The subject of men and singleness came up first with me and Zsuzsa. Tanya wanted a man too, but she took longer to admit it to me. Marion, it turned out, had been married and was quite happy never to be so again. It seemed like the world of women over forty was mainly divided into two groups: those who never got married and would have liked to, and those who had been married and were relieved not to be any more. Of course, there were the few who'd married lovely partners at twenty-five and were still married, but they appeared to live in a different world, a paradise untram-melled by the fear and loneliness that accompanied me day by day.

Zsuzsa and Tanya and Marion and I played Scrabble, ate gourmet home-cooked meals, went out to dinner, drank far too much red wine, smoked cigs (well, that was me and Tanya, and I only smoked OPs—Other People's), talked about our personal lives, and became friends.

Despite my fourth place in the 1996 New South Wales Scrabble Tournament, I was beaten—regularly, comprehensively and undeniably—by Zsuzsa. I used to grind my teeth as the games reached their conclusion, with Zsuzsa homing in on me and edging me off the board, narrowly but surely. This was a woman whose second language—no wait, whose third language—was English. The second was German. Oh, and French.

15

Christian John was a lovely fellow to work with, a real sweetheart. We tried to stay out of the bookings and customer-service area, where Leonard's peculiar demands created chaos and stress.

Leonard was a combination of mad and charming. He had the most extraordinary beliefs, and not the slightest sense that they were in any way unusual. There was a hotel incident book in which the customer-service people had to write up any problems that occurred so the folks doing the next shift would know about it. On one occasion, a Thai couple had turned up and claimed to have made a booking. They weren't in the system and the hotel was full. The couple were very annoyed and expressed it. Amanda, the purple-haired receptionist, had suggested to Leonard that she try to get them a room at Jana's hotel across the street. But Leonard had taken against them and said he didn't believe they'd booked and sent them away. Amanda wrote in the book 'Leonard said he wasn't going to help them because he doesn't like Thais'. Leonard wrote underneath, '*THIS ISN'T TRUE*. It's the *Chinese* I don't like! Thais are fine.'

I became more and more drawn in to the hotel side of the business, though, despite my best efforts to steer clear. On one occasion, The Three Bells was in the grip of a plague of fruit flies, which had got into the guests' rooms. Leonard, a fanatical vegan and animal lover, refused to let Dita kill them and demanded she wave them out the window. When a guest complained and insisted we use insecticide, Leonard said he'd kill the guest rather than a fruit fly.

Dita was in tears. 'What can I do? Mr Gunther keeps calling me!'

'How about I go up and see what the situation is?' I said, because years as an administrator have made me good with people and complaints.

I came back down in ten minutes. 'All sorted.'

'Wow, really? What did you do?'

'I killed them, of course. Christ . . .' Christian John winced. 'Sorry, John. Don't listen to Leonard. This is a paying guest. It's ludicrous.'

Dita had just returned from sick leave, but she didn't look well and kept having to go back to her doctor. She seemed to have some mysterious pain in her stomach that was excruciating and getting worse, not better. She worried herself sick over Leonard's demands which were, quite frankly, insane. In the chaos, I asked her about my visa.

'Leonard said he'd get you a visa? He didn't say that to me.'

'Well, could you check it out, please? I need to get one now that Schengen is coming in.'

I'd been forced into taking notice of the new rules around Schengen. My efforts to become an editor had all been thwarted because no-one would hire me without a *živno*. The *živno*, it turned out, was a register you had to get on before you could get your visa. You'd register as a worker, then you could get your visa and then you were sorted. Employers (and Leonard was one of them) insisted on employing foreigners as contractors so they could get out of having to pay their employee tax and health insurance. The trouble for me was that both processes, the getting on the *živnostenský* list (getting your *živno*) and the subsequent receiving of the visa (which only lasted a year but was still considered long-term), involved incredibly complex paperwork, all in Czech and all very expensive. I needed Dita, who spoke Czech and had a deep understanding of Czech bureaucracy, to figure it all out for me.

'Okay,' said Dita, not really paying attention. She was distracted by Leonard's latest scheme—a vegan restaurant servicing the hotel.

'So, we're going to give them a vegan breakfast?' Christian John asked. 'What is that, exactly?'

Atheist John exploded. 'People aren't going to think a vegan breakfast is "breakfast included". They expect eggs at the very least, certainly butter and milk. I mean, *JESUS CHRIST*!' Christian John flinched. 'Could he not have a vegetarian restaurant?? Does everything have to be so insane?'

'So you'll check about the visa?' I asked Dita again.

She looked harassed. 'How about you find out what is needed.'

135

I sighed. The very thing I didn't want to do. Find out how to get a fucking visa in Czech. 'Right, right.'

'I just don't understand what he wants,' Dita muttered. 'What does this mean? "Find the Risbach invoices". What is Risbach?'

'Who is Risbach, maybe?'

Dita kept staring at the invoices, her eyebrows knitted, pain written on her every feature. I returned to my desk.

I kept up my best efforts not to have anything to do with the guests. This was mainly because Leonard had a lot to do with the people who *did* have something to do with the guests, and the atmosphere around them was palpably tense. There was a rapidly rotating field of customer-service personnel. I hadn't been there a week before two people left after a screaming match with Leonard right in the middle of the office.

He seemed inordinately suspicious, Leonard. He liked me, so more than once I'd be coming up the stairs at work and I'd hear a 'Hsss' above me and look up to see him waving a frantic, secretive arm.

He was doing this one morning, a couple of months after I started.

'Come up here,' he hissed.

'What?' I said.

'SHHHHH!' bellowed Leonard, followed by 'Come up here!' in a hoarse whisper. I went past the front door of the office and saw Amanda glancing my way. She winked. When I got up to Leonard, he grabbed my elbow and dragged me out into the garden.

'Come here where they can't hear us. I don't want anyone to know something's going on. It upsets the staff.'

The Ukrainian cleaners looked at us out of the window above, curious. Being his most vulnerable employees, they kept a close eye on Leonard's behaviour, always watching for danger signals. Their relationship to him was more intimate than the rest of ours—and perhaps because they had fewer options, he trusted them more. Leonard had twelve cats living with him, animals he loved more than any human being. The Ukrainian cleaners were the only people who were allowed into his apartment, where their job was not to clean but to feed his cats and make sure they were comfortable when he was at work.

Leonard's jaw worked. 'Atheist John is selling customers to Jana,' he said.

'What?' Jana owned a rival hotel across the road. Hers operated the same as Leonard's—she had a couple of houses full of apartments that she let out like hotel rooms. Sometimes, it was true, our guests ended up at Jana's and she didn't bother telling them they were at the wrong hotel. And occasionally we did the same to her. But selling customers? That seemed an order of magnitude further along the organised crime continuum than seemed credible.

'Atheist John. He's slippery. You can't trust him. I happen to know he's been selling our customer details to Jana. He thinks I don't know, but I do.'

'Gosh, are you sure? He seems so committed to things working well here.'

'He's got an attitude problem.'

'But he's working so hard in the restaurant.'

This was true. Against all the odds, Atheist John had been making the vegan breakfast work with the hotel's guests. He had a New Yorker's ability to make a vegan restaurant seem cool and virtuous. He had ordered special breads and spreads; he had money to spend, because Leonard's idea was that the restaurant was a way of collecting information on customer satisfaction.

But Atheist John had his own problems, mostly with Leonard. 'He keeps coming in each morning and sitting right next to people,' he told me one day, 'demanding they tell him what they liked or didn't like about the hotel.'

'He doesn't!'

'He does,' Atheist John continued. 'If he'd just *STAY AWAY* I could run the place. Oh, ha ha ha, I didn't tell you, he wants the girls to force guests to fill in satisfaction cards. I said people really don't want to in the morning over their breakfast. But he insisted. He reads them all. If they mention one tiny thing wrong, he's yelling and upset. Yesterday we got one that said, "It was all great, apart from the annoying manager who insisted on interrupting our breakfast." Didn't hear a peep out of him on that. I loved that one.'

Atheist John and Leonard had been fighting constantly. However, up until now, it had seemed nothing more than a battle of two strong wills. But I'd noticed that lately Leonard had become increasingly upset. At one of our secret garden meetings, he'd said, almost crying he was so wound up, 'He has to understand who's boss. I'm boss.'

'He is very forthright,' I said, diplomatically, soothing, 'but he has the hotel's best interest at heart. I just think he's an American and a New Yorker and this is how they express themselves.'

Today, however, their conflict seemed to have reached a

critical juncture. Leonard's eyes glittered in battle triumph. 'I've got him now. All I need is the evidence. He's been stealing from me.'

I sensed the end of the road for diplomacy and instead said, 'Well, I'm very sorry if that turns out to be true . . .'

'Oh, it's true alright!'

'He really does work so hard.'

'Yes—hard at stealing! He hates me and he can't wait to do me over.'

I wondered if Leonard had a streak of paranoia.

From there it all happened very fast. Within minutes, it seemed, I was back at my workstation and Leonard was screaming at John, and John was white and grim. And then John was gone.

Leonard, sweaty, eyelid twitching, snatched up his battered leather satchel and flicked his eyes around the office—at me and Christian John and Amanda, all of us pretending to be glued to our screens. The shrieked accusations of theft and the outraged American's innocence had been apparently unheard in our concentration on our bookings and search for information on beer festivals.

Out of the corner of my eye I caught Leonard's awkward pose. His self-justification was at the ready, should anyone demand it. We didn't. Then he stalked from the room, his satchel bouncing off his bottom.

Later, in the garden, while I caught the occasional flash of a Ukrainian cleaner's eye coming at me out of the window of the Mozart Rooms, Leonard told me, 'He was a good worker, John, but he had an attitude problem. He thought he could get one over on me. Americans.'

Seeing as John was now gone and there was no saving him, I decided not to stand on principle. 'Yes, yes, oh well . . .' I tried to sound non-committal, and didn't feel too cowardly and unprincipled. I needed Leonard's good will.

16

Once I'd moved into my flat, the problem of furnishing it became urgent. I slept on my camping mat in a sleeping bag for a while. On the wooden floor. I decided that only beautiful things should enter my home; after having spent the first half of my life amid creaking, badly painted IKEA bookshelves, and forks with hideous plastic handles, I knew I wanted a complete change.

I knew that the secret was not to say, 'I'll get these ugly chairs in the interim, while I keep an eye out for something more elegant', because the eye becomes used to dingy furniture.

For several weeks I lived in my empty apartment, paralysed by my need to get beautiful things. Anna took me to antique shops, where I bought a battered leather-topped desk in dark wood, a 1960s repro. Some may turn their noses up at this but although I wanted beautiful things, I didn't need authentic. I'm not that mad. Besides, I had no money anymore.

I had bought a washing machine, but that was easy—I'd been able to do it over the net. When the movers came to install it, and saw the size of the space they had to squeeze it into, they baulked.

One of them said, 'So small!' They looked at each other.

The other one said, hoping I'd get the hint, 'We may not be able to get it in.'

Since I knew it fitted, I metaphorically put a hand in the small of his back and urged him forward to the job.

The first one sucked on his teeth. 'I don't think we can do it,' he said. I only really caught 'can't' in Czech, but that and his tooth-sucking were backed up by a pair of eyes that said, 'If I stand here and complain, and look as if it can't be done, she won't make me'.

Fools. Little did they know who they were dealing with. I waited patiently, smiling and inexorable, until they decided that whining wasn't going to work, so they'd better get on with it. They managed to get it in but not quite up to the wall and then they decided that lifting it was something they could definitely say was impossible. So they didn't, and I conceded. I could live with it not perfectly flush.

Marion lent me a single wooden bed with a rubber mattress when she saw my camping mat. Even though it was a top-of-the-line thermal camping mat, it was super narrow and not the most cosy sleep I'd ever had.

I had a couple of pots and pans I'd brought from Australia, but as I had ditched the white plastic cutlery with its white plastic stand, I had no eating implements. My first trawl of antique stores failed to reveal any knives and forks, but I did find a delightful set of silver teaspoons, engraved with someone else's initials. It's amazing how long you can survive with just teaspoons to cook with. I became quite adept at using them to make stir fries.

I really wanted an antique bed, but it turns out they're a pain in the neck. The springs are pre-modern technology and horrible. No matter how wedded you are to the ancient, with a bed you should be grateful for technology. I rejected one rusty bedstead after another as they leant upright in dark corners of antique store basements, and then Anna told me that modern mattresses don't fit them anyway, so I got an iron bed from IKEA. Then came the saga of the mattress.

I am particular about mattresses. I couldn't just get a cheap IKEA mattress because I need the highest quality. For me, a comfortable night is the difference between a happy and a miserable life and I will pay anything for a mattress that will give me a decent sleep. I wandered around town for a bit, looking for a bed shop, but nothing materialised. Following my success with the washing machine, I tried to find a mattress store near me online but none of them translated their websites into English and I couldn't tell where they were or whether they even sold what I needed.

Buying anything is exhausting work. I bought an iron from an electrical goods store in the centre of the city. Later, I thought I'd practise my Czech by reading the instructions. There was a page of the stuff and it took me ten laborious minutes to translate the first sentence. It wasn't anything useful like 'Use this setting for silk' or 'Use water for this setting', but 'Do not touch the metal plate of the iron while the iron is on.' This was followed by 'Do not immerse the iron in water while the iron is plugged in'.

A certain sense of futility—more than the ordinary sense of fruitlessness in struggling over a language that only ten million people speak—came over me. Not only was it not telling me anything, I was getting irritated by the vacuity of the instructions. At this rate it would take six months before I got to anything useful like 'This button is for steam'. I played with it and, as I do with all appliances, ultimately used one setting for everything.

So I was immensely grateful to Anna when she found me a mattress store in my neighbourhood that appeared to specialise in high-end beds. I went there one Friday.

The shop was on a main road off my little tree-lined avenue. On this main road there was an Erotic City, of course, and on every block a dingy pub. There were second-hand electrical stores and what appeared to be a wholesale cheese seller, specialising in Dutch cheese. It was as though the street, as a shopping street, was straining to come to life—it was shooting up buds here and there, some that browned into porn shops and some that tried desperately to become exotic blooms.

The mattress store had a modest front but was surprisingly lavish inside. Beds were set out so as to display the different mattress types and sizes, and the different bed suites they had for sale—all rather nicely done in wood and iron. I already had my bed, so I had to disappoint the very lovely sales lady, who was thin and middle-aged and wearing a cardigan. I didn't want a bed; I wanted a mattress. She didn't speak a lot of English, but by this time I could speak moderate Czech. Not great Czech, but I had a few opposing adjectives down—hard, soft; wide, narrow; high, low—just enough vocabulary and ability to string a sentence together to buy a mattress with the aid of the brochures she could point to.

Mattresses are made from various materials. I had already spurned the memory-foam crap, a fad that will last as long as futons did. At the end of our days, all of us will end up in physio for our bad backs and cricked necks, or on anti-depressants— not because anything's wrong with us, but because we haven't had a decent kip in years. We'll wonder what on earth we were thinking about when we paid vast amounts of money for that memory-foam snake-oil. *Plus ça change.*

I am proud to say that the thin lovely lady and I managed to discuss my contempt for foam and my adamant loyalty to ensembles and traditional mattresses (*tradiční matrace*, so not that hard, but you'd be surprised how confused she'd have got if I'd said just one letter of an ending wrong, *tradične matraci*, for instance). We then moved on to exactly what sort of mattress I would like. She opened up booklets and explained how the different materials made it harder or softer and we discussed the size I would need—a small double to fit into my tiny apartment.

I lay on one bed and then another, and then the first one again. She served another customer and left me to it. In the end, I knew which materials I wanted in the mattress, and had the brand down, but I needed to go home and measure the space to make sure I was getting the right size.

'Okay,' she said. 'We are open all weekend.'

In the end, I never made it back that weekend. It was summer and much time must be spent in the beer gardens in summer, until late into the light, warm, welcoming nights with all the other gentle drunks in Prague. It was a week later before I got back to the mattress shop. To my disappointment, the thin lady with whom I had bonded on the subject of quality mattress material wasn't there.

A young, blond man was there instead. My heart sank. I almost left to come back another day, but the thought of going another night on the camp bed kept me strong. Perhaps it would be okay.

'*Mluvíte anglicky?*' Do you speak English?

He did not. However, he told me this by giving me a charming, boyish smile and holding his thumb and forefinger close together, 'Little, little.'

I twinkled back at him. '*To je v pořádku. Mluvím trochu.*' It's okay, I speak a little.

Conducting the entire conversation in Czech wasn't going to be easy but on the other hand I knew which mattress I wanted, so I didn't really have to say that much, and anyway he was nice. He wasn't a surly, bitter Czech, he was a young one, in a clean shirt, crisp even. Young and clean-shaven, nice haircut, rather pleased with himself. I imagined him with a pretty wife, or several girlfriends (no, a wife; there's a ring). He looked like a young man who'd left school and not gone to university, but was going to make a go of being a bed salesman. He had salesman written all over him. I liked him.

But now, if I was committed to buying this bed in Czech, I needed to concentrate hard. I turned over my opening Czech sentence in my head, and then, satisfied I had it about right, said,

'*Chtěla bych si koupit matraci.*' I would like to buy a mattress.

146

'*Máme mnoho matrací*,' he said, indicating the shop with a sweep of his hand and grinning at me. We have something-something mattresses . . . *mnoho*? Many, perhaps? Yes! We have many mattresses.

I looked up at him, startled out of my frowning concentration on Czech vocabulary. He was looking at me, giving me a teasing smile. Oh, he was making a joke! How sweet! I ask for a mattress and he looks around and says, in effect, 'Yup, mattresses we got.'

I smiled back, then screwed up my eyes to churn out the next sentence: '*Ráda bych tuto matraci*.' I would like this mattress.

'*To je velmi dobrá matrace*,' he said, approvingly. This is a very good mattress. '*Potřebujete postel stejné velikosti?*' Do you need a bed something-something-or-other?

'*Ne, nepotřebuji postel. Jen matraci*.' No, I don't need a bed. Just a mattress.

Ooh. Some of that even flowed off my tongue. I felt quite chuffed. Could this be easy?

'*Už jste se dívala na některé z pěnových matrací?*' he asked.

No, it couldn't. He saw the look of blank panic and incomprehension in my eyes and smiled again. '*To nevadi. Tato matrace?*' Never mind. This mattress?

I sighed with relief. 'Yes, this mattress,' I said in Czech as we continued to battle on with simpler sentences.

'Good.'

'I have one question.'

'Sure!' He really was lovely, this guy. Always smiling, such a lovely manner.

'I don't know if I need the . . . the . . . the . . . small . . . mattress or the medium mattress.' *Dang, I'm pretty sure I*

147

mixed up my endings there. Oh well. I took a breath. 'Small mattress . . . looks . . . very small.' I did some more mental translation, word by word. *'Je to dvojí? Vypadá to jako jeden.'* Is it a double? It looks like a single.

'To je dvojítá.' It is a double.

The trouble with the small double is that it looked really, really small. It was hard to believe you could really get two people onto it, but apparently lots of Czech couples had the small doubles—we were all squished into such small spaces.

My own flat was hardly going to take anything bigger without flinging me out the window if I turned over too fast, but could I fit another person in there? It seemed unlikely. Moot point anyway, said a bitter voice inside me, but still one must plan for a happy future, no matter how unlikely it looked.

He broke into my contemplation. 'May I ask you a question?'

'Sure.'

'Mohu se zeptat, spíte sama?' Something-something to sleep something . . . *sama?* . . . Now what's *'sama'* again? Alone! *Sama* means alone! Hey I understand this! Something-something sleep alone. *Wait . . . What? . . . Do I sleep alone?*

'Uh . . . uh . . .' I began. But should he be asking me that? 'Uh . . . yeah . . .'

'It's just that . . .' And he continued in Czech that I only barely followed; well I didn't really follow at all. But he was explaining something about the way the mattress was designed and his face looked quite scientific, and anyway the Czechs ask those sorts of questions all the time without blinking— they take mixed saunas together, for god's sake. So I decided that his question must have been alright. Perfectly legitimate conversation to have in a mattress shop.

'Oh, I see,' I nodded sagely, as though I'd followed every word. 'Yes, perhaps it is enough.' Although some part of me thought *Shouldn't I at least live in hope? If I buy this small bed, perhaps the universe will give up on finding me anyone. Shouldn't I buy a big bed—one that invites companionship? Oh shut up! Get the small bed. You can get a small lover to follow.*

'Your Czech is very good,' he said, in Czech.

That was kind of him. And untrue. But it was getting better.

'Thanks.'

'It's hard, Czech. Not many people speak it. Do you live here?'

'Yes, I . . .' And we entered into a relatively easy conversation—one I'd had a few times, so I could do it quite smoothly. Where was I from? How long would I be here? Had he learnt English at school? Did I like the beer? What did I think of the country? It was very pleasant. Easy conversations were easy until they got hard—the moment my stock of opposing adjectives and entry visa questions ran out, and we were beyond such pleasantries as 'I like dark beer' and 'Where does your sister live?'

But I was saved at this point by the clink of the door. The young, blond man excused himself and went off to see to another customer and I lay down on the mattress to make sure I really did like it.

When he came back, I told him that I had chosen this mattress last Friday.

'Are you sure were here last Friday?' he asked.

It seemed an odd question. Had I misunderstood him? Why wouldn't I be sure? I'd been there last Friday, hadn't I? Perhaps it was Saturday . . . No, no I'm sure it was Friday. Oh lordy, had he just used a colloquialism, using the word for 'sure' which meant something entirely different? Have I reached the limit of my Czech and now it's going to be all misery and *çěřďšňňž* from here on in?

'Yes, I'm sure,' I said, uncertainly.

'It's just that I was here on Friday and I'd have remembered you.'

Hey, that was a really long sentence and I understood it! *Was I here on Friday? No I guess it must have been Saturday, if he was here on Friday. Oh well.*

'I will definitely buy this mattress,' I said, pleased that all this Czech was going so well.

We went over to his desk and he showed me the mattress brochure so I could see the catalogue number and be sure I was getting the right one. He really was a terribly thoughtful guy. I imagined he must be one of those guys who had a pretty young wife. He seemed to be someone whose life would always work out.

He started to take my details.

'What's your name?'

'Rachael.' Well, that's quite an easy one.

'That's a pretty name.'

'Thanks!' Gosh, I still understand him.

It was only when I was leaving the shop and noticed a faintly puzzled look in the guy's eyes . . . It was only as I was standing outside, as the door clicked to . . . that it all suddenly fell into place. *He was flirting with me! And I'd missed it!* I put my hand on the door . . . But no. Sometimes when you've missed it, you've missed it.

I began to hope he'd deliver the mattress himself. When I wrote my horoscopes that week for Cancer (me), I wrote: 'A chance encounter could develop into the excitement you have been craving.'

17

Within a few months my work with Leonard became pretty much anything Leonard wanted me to do. Shortly after I started on the horoscopes, he commanded me to hire a photographer. He had run an ad and then couldn't be bothered wading through the responses, so he told me to do it. He wanted someone to come and take professional shots of the hotel rooms.

'What's wrong with the ones we already have?'

'They're *terrible*,' squealed Leonard. 'They're the worst.'

'They look alright to me.'

'Are you mad? We can't go on with them the way they are.'

'So what do you want me to do?'

'Just choose a few of the best photographers and give me a list. I'll interview them next week.'

'Uh. Okay. So . . . what are you looking for?'

'You'll know it when you see it,' said Leonard, impatiently. 'Anyone can do it. Just pick the best.'

'Okay.' I'd learned by now not to claim that I wasn't an expert. Leonard liked to say 'Anyone can do it' and then criticise everyone who did anything and state, while sighing loudly, that he'd just have to do it himself.

I started flipping through the applications. I really had no idea what was a good photo and what wasn't, so in the end I just organised them all into portfolios of printed-out material to let Leonard choose.

There was only one I thought about omitting—an Englishman who'd included pictures of half-naked women, with more than a faint suggestion of bondage. I'm not against being leather-clad for a night on the town, but I query whether it's entirely appropriate to include your soft porn shots in an application for real-estate work. It seemed creepy. There was something about his whole portfolio that made my skin crawl. But I left him in and regretted it when Leonard decided he was one of the best.

'You don't think the naked-chick shots are kinda spooky?' I queried.

'Don't be so judgemental,' said the most judgemental guy on Earth, outraged. 'It would be illegal to exclude him because of your feminist biases.' He pursed his lips primly.

I grinned at him. 'Okay, if you say so.'

Four photographers were invited to come and take test shots, including the creepy English guy, Don. I wasn't there when he arrived so it was Dita who took him to the Oak Room for his test run. When I got into the office later, she said, 'You're not really going to hire that guy, are you?'

She was looking appalled. He'd apparently stared down her cleavage and asked her to go up to the room with him. When she showed him the way, he tried to get her to come and pose in the picture, saying it would add realism.

Dita and I shivered, and I mentally struck him off the list. I told Leonard what he'd done and even Leonard agreed it might be a bit much to hire him.

Don sent his photos and, thinking I should at least let Leonard see them, I wrote the following email:

'Leonard, this is the horrible Englishman, but you might like his photos.'

And then, in one of those regrettable moments so beloved of comedy writers, I hit Reply instead of Forward.

I owned up straight away to Leonard. It was just as well, because the horrible Englishman then sent a very stiff (and, I was pleased to note, barely literate) email to him demanding an explanation and signing himself off as 'The one who was at least professional.'

Leonard shouted at me, but I soothed him and wrote a draft reply, apologising for any hurt or distress caused and agreeing that I'd been rude. I was rather proud of my response—it apologised without committing us to seeing him again and made it clear, without actually saying so, that there would be no subsequent interview. A bit of a literary masterpiece, I thought.

So I was the tiniest bit surprised when Leonard cried, 'Oh, no, no, this is no good!'

'Why not?'

'Because it doesn't say why you thought he was horrible.'

Sometimes he left me utterly clueless as to his inner

workings. 'Leonard, I'm fairly sure he doesn't want to know why I think he's horrible.'

'Of course he does. Now listen, I've written my own response: "Dear Don, I am very sorry that Rachael was so rude to you. Dita said that you were very charming and she was quite bewildered as to why Rachael would be so horrible. Rachael is an extreme feminist and can be very caustic about men sometimes. I think she might have been attracted to you and then upset when you weren't attracted to her."'

I *begged* him to send it. And indeed he did, but only after he decided to leave out the bit about me being attracted to Don, because 'He might not believe that, what do you think?' I agreed that Don might find that a bit far-fetched.

However, I might have given Don too much credit because he wrote back to Leonard agreeing that feminists were difficult but he'd still consider the job. Leonard wrote back saying that I was more difficult than most, was twice-divorced and had attacked my last husband with a screwdriver when I discovered he was having an affair, so perhaps we'd better let it go.

It was episodes like this that kept my heart interested in Leonard, even though his unsuitability was more extreme than most. He showed no interest in women, except in the most puerile, misogynist way. He became hysterical when crossed, even with the most minor infractions, and developed instant and implacable hatreds for people, his employees most of all. He was forever conniving and scheming to do other people down and saw people working against him wherever he looked, yet he failed to connect these two things. And yet he was super smart, and hilarious with it when he was in a good mood. I had the upper hand with him because I just pulled out my Australian-ness whenever he got out of control, giving him a bit of a grin and getting on with whatever I was doing. But in the back of my mind I had a sense that one day my time would come. It had to.

He turned on everyone else, so why not me? He smelled strange and he didn't wash his clothes and he spat when he got excited, which was most of the time. I found the thought of sex with him repulsive, and yet I *still* dreamed of us together, in a teenage, hair-twisting kind of a way. My loneliness was a problem I didn't seem to be able to control.

18

Until my first trip to Prague, I'd never seen anything like a European autumn. Prague is a tremendously green place and slowly, very slowly, the trees turn to gold and red. The red is really extraordinary. I had no idea a green tree could turn so completely into its polar opposite. I watched the change from my window, from where I could see entire hills changing colour.

Hiking in this weather is beautiful. The change is so slow that you can see the first leaf turning—a green tree with just one gold leaf. I found myself very touched by those leaves, the first ones to go. How do they decide that they're the ones who will have to take the plunge and start the change? Do they change colour, then nervously look around to see if the rest are following? I would—I'd be sweating on it.

It's such a slow process that there'd be at least a couple of days when that first leaf, glowing gold all on its own, is thinking, 'Uh-oh. It *is* October, right?' It was beautiful, but cold. *Nine* degrees Celsius. Curses, curses, and I was *freezing*.

Autumn brought with it the Jewish High Holy Days, my first at the Spanish Synagogue. The High Holy Days are the pinnacle of the Jewish religious calendar. There is a ten-day period of rituals, the peak of which is Yom Kippur, or the Day of Atonement, when we apologise to God for all the wrongs of the past year.

Given that Jews apologise only once a year, while Catholics have to do it every week, the Day of Atonement is appropriately dramatic. You have to abstain from all food and drink for twenty-four hours; you don't wash and you stand in shul for most of that time, reading through sections of the Old Testament. There are five back-to-back services, all involving a lot of sermons, mournful singing, praying, standing in silence and reflecting on our bad behaviour. We are *really* sorry.

During my days studying to convert I had given the fasting a go several times and failed. You're not supposed to have water but I just couldn't come at that. What I usually did was agree not to eat during the day. The no washing didn't stand a chance. I'm a two-shower-a-day person with a healthy respect for germs. There was no way I was apologising with greasy hair.

Everyone, but *everyone*, goes to Temple on Yom Kippur. Even my father goes every year. It's the time of the year when a small congregation of six, like ours, can turn magically into hundreds. The Spanish Synagogue was packed. Peter knew almost all the attendees because he regularly pressed many of them for contacts, references, time and donations.

Peter valiantly conducted most of the five services but for Yom Kippur what is required is a rabbi. There's no getting away from it—if you're a practising shul, no matter how small, you need a rabbi for the High Holy Days. The rabbi mentioned in the ad I'd first seen for the Spanish Synagogue, Rabbi Morton Narrowe, had long gone. I never quite got to the bottom of what had happened with him but by the time I got there he was history.

Anna told me that the year before they'd found a great rabbi and occasionally he came back from the States to give an inspiring sermon. Unfortunately, this year he'd been snaffled by some other impecunious shul. So Peter had scoured his address book and come up with a retired rabbi who had agreed to help us out.

I was quite looking forward to a stirring Yom Kippur sermon. It's usually the pinnacle of a rabbi's speaking calendar, an occasion when he can break out his poetic best, a time for profound and moving oration, rousing speeches exploring universal themes and reflecting on the deepest aspects of our humanity . . .

You know those occasions when a speaker begins, and you think, 'Hmm, this is a bit under-rehearsed, but not too bad,' and then, gradually, it gets worse and worse until you're gripping your seat in embarrassment? This was one of those occasions.

The elderly rabbi started by saying he was going to talk about the great change the Jewish people have undergone from being warriors (in the Roman Empire—hard to believe, I know) to thinkers; and I'm thinking, 'Yes, this is good. He's going to talk about the Gaza pull-out, and quite rightly too.'

He carried on about the Jews as warriors for a while—quite a while actually, and not very coherently. There was a nice young man simultaneously translating the sermon into Czech, a process that rather unfortunately highlighted its rambling aspects. Anna might have cut out some of the repetition and half-sentences, but her replacement wasn't as linguistically skilled, so he translated every word as the rabbi said things such as:

'The Jews were great warriors, yes very great, very great warriors, with swords and tridents and they were particularly skilled with tridents, not many people know that. They were very skilled, very skilled indeed with tridents. Yes, skilled, skilled and strong. The Jews were the bravest soldiers in the Roman Empire and tridents were the main skill and Caesar had Jewish soldiers because of their very great skill as soldiers.'

We were all waiting for him to get to the bit where the Jews drop the sword for the book and *change*—surely the point of the sermon—but he seemed fixated by Julius Caesar's Jewish mercenaries. It was one tedious story of Jewish bravery and blood thirstiness after another, which the poor translator struggled to make fascinating in Czech.

Time ticked on and heads began to droop. I certainly had reached the stage when staying awake was physically painful and required the application of nails into palms. We were all in various stages of pre-sleep when the rabbi said, 'One of my favourite stories concerns the time a yeshiva student in New York ran over a black woman and killed her.'

The English speakers in the audience leapt awake and I thought to myself, 'Yes, that could have been put better, but at least we've moved into the twentieth century, we must be getting close to the end.' The translator too was briefly gobsmacked but he collected himself together and translated. I watched the Czechs jump in their seats.

The rabbi continued, 'There were riots and five black people were killed, and all the black people . . .' *Shouldn't he be saying 'African-American' people?* I could see the translator was worried about this too. It's *very* rude to say 'black' in Czech. '. . . er, all the Africo-Americos . . .' *Ah, he's remembered now, in a way.* '. . . all the black . . . Afric-Afri-o-Americo . . .' He gave up, let the term die away and continued on. 'They all claimed that the Jews were being favoured by the police. The police and the politicians and the Jewish community said, no, everyone was being treated equally . . .' and the audience nodded, thinking, 'Quite right too. Equality under the law, is that what this rabbi is getting at?' (Except me. I was thinking, 'Is that what this *idiot* is getting at?') But no, it wasn't, because he continued, '. . . but in private, the police admitted that they *were* favouring the Jews because, if you're walking down a dark alley, and you hear footsteps behind you, and you turn around and see it's a yeshiva student . . . well you know you're safe!'

There was a long, expectant silence. The rabbi looked triumphantly around the shul. We looked back at the rabbi. The nice translator finished his Czech translation and looked at the rabbi. We were all waiting for the punch line. And then, horribly, it dawned on us that that *was* the punch line. This lame, sordid story was the rabbi's favourite tale. He liked it so much he used it as the centrepiece of his Yom Kippur sermon.

But it didn't finish there. Seeing our blank faces and wide-open mouths and eyes, the rabbi deduced not that we were stunned, but that this congregation was too stupid to get the point. So he spelled it out for us. 'You see,' he said, a touch impatiently, 'I know of many Africo-black doctors and engineers and . . . and . . . doctors . . . so if *even the blacks* can change, then *anyone* can change for the better.'

Well, I thought the poor translator was going to pass out. He blushed. He cleared his throat. He looked up, trying to get help from a higher source, then finally he decided to go against a lifetime of training and ignore a rabbi. He skipped all the stuff about doctors and blacks and just said, 'We can all change.'

That, I'm afraid to say, wasn't the end of it. We had twenty more minutes of insane ranting, the kind you'd generally only hear in a nursing home. 'There's sex everywhere . . . violence on our doorstep . . . can't walk the streets . . . teenagers going wild.' This, in Prague, where there's been one murder in the last four years, where teenagers obey any old lady who cares to order them about, and where you can walk about alone at two in the morning in perfect safety.

The translator's translations got shorter and shorter until a three-minute tirade from the rabbi was translated to 'Violence is bad.' The Czechs in the audience were looking increasingly puzzled and the translator was in agony. I really wanted to applaud him—he had done such a good job under extraordinarily difficult circumstances.

19

By the time of Yom Kippur, I was well-entrenched in the Spanish Synagogue community and friendships in other areas were blossoming too. Through my study-buddy Andy I met Debra, an Australian who became my closest friend. Debra was a poet, a strict vegan, a woman who drifted through the world focused on her dreaming, inner life. She could barely operate a tin opener.

How she survived in Prague was beyond me. It was hard enough to be someone like me who couldn't bear paperwork; but to be someone who can't bear paperwork, can't eat meat or fish, and can't seem to get through the day without losing her phone or tangling herself in trailing laptop cords—it seemed incredible. And yet, not only did she survive Prague, she had survived—all on her own—Russia. Yes, Russia—surely a far more violent, depressed, miserable and narrow place.

I met Debra on the night the Australian Labor Party regained office, in October 2007. She came to a party at Andy and Barbara's place with her dad, who was visiting her from Australia. I didn't know either of them, but we hugged and kissed and got excited about the new government. I'd just assumed—correctly, in this case—that she'd be as glad as I was to be rid of eleven years of Liberal shame. The trouble with being an expat Australian is that you can't bag your own political leaders. You just can't. It's no good saying 'But I didn't vote for them' when people say to you, 'How can your government send refugees who are fleeing oppression on flimsy boats to prisons in the middle of the desert? How can they do that to children?'

When you're an expat, you have no choice but to defend your country. You accept all the benefits of the Australian reputation ('Australians are so friendly, I've never met one I didn't like') and you can travel anywhere, because you're judged to be harmless. So, if your country's reputation suddenly gets worse, you have to accept that too and offer some fairly feeble explanation like: 'We've got a big coastline. We have a huge refugee intake. I know they're desperate, but so are all refugees. We can't take them all. Yes, the prison thing is shocking.'

It had been embarrassing and shameful to be an Australian having to defend Howard's refugee policies, his frankly White Australia outlook and his dog-whistle of terror making Australians snap with fear. It was bloody awful but I did it, because I'm a patriot. Living among strangers does that for you—it makes you a patriot. It's a strange thing for an Australian to be but there's no getting away from it, that's what living overseas does to you.

So, when Labor finally made it back to power, I cried with relief. So did Debra and so did her dad.

After that party, Debra and I met a few times around the traps; the expat community in Prague is small and interconnected. Debra was an extraordinarily thin, pale girl, shaped like the letter S. She had amazingly beautiful hair—it was very thick and dark brown, falling in long waves over her shoulders—and chocolate-brown eyes under Andie MacDowell eyebrows. She worked as an editor for a legal firm.

'I work at The Three Bells,' I told her.

'Everyone's worked there at one time or another. How long've you been there?'

'About six months.'

'A year is all anyone lasts.'

It turned out that she was an ex-girlfriend of Leonard. I thought she could have done way better than that. She told me how his career in hospitality had started. She'd come home from a conference one afternoon and found that he had rented out their bedroom to stranded tourists and was sleeping on the floor next to the oven.

'The floor. Not a mattress. The floor. And the oven was on because it was winter. Our bedroom had become a hotel. Still, you have to give it to him—he made that business work. Turns out lots of tourists wanted to stay in apartments rather than hotels.'

I asked her about the legal editing.

'Don't do it. It's hell. But it's all I can do unless I want to be an English teacher . . .' We grimaced at each other—who'd want that? '. . . and I speak Czech, but not well enough to get a job as anything interesting.'

Editing, though, did seem to be the sort of thing that you could make a decent living at. I had given up looking for editing work shortly after failing the legal editing test. I'd contacted one or two other companies, but editing turned out to be the sort of job you needed a *živno* for. No-one hired for cash; annoyingly, they all required legal status. It was one more reason to keep pressing Dita to get cracking on making me legal. Leonard was becoming more and more erratic. Editing might be calmer. And I could do it in my pyjamas.

Debra told me she wrote poetry.

'Oh, ah, lovely, I must read some some day.'

'I'll send you some.'

Oh, god, please don't! 'Lovely, I'd love to read it.' *Sigh.*

The trouble with poetry is that unless it moves me I really don't want to read it. And I've got very particular tastes in poetry. I love *Ozymandias*, I love Browning. I pretty much can't stand anything else. I have read swathes of the stuff, and completely could not care less, but then *one* comes along that makes me jump—the snowy evening one by Frost, the one about welcoming a stranger by Walcott. But not very many. I think of myself as a philistine and I don't care. People are always raving about how moved they are, but I rarely am. On the other hand, *Porphyria's Lover* is great, because you don't expect him to kill her. I love a twist.

Debra did email me a poem and I avoided opening it for weeks. Then she emailed me again to ask if I'd managed to read it. I claimed super-busyness, but the time had come. I opened her poem and read it. It was called 'Where'.

I loved it. I have it on the wall of every office I ever work in, so I can read it over and over again. Debra was a really, really good poet. Really amazingly good.

I asked her if she wanted to start a writing group with me.

20

One day, just as winter was beginning, Leonard came stomping into the hotel and ordered me to refurnish the office.

'It looks fine, what do you want changed?'

'IT'S NOT FINE! I want a complete change!'

Leonard could be sensitive to the slightest suggestion that you might be about to question his orders. I couldn't get out of him what exactly he wanted to change, but at one point he said 'We have to spend 200,000 crowns!' That was around ten thousand dollars. I took it from that that his real motive was something to do with the Tax Office. Leonard was on a lifelong quest to keep as much of his money as he could, even if, as on this occasion, it meant spending it on something completely pointless.

I took advantage of this order to trawl around town looking at furniture stores. Leonard, once he got a project in mind, became obsessed with it, so it was easy to leave work, where Leonard was increasingly reminding me of Basil Fawlty having a meltdown, and waste time amusing myself by hunting down furniture suppliers and going to look at their wares.

Leonard's hysterics, his suspicions and tantrums and his endless insane projects, which he'd drop on any of us at any time, were beginning to really get to me. I tried hard to remain separate and calm but after Atheist John left, I couldn't help noticing that Leonard didn't seem to relax any more and his humorous flashes had completely disappeared. Now that he'd discovered a thief, he started hinting that Antoine, another American in the office, was cheating him in some unspecified way.

Antoine was a muscle-bound and incredibly gentle guy who'd left America to work out his inner demons in peace, having, as he once said to me, 'received the double whammy of being gay *and* black'. He'd been employed by Leonard longer than any of us. He worked on reception and was the only person in the office who truly knew how the PCs worked. His patience with the guests and with Leonard was legendary. The idea that Antoine might be cheating him was ludicrous but Leonard lived in a permanent lather of paranoia and it caused us all to feel jumpy and nervous at work.

The morning Leonard announced his new-found desire for a complete refit of the office, I had checked in two lots of guests. I loathed checking in guests. I'd have enjoyed it in any other hotel, but here the name of the game was keeping out of anything to do with Leonard, and checking in the guests was fraught with potential pitfalls. If there was a complaint, and you were fingered, Leonard could keep on at you for months at a time. He would not just remind you of the fault, but somehow convey the belief that you had deliberately annoyed the guest so as to undermine him and The Three Bells. That morning I couldn't get out of it, because Amanda and Antoine were out settling in other people.

I was at my computer when a couple arrived, wanting their room. I thought about making them wait, but after a few minutes they were getting restless, understandably, and it seemed reasonable to take care of them. Unfortunately, when I escorted them to their room I walked in on Halyna, one of the Ukrainian cleaners, still mopping out the bathroom. She looked put out, as well she might, since this was the very thing that guests were likely to write about in their TripAdvisor reviews and start Leonard on the hunt for the culprit. I quickly closed the door and kept the couple entertained until she'd finished. Halyna came out with her bucket, looking displeased and scowling at me. I smiled at her, trying to convey innocence and to avert a scene, and hustled the guests in while chatting amiably, hoping they'd not noticed her face.

I went back to the office and prayed Amanda and Antoine would hurry up and get back. Hardly had I started on my website (Czech hiking trails) when another couple appeared, wanting to check in. Slightly desperately I tried to persuade them to leave their bags and come back later, but they were tired and needed a shower and a lie down, so I was forced to take them to their rooms. They were greeted by a room in complete disarray—towels on the floor, dirty sheets on the bed. Even worse, it too was being cleaned by Halyna. This time she couldn't contain herself. She started yelling at me in Czech. I couldn't understand a word.

'Halyna, please, just tell me when it's going to be clean!' I pointed to my watch to mime time.

'Hour! Hour! Why you here? Why you here?'

She kept on shouting 'Why you here?' And I found myself shouting back, 'Because we are! For God's sake, Halyna, will you shut up?'

She was very upset, poor girl, but this too was like a scene from *Fawlty Towers*, both of us stressed out of our minds and losing control. The guests tried to sneak past us out of the room while we were bellowing at each other in a mixture of Czech, English and Ukrainian.

So it was good to have a bona fide excuse to get out of the overheated atmosphere of the hotel. After a couple of days of visiting furniture showrooms, I took a lot of options back to Leonard.

'This is no good!' he said as he flicked through my photos and brochures. 'Oh no, no, no . . . What were you thinking? This isn't what I want! . . . This is terrible . . . Is this a chair? . . . I don't like this.' And so on.

Patiently, I got him to describe what he did want. 'Well, something like this,' he said, gesturing around the room.

'You want what we've already got?'

'Not *exactly* what we've got, but something like it.'

What we had was IKEA, so my next trip was to the IKEA store. I brought back some brochures, marked with suggestions.

'Yes, this is more like it. I like that one. In beige.'

I looked around the room. He'd chosen exactly the same furniture as the furniture we already had. With my fight with Halyna fresh in my mind, I kept my mouth shut and took out the measuring tape. After several more visits to IKEA and some more back and forth with Leonard ('How about the maple?' 'No, I want the beige.'), and when we'd finally decided on the exact order—precisely what we already had—I revisited IKEA.

Leonard didn't have enough credit on his card so I carried, like a millstone around my neck, 200,000 crowns in cash, more than twice the average annual—yes, *annual*—wage. I had to catch the metro out to a god-forsaken place called Zličín, the end of the line, and then a bus in the freezing winter late afternoon, midnight-dark by 4 pm, in poor, benighted, deserted streets while carrying a kilo or two of cash.

When I'd told Leonard I'd rather go with Antoine, saying, 'Don't you think I'd be safer if I had a big, black man with me?' he replied, 'Oh, you'll be alright. You're Australian.'

At every stop on the metro the voiceover tells you, in Czech, what stop you're at, what the next stop is, and sometimes other useful information, such as that the platform is on the right of the train, that you can alight here to join the main trains, etc. You'd think they'd translate this into English for all the tourists who might want to get around but, no, it's all in Czech until you get to the last stop, Zličín, where they bother to translate one thing: 'Terminus. Please leave the train.' One piece of information, and that one will only strand you in a freezing, communist-built hell. It always sounded like the voiceover really wanted to say: 'Get off the fucking train.'

I made it to IKEA without being mugged, bought the exact same furniture we already had, then stood at the cash desk ready to hand over the most fantastic amounts of cash. The only thing stranger than this in the whole strange episode was that the cashier at the till accepted the 200,000 crowns without a blink. In Prague, cash is god.

By the time Leonard had finally made his choice, winter was in full swing. Christmas was closing in, the days were dark and the snow fell in massive drifts. Since the first time I'd seen it at age nineteen, I was still incredibly excited by snow. I was in the office when I noticed the first flakes.

'Oh my god!—Sorry John—Snow!' I stood pressed to the picture window, trying to see as much of the street scene as I could, as the snow fell faster and thicker. It was so exciting.

'Spot the Australian,' laughed Amanda.

I spent Christmas with Tanya, Marion and Zsuzsa in Tanya's vast apartment. She'd bought, as she did every year, the biggest tree she could possibly find and had climbed into her apartment loft to retrieve her thousands of decorations. The four of us drank champagne and sang Christmas carols at the tops of our voices while we strewed the tree with tinsel and Tanya's collection of baubles, built up over years of travelling. The final touch to the tree was her tall white wax candles that perched, lit, on each branch, using counterweights to stay upright. Christmas dinner was a party of eighteen around Tanya's oak dining table. It was the first truly traditional white Christmas I'd ever experienced and it was wonderful.

21

In the middle of this winter, Anna took me to my first Czech sauna.

'They are a Czech tradition,' she told me. 'You can't miss this, especially not now it's snowing.' I didn't quite understand the last bit but went along with her, keen to try any tradition. She took me to the sauna at the Hotel Olšanská, a delightful 1970s building constructed for the party faithful. It had been the last word in seventies glam and had not been updated since. The sauna was at the top of the hotel. Like all Czech saunas, it was mixed, so men and women swanned about naked, sweating in the sauna rooms together. It's amazing how quickly that becomes easy and natural.

I don't take to heat too well, so it was only half an hour before I was saying to Anna, 'Where's the pool room?'

She grinned. 'Ah. That is the best thing about Olšanská. Come with me.'

We left the sauna and walked, naked, down a corridor, through a small door, then a smaller door, then up some metal stairs and out a third door . . . onto the roof.

'You're kidding me.'

'Come on!' cried Anna. 'You'll love it!'

The cool-down pool was banked in snow. Sitting in the icy water, the snow falling on our heads, was about the most freezing I've ever been, but strangely exhilarating. She was right—I did love it.

The sauna had a bar, another Czech tradition. When we had cooled down we wrapped ourselves in towels—etiquette dictated you didn't go to the sauna bar naked—and sat down. I saw two men looking at us. After a few moments, one of them said something to Anna, who grinned and replied. She turned back to me. 'They are saying how odd it is that we are sisters, and yet one of us has an overbite and the other does not. I have explained we are not sisters.'

I still have difficulty decoding this conversation. My overbite was not a physical feature I'd ever given much thought to. Here we were at a bar, wrapped only in towels, and the feature that drew comment was a facial flaw. The Czechs have no hang-ups about sex or nudity, but they do like women to be beautiful. And they had no qualms about pointing out a perceived flaw. Czech ideas on rudeness are unlike anyone else's (except, possibly, Russians').

Czech shopkeepers are famous for their rudeness and surliness. Expats tended to respond to this in a variety of ways. Some were rich enough not to care—they didn't have to shop where Czechs shopped (the Czechs were as rude to each other as they were to anyone else) and they had Czech functionaries in their offices to deal with the Czech bureaucracy. Some were tough enough not to care—quite a few of the British male expats thought it was amusing. Mike from the Lazy Vinohradians said he enjoyed provoking even more appalling rudeness from shopkeepers by making demands he knew would infuriate them.

Many—and I was one of these—found that this persistent misery and horribleness gradually wore you down. I could never understand why no-one smiled, in fact they seemed to go out of their way to make you feel you were inconveniencing them. I shopped in Vietnamese-owned grocery stores whenever possible and was intensely relieved that my corner store in Zelenky-Hajského was run by a Vietnamese family. They were surprised and delighted when I smiled at them—it was clearly something they weren't expecting, since customers are as surly as sellers—and we quickly bonded.

Exposed mainly to Czech officials and shopkeepers, I began to wonder if this was the Czech character. It was Eva, the previous owner of my flat, who introduced me to a side of the Czechs that had previously been invisible to me. She invited me to an art gallery event to see an exhibition her sister was mounting. Because of Eva's very small store of English and my equally small store of Czech, I was unclear about what to expect—I thought I would just turn up, do a tour of the paintings, express enthusiasm for her sister's talent and leave. However, when I got there I found myself not in a gallery but in a tea house.

This was a trend that was growing in Prague. These tea houses were springing up everywhere, serving exotic high-quality teas in graceful, Japanese-themed teapots, which you could drink while kneeling at a low table. The upper gallery of the tea house had been converted into a stage with the chairs set in semi-circles. Eva guided me in and sat me down and I was soon hemmed in by a crowd of young, chirpy, friendly and unbelievably sweet Czechs, all trying to make me feel at home. Where did these Czechs normally spend their time? Not in the shops, that's for sure.

This, it transpired, was going to be a performance. At one corner of the stage was a large bongo drum. A young bloke, wearing nothing but a sarong and an impressive head of dreads, started with an enthusiastic bongo drum solo. After that came a display of Bolivian dance, then a rock band, a pan-pipes recital, a poetry reading and, finally, a fella playing a didgeridoo. Yes, a didgeridoo.

The concert seemed to express the yearnings of Czech youth who were straining to get out from under the yoke of their miserable parents. Given freedom, young Czechs were travelling and bringing back to their country anything foreign they could lay their hands on, and celebrating it like crazy. This wasn't a themed concert—it was a freedom concert, an enthusiastic and unfiltered embrace of everything that was foreign.

The paintings themselves I can barely remember. But I left knowing there was an underground swell of youthful, dread-locked, yoga-practising joy beneath the miserable bureaucracy and sullen shopkeepers.

———

Anna and I were having enormous fun trailing around antique stores, equipping the flat. I bought a pair of old brass scales with a box of weights that dated back to before the war. It was ages before I found knives and forks I was happy using; although many were very beautiful, because the silver plating had worn off they made food taste slightly metallic. I had some plates I'd brought with me from Sydney—a white set my sister had given me, which had replaced the mishmash of chipped crockery I'd had since a student. I was finally gathering things to make a home.

Anna also helped me navigate the mysteries of the electricity and gas companies. I'd been on a 36 kilobyte-per-second dial-up connection at Dad's place and longed for ADSL, but when I tried to sign up I was told I had to be a permanent resident before I could purchase the card. I lied, of course, and said that I was, but that wasn't good enough. They wanted me to produce my passport with the correct rubber stamps and, since I was technically only on a tourist visa, I couldn't. So Anna put it under her name.

The Czech Republic had joined the European Union in 2004 but it was only now that the EU regulations were beginning to come into force. Lifts were being replaced all round town to comply with the EU regs. In the expat community, we knew that it was going to impact on visa regs soon.

I felt the first stirrings of the EU beast shortly after moving into the flat. I was cooking with my antique monogrammed teaspoon one evening when there was a knock on the door. Since it was on my posh double doors, and not a buzz from the street, I thought it must have been one of the neighbours.

I opened the door to see three men in overalls. One of them began speaking to me. By this time, I was feeling quite confident in my Czech. My lessons were going well and I had enough, generally, to get by in most basic situations. I could certainly understand greetings and yet, from the moment the man opened his mouth I had no earthly idea what he was saying. He, however, seemed to think he had every right to come in, and his two mates hovered behind him wondering what the unusual hitch was.

The first man, a biggish fellow, blond and clearly fond of his beer and sausages, saw my puzzled face and pulled out of his overalls a piece of paper with official stamps all over it. He handed it to me and pointed to my bathroom, talking unintelligibly all the while. I hesitated to let them in but saw the EU symbol and dimly recalled Eva saying that something was about to happen to all the bathrooms. What clinched it was Mr Konečný's name and signature on the paper. I trusted Mr Konečný implicitly, so I allowed the three men inside.

The bigger man, after tapping pipes, staring up at the ceiling and conferring with his fellow tradesmen, came back to me with more incomprehensible talk. It was while trying to untangle this bit of the conversation that I discovered two things. One, my pipes were all going to be ripped out and replaced; and two, the reason I couldn't understand the plumbers was that they were Ukrainian, so they were speaking with an accent.

They were coming back 'later' to start work and would only take a couple of hours. That was good. I could survive a couple of hours of plumbing work.

Two days later I had a house full of Ukrainian plumbers tearing down my bathroom walls and covering the place in plaster dust and I was feeling just the tiniest bit fed up with the EU. Why must they interfere in my life? I *liked* the old lifts; I didn't want all this updating. The Ukrainians seemed nice fellows, although they did spend much of the day berating each other fiercely in Ukrainian. They seemed anxious to do a good job. I suspected they were frightened of Mr Konečný— as well they should be. The 'couple of hours' turned into a full day, and that was just to rip down the walls, so I supposed this was going to take another half century or so before the EU was satisfied. At the end of the day, the nice Ukrainians nervously showed me the bathroom, which I could see they'd done their level best to clean.

I smiled and said, 'Yes, fine, it's lovely and clean, thank you.' I was lying. But they'd done their best without their wives there to show them how.

When they left, I got out my mop. Tip for young players: plaster dust is immune to water—you need to use detergent. Further tip for young players: don't use too much, or you'll spend half your night trying to clean up the soap suds.

I expected them to show up the next day, and the next, but there was no sign of them. Occasionally cement fell in chunks from the chopped-out walls around the pipes and exploded on the floor.

'Should it be doing that?' I wondered. I peered into the glass of water on my desk and saw brick dust at the bottom. *Sigh.*

A week after the plumbers first knocked on my door, with still with no sign of them returning, I ran a shower and was immediately ankle deep in soapy water—the drain had stopped working in my bath. Half an hour passed and the bath was still slowly, slowly draining. I couldn't help feeling this was bad news. The plumbers were banging away in the flat above me and fine plaster was raining down on me.

Two weeks after they had first arrived and left again, to be heard only as ghostlike presences in other apartments, banging on walls and sending cement bombs flying, the plumbers returned. Their demeanour had changed. They looked as though they were getting sick of the job and they didn't seem as afraid of Mr Konečný as I'd have liked them to be. They started murdering the bathroom walls without putting down any protection. I feared my washing machine might not survive the assault. I went back to work, sitting there in a fine hail of plaster and brick dust.

An hour after they began, I went out to inspect the damage. It was terrifying. Walls that appeared to have nothing at all to do with my pipes were falling apart. I was at the mercy of Ukrainian tradesmen. I was doomed.

The next day (and note how far from 'a couple of hours' this is), the Ukrainians informed me that I would have no water for two days. None. Apparently, they had tried to tell me this the day before. Looking back, I did remember some reference to buckets but as I was too busy trying to establish whether or not they intended to replace the walls they'd demolished I wasn't really concentrating on this seemingly pointless talk.

If I had understood their mangled Ukrainian Czech better, I might have appreciated that I was going to be living in refugee camp conditions for the rest of that week. I am a woman who needs two showers a day. I am clean. I like clean.

Clean is important to me. And now I would have to make do with two bottles of sparkling water I got from the Vietnamese corner store.

The following days were spent with my head in my hands, desperate to make it through to the end in one piece. The plumbers were merrily destroying the tiles in my bathroom and the smell of ammonia was pervading. It turned out that not only did the big blond plumber speak with a Ukrainian accent, he had a speech impediment—he lisped. And he also wasn't speaking Czech—he was speaking Slovak, a similar but different language. That helped to explain why I didn't know what was going on.

I remained as patient as I could, plying them with coffee and nodding and smiling even in my total incomprehension, while willing them to finish and praying fervently that my apartment would survive the assault. What on earth was Eva's divine bathroom going to look like after this? How about my foyer and my lovely tiles? The plumbers began to turn up erratically, with no explanation as to their absences, or at least no explanation that I could understand in lisped, Ukrainian-accented Slovak. The weeks dragged on.

And then one Monday night I had gone out with a couple of friends. As one of them was Irish Pam and the inevitable *craic* had been had, I'd woken up Tuesday morning murderously hungover. P. G. Wodehouse has a lexicon of hangovers; this one was a Broken Compass. I lay in bed, willing myself to get out. Then the plumbers forced the issue by ringing the bell and, when the door wasn't immediately answered, bashing on it.

'Yes, yes,' I cried weakly from the bedroom as I crawled around trying to find my jeans, 'I'm coming.'

Bash, bash, bash.

'Errrrrrgh. Yes, yes, in a minute.'

I answered the door, my head hanging from its stalk, and the lisping Ukrainian plumber grinned at me. 'Are you sick?'

I toyed with the idea of agreeing that I was sick, but I was too sick. 'No, I have a hangover.'

His grin widened—he knew it! And since they all probably had hangovers too, being Ukrainian, we rather bonded that morning, which turned out to be their last. Yes, they were finished.

I had concrete where my lovely red and white tiles used to be, and concrete blotches where once I had paint. But they'd put my walls back, I had water again and a toilet I could flush. Best of all, I wouldn't have to live in a fine spray of plaster dust anymore. I'd been living a life where every day I had to get down on my hands and knees and squeegee the floor in an almost entirely vain effort to keep the air particle-free. I'd spent my days coughing and wheezing and trying not to think about lung cancer. Now I could squeegee my last.

I gave the place a thorough spring-clean the next day and was about to replace the bathroom fittings when I got another visitor: the tiler. Astoundingly, it turned out that they weren't going to leave me to re-tile on my own. Not only that but, by some miracle, the tiler had white tiles exactly like mine. Well, mine were square, white bathroom tiles, not exactly bespoke, but still . . . I'm in Prague.

He apologised for not having any red tiles. I told him that having any tiles was brilliant—no apology required. I asked if a painter was dropping by but there, I fear, I was being too optimistic. The paint I'd have to do myself. At least I had a functioning, tiled bathroom.

A neighbour dropped by and asked to see it. I showed her around and she was suitably impressed, bless her. Then she asked how I'd managed to get it done so fast. She rubbed her thumb and middle finger together. Bribery? No, I hadn't bribed them, I said. And then I wondered if maybe I should have. I only gave them coffee. And I was nice to them. But that's not enough to get the quick service, is it?

But then I realised she thought the renovations were all new. I hastened to assure her that the bathroom had looked like that before. She went on to tell me the tale of her reno-vations, which were taking forever. It sounded ghastly. This entire conversation took place in Czech and I began to feel more confident after the knock I had taken with the plumbers.

I passed Mrs Kohoutková on the ground floor, sweeping plaster dust out of her front door. With my renewed confi-dence in Czech, I asked her how her bedroom was looking.

'*Prosím?*' Come again?

'How's the bedroom going?

'Oh, you mean the bathroom?'

D'oh! 'Yes, the bathroom.'

She invited me in to have a look, and we discussed the expense of new tiles and how long it was all taking. Now that it was no longer happening to me but to other people, this whole pipe-replacement project became something of a bonding experience for me with my neighbours. I started to quite enjoy it.

Czechs generally keep themselves to themselves. My father had coached me that although they might be appallingly rude when they were serving you, in your block of flats you must always say hello when you passed by people. So my neighbours and I had always exchanged friendly hellos in the hall, although we never stopped to talk. This was true even of those neighbours I knew slightly, like Mrs Kohoutková and Mr Konečný.

The only neighbour who ever really engaged me in conversation, with no reservations at all, was Mrs Cakes. Czech names are mostly derived from real words. Mrs Kohoutková's name meant 'Mrs Rooster', for instance, and Mr Konečný was 'Mr End'. Mrs Cakes' real name was Mrs Koláčková, but her personality was so exactly suited to her name that I forever thought of her as Mrs Cakes. She was a tiny, rubicund woman, with cheery apple cheeks and blue eyes. When I first said hello to her in the hall, she didn't just reply with a pleasant *Dobrý den!* while walking on, but stopped and asked me about myself ('Australia! You have seen a kangaroo?') and then introduced herself at some length.

Mrs Cakes was very old. She was in her nineties and her hip was playing up, but her doctor had said that if she kept walking she'd be alright. So on that particular morning she was off to the shops and she thought in a few months she'd be fit enough to ride a bike—yes, a bike! Her doctor didn't believe her, but she was adamant.

Mrs Cakes told me that she had lived in the apartment block since the 1940s, that she liked the area very well and what a pleasure it was to see new faces. All the young folk, they moved all the time, not like in her day—but it was good to try new things, wasn't it, and it was fun to see the new faces, all the new young faces. Yes, Mrs Cakes liked to have the young about her. Well, she must be off, had to get her exercise. She was going to see if they had any bikes in the shop on Koněvova Street. She wished me goodbye, remarking that it was a beautiful day, and then tottered off, a bundle of cheery optimism.

I adored her at once. It became clear, through our conversations, that Mrs Cakes had no-one left in the world, no children or relatives. Another day I met her as she was coming out of her apartment. I caught a glimpse of a thick layer of dust and the distinct smell of decay and unwashed clothes. I suddenly realised that she was struggling to stay on top of her life, and chided myself for having gotten too caught up in my own.

Mrs Cakes was careful not to let me see inside, closing her door quickly behind her. I could think of no way of saying to her, 'Let me clean it for you!' without shaming her, but I resolved from then on to keep a closer eye on her.

22

'I need you to do something.'

Leonard had dragged me once more into the garden to have one of our 'secret' discussions. 'I asked Christian John, but he refused. Ridiculous—it's not like everyone else isn't doing it. It does require some writing skill, though, so actually I'd rather you did it. Have you heard of TripAdvisor? It's a traveller's rating site connected with Lonely Planet. You know—the Australians. Your lot.'

'Yes, I . . .'

'People recommend hotels on TripAdvisor. Now it's vitally important that we get a lot of recommendations, but it's also important that the good reviews are rated as helpful and the bad reviews as unhelpful. The helpful ones get put to the top of the list, see?'

'Right . . .'

'And so that puts us at the top of the list, see?'

'Right, so you want me to write reviews for the hotel?'

'Yes, as if you were a traveller.'

'It doesn't seem very . . . aren't they supposed to be real reviews?'

'Oh grow up! They're all fakes put there by hotel owners.'

'O-kay. I guess I could do that.'

'But I don't want you to do it at the office—you'll need to do it from home. I don't want people seeing what you're up to. They may not like it. Christian John seemed to think it was criminal.'

'Ah.'

'But I knew I could trust you.'

Was it criminal? Somewhere inside of me, I thought, *It's a bit dishonest, isn't it? Oh well, I suppose everyone's doing it.* 'So, you want me to do this from home?'

'Yes, but there's one more thing. TripAdvisor can identify the address of the PC you use, so you'll need to create a whole lot of identities and then you should set up a proxy server, so no-one can tell where you're writing from.'

'What?! What do you mean—they know where you're writing from?'

'All PCs have addresses—you knew that, surely?'

I didn't. I didn't know anything about technology. I was the creative type.

'So they're aware of people writing their own fake reviews and if they see the same PC address being used they'll block you.'

'I'm not doing this from my home PC. I don't mind writing fake reviews but I don't want my personal space contaminated.' Having my own computer marked out as a liar, I couldn't bear it.

'But you can set up a proxy server!'

'No I can't, I don't know how.'

'I'll show you, it's easy.'

'Why can't I just do this at work? No-one will know what I'm doing. I can just say I'm reading the reviews and responding to them.'

'No, Christian John is already suspicious.'

It seemed to me that if he was afraid of suspicion, there may well be something more to this than just industry-wide accepted creativity. Trouble was, I needed a job.

'Look, how about I do it at work when Christian John isn't there?'

'I don't see what your problem is. You're Australian. You're all thieves. Why do you care?'

'I just don't want my personal space compromised.'

'Now you sound like Christian John,' he said pettishly.

I automatically soothed him. 'It's not that I don't want to do it; I just don't want to do it at home.'

Leonard chose to be mollified. 'I think it's ridiculous. How about an internet café?'

'Fine,' I replied. 'I'll do it at a café.'

At once his mood lifted. 'When you do this, you have to be careful. You can't just come in and say "Ooh, The Three Bells is wonderful." You have to set the scene. First, comment on a trip in Spain, for example. Pick a hotel and say nasty things about it. Then later you might do one on Newcastle, and then, when you become a trusted source, you do one about The Three Bells. I'd suggest you write a nasty one about Jana, but she may get suspicious.'

And so I began to write reviews. It was quite tricky. I had

to come up with a convincing name, an identity (single, couple with kids, romantic holiday, pet owner) and then invent trips all over the world. Leonard showed me how to set up a proxy server and I started laying down my trail, all the time with him shouting that I wasn't working fast enough.

I told Mathematics Neil about it one day when we were out hiking. He looked dubious.

'That doesn't seem right.'

'No, it doesn't, does it. But I need the job.'

My conscience began to make me sweat and keep me awake at night. I was adamant I wouldn't do it from home.

'But it makes no sense,' shouted Leonard. 'I had no idea you'd be so mealy.'

'Mealy?'

'Yes, mealy.'

I had to keep a spreadsheet of my identities and their logins and passwords ('Use different ones every time, because they can track that too.'), all the time protesting to Leonard: Get someone else to do this/I'm not cut out for it/I'm the straight-forward type/I'm no good at subterfuge.

And then one day he commanded me to write a fake review of a travel company we actually did business with. They knew that I was the communications person at The Three Bells. I thought it was risky. He was in a bad mood and harassing me to get it done, so instead of setting up a fake ID I wrote from my personal email account as 'Rachael Winslow', completely forgetting that my email would automatically give my full name. The travel company wrote an ironic reply to 'Rachael Winslow'.

In some distress, which had just increased monumentally, I told Leonard what had happened.

'Why would you do that? Why would you write from your personal email?'

'I didn't realise it automatically sent my full name.'

'I don't understand why you'd deliberately jeopardise the company.'

'That's completely unfair! I told you I was no good at lying, but you wouldn't listen to me. Some people can and some people can't. I'm one who can't. My god, I'm not boasting about this—I wish I could be devious, but I don't have the skills for it.'

That was a language Leonard understood. But he was still angry and a mote of suspicion had been lodged in his brain. I could see he was wondering if he could trust me. I'd have to work hard to get him back to cosy chats in the garden.

Leonard decided he'd taken enough of a risk with the reviews. A week later, though, he had another scheme. He must have still trusted me, because he called another 'secret' meeting, this time in the vegan café.

These secret meetings would have been more effective if Leonard didn't habitually behave like Inspector Clouseau. Antoine happened to come into the café while we were conducting our 'secret' business. He'd hustled me into a dark corner 'where no-one can see us' and, when Antoine came in and gave us a cheery 'Hi!' as he passed, Leonard hissed at me. 'Pretend we're talking about the guest comments!' Then said very loudly, 'I see they like our artisan bread!'

I saw Antoine grin.

Tucked into the dark corner, Leonard explained his new stratagem: 'There are these programmes that measure how many times something's been mentioned. So, for instance, if you review The Three Bells—' I opened my mouth. 'Don't worry, I'm not going to get you to write reviews! But when you mention a name, then these programmes pick up the name and count it. And the more times it's mentioned, the hotter it is, so the site gets moved up. See, when people search on Google, you want the hotel to come up if they write 'Three Bells' or, even better, 'hotel in Prague'. Do you follow me?'

'Y-e-e-s.' I did but I didn't like the sound of it.

'So you have to go onto sites, chats and things, you know, and mention the hotel.'

He seemed to think he'd made it all perfectly clear and looked at me expectantly.

'Uh, right, but what sites?' I asked.

Leonard *tch*-ed. Was I slow or just being deliberately annoying? I could sense that the vague idea was occurring to him that I had an attitude problem.

'*Any* site. You can do this on any site. Look, you can start with the travel chat sites, but then you can go onto anything. Say you have a technical problem with Word—you can go onto the Word site and write "I work for The Three Bells and I have a problem with . . . whatever." It has to be a real problem of course or they'll know what you're up to.'

'Oh my god.' Not this again.

'But it's easy! You can just cut and paste from some other technical site.'

'I don't know,' I said. *For fuck's sake, are you mad?* 'I can't do this. I have no technical skills—you know I don't!—and it makes me nervous doing things where I could get found out. Things that involve being found out are usually wrong. I just can't do it.'

'Nonsense. Of course you can. You can't do it in the office, though.'

I sighed and agreed. I needed the job.

⸻

Meanwhile, my visa situation hadn't improved. Dita was momentarily back in hospital with her mysterious complaint after some weeks of deteriorating health, culminating in her having to pee through a self-inserted catheter. She provided graphic descriptions of this procedure to me and Amanda— we crossed our legs every time Dita told us about it.

She was suffering from some dire malady that prevented her bladder muscles working. And her oesophagus. She could no longer eat. Dita soldiered on, but mostly I wished she wouldn't. I just wanted her to stay in hospital until it was fixed and reserve all her energies for my visa. But she kept coming into the office and instead of doing any work she'd give us a blow-by-blow description of her efforts to have a wee that morning. And her battles with the catheter.

'It's so small down there I have to force it up. I was screaming with the pain.'

'Right, right,' I said, my eyes watering. 'That sounds terrible.' But somehow I couldn't stop myself from asking, 'I don't suppose you've found out about my visa yet, have you?'

23

Although work was becoming increasingly painful, my life in the Spanish Synagogue flourished. There I had found the security I needed. I got tremendous satisfaction from helping to keep the tiny community going, but occasionally I felt the precariousness of European Jewish communities. Every so often, neo-Nazis took to the streets to claim that the holocaust never happened and march with swastikas in the name of free speech. The anarchists loved marching on the same day, hoping to get into a fight.

The mood in the synagogue on those occasions was sombre. Neo-Nazis were never given permission to march through the Jewish quarter, although they always asked for it, and marched anyway. The police were on the side of the Jews—something I hadn't necessarily taken for granted.

I guess no-one likes a neo-Nazi, especially not in central

Europe. People were divided on the communists, as for some the life had been easy under communism and considerably more challenging under democracy. They were united in their view of life under the Nazis, however.

During these marches, people decided whether to stay away or line the streets, waiting. The decision to go out or stay in showed me more than ever the undercurrent of hatred towards Jews in Europe. No-one blamed those who stayed in; it was a tough decision to stand up to the neo-Nazis. Violence could so easily break out, particularly if the anarchists were there. Coming face to face with the hatred was a brave thing to do. Anna, of course, was on the streets, and so was Peter. I had to really think about it.

Protesting in Australia—with placards and loud hailers— was something I'd done many times before. I'd marched with thousands against the Iraq War and for Reclaim the Night, I'd handed out leaflets with a ragged few outside the Healthcare Commission (a whistleblower case being swept under the carpet). In the days when I taught school leavers how to be PAs, I took a class of mine to the wharves to see worker power in action (one of the young male students linked arms with one of the wharfies and I did wonder if I'd been quite wise). However, facing neo-Nazis in the Jewish quarter in Prague had an air of menace to it that I had never experienced before.

'I will go,' Peter had said, although he looked white. 'I am a leader. I must go.'

Anna had been less worried, possibly thinking that her gender would save her from any unpleasantness. I felt that my gender made me more vulnerable to unpleasantness, but I agreed to go. How could I not? I hadn't left my home country to huddle indoors at the first sign of difficulty, much as I might want to.

In the end, the neo-Nazis did not enter the Jewish quarter. They tried to get to Wenceslas Square and scuffled a bit with the anarchists, who seemed to be having a hugely enjoyable time, but the neo-Nazis ended up being a much smaller and less threatening rabble than their pre-publicity had suggested. They were reported to have come from Germany, a well-drilled army of the young and disaffected. In the end they were a bunch of dimwits: disaffected, yes, but more like the anarchists—hoping for a bit of biffo on a dull Saturday.

Quite a few people had turned up—members of our community and sympathisers—but the word quickly got around that most of the Neo-Nazis were actually football lads, and they'd been diverted by the ever-helpful anarchists. At that, a palpable relief swept through the quarter and we waited around for a bit, our shoulders noticeably less tense, then drifted off to pubs and home.

Over the last few months, my life in the synagogue community had become richer, partly as a function of being in a tiny group of people that needed all hands on deck, and partly out of love of Anna. Anna's energy and output were incredible. She translated academic books professionally and wrote journal articles on the side. In her spare time she stripped down and restored antique furniture, crocheted her own table linen, made jam, kept up her grandmother's garden, travelled and learned Krav Maga (an Israeli martial art).

She and I started a choir together. I had come up with the idea of a choir because I had so loved the choirs on High Holy Days back in Sydney, led by our gay choir master. I had seriously underestimated how different a choir can be if it's run by me, and not by a gifted musician. Most of my wannabe choristers could barely hold a note, let alone sing a scale or harmonise. And Anna didn't make it any easier by wanting to spend obsessive hours with the choir so they could get the Hebrew pronunciation just so. They grew weary of my inability to deliver a singalong, and by Anna's mad interruptions.

'It's not AY it's AH!!' She had halted the entire song to tell us this.

'Does it really matter?'

'It changes the meaning!'

'It's Hebrew—who's going to know the meaning?'

'Someone might. I can't bear it.'

And so we would all have to stand around for two hours being coached in the exact pronunciation of a song that I would have been happy if they'd been able to sing without sounding like seven people singing different songs simultaneously. We got as far as two recitals in the shul before we gave it away as one of my projects that wasn't going to fly.

One project that did fly, however, was the new siddur (prayer book), which Anna and I worked on together, along with a few other people. Anna did all the translations and I did the editing of the English. To this day, my name appears in the acknowledgements in the siddur used by the Spanish Synagogue in Prague. I'm immensely pleased with myself about that.

One evening when we were planning the new siddur I went around to Anna's place for a pot-luck dinner. She had whipped up a loaf of bread, which was so delicious that I could have eaten the lot, and nearly did. I brought my usual—cherries and grapes from a Vietnamese shop in Újezd that Marion had introduced me to. It was the only place in the whole of Prague where the fruit and vegetables could be said to be reliably fresh. It was here, and only here, that you could get white crisp cauliflower, instead of the grey dying stuff. You could also get 'exotic' fruit and veg. The fennel was so unusual to my sight and taste that I could almost have cried at its fragrant presence on the shelf. Cherries, strawberries, grapes—these were all to be had in abundance. You could barely move for the expats, weeping in joy and crowding the place out.

Anna and I were meeting to discuss the printing of the siddur, a matter that was threatening to turn into a months-long barney among the committee responsible for it. What everyone wanted was a glossy, gorgeous, illustrated siddur. What they wanted to pay for it would give us something printed on butcher's paper, held together with string. Anna and I said we'd make an executive decision and spent an hour beavering about in the gritty details of how it should be printed, on what paper, how much each option would cost, cost-benefit analyses. Then we got bored, made a quick decision and emailed it off to the rest of the committee to bicker over.

After that, we opened a bottle of wine and chatted about this and that. Then Anna suddenly said to me, 'My twin sister, Marie, knew a Weiss in Bosnia. Would that be your brother?'

My brother had spent some time in Bosnia with the UN but his knowing Anna's twin sister seemed a bit far-fetched, even for a woman who'd had three glasses of wine.

'Well, there are lots of Weisses, so probably not.'

'Yeah, yeah, I think maybe. He was about the right age. Your brother's a year younger than you, right?'

'Yes.'

'Yes, so was this one. About 1991?'

Actually my brother had been in Bosnia about 1991, reporting on the war there. 'Medium height, blond hair, blue eyes, deep voice. Does that sound like this guy?'

'Yes! His name was Karel, I've remembered now.'

'My brother's middle name is Karel. His first name is Gordon.'

'Yes, that's the one. Gordon. Karel was his grandfather's name.'

'That's right. My god. Your sister knows my brother.' It was absolutely astonishing.

And then it became even more peculiar.

'Marie told me about your grandfather.'

'Right. Terezín.' My grandfather had been interned in the Terezín concentration camp in Czechoslovakia.

'And Auschwitz, and dying on the forced march.'

'What?'

'He was in Auschwitz.' Anna looked at me. 'Didn't you know?'

'No. I never knew how he died.'

'How could you not know?'

'We never talk about these things in our family.'

But amazingly, Gordon had told Marie the whole story. He had discovered that our grandfather had died of dysentery on a forced march from Auschwitz. When Gordon had gone to a talk about the holocaust in Sydney, he had met a man who'd been on the march with our grandfather. This man had been talking about the people he'd known during that time, and had mentioned Weiss. They established that it was the same man.

My brother had gripped the man's coat. 'Do you know what happened to him?'

'Shit! He died of shit under a tree!'

And then the old man had pulled himself away and disappeared into the crowd.

My brother had never told me about this encounter but he had told Marie while being bombed in Bosnia.

'I can't believe you didn't know,' Anna was incredulous.

But that's how it is in families where the survivor chooses silence. You never know, until a senile old man shouts 'Shit under a tree!' at you in a gleaming theatre in Sydney. Or when you hear about it third-hand on the other side of the world.

24

Leonard was unhappy with our rate of site creation. According to him, Christian John and I should have been producing a site a day.

'Don't mess about with getting it pretty and right—just get it up! We have to get on with this.' He seemed to have dismissed from his mind his ambition for 'long-term' projects and was impatient for results.

'What do you *do* all day?' he said to me. Accustomed as I was to the politics of the office, I'd seen this one coming from the increasingly sour look on his face whenever he inspected our work.

I whipped out the list of tasks I'd been keeping. 'Well, it's interesting that you should ask, because I've been a bit worried about the amount of time I spend on guests. I've been keeping a note. Let's look at yesterday. I welcomed a guest to the

Mozart Rooms, then another one to the Palace Suites. Then the restaurant called because a guest had left their luggage in the lobby and they wanted it up at No. 54, so I took that up. Then the photographer came by and needed to get the shots you left him and it took us half an hour to find them. Then I wrote some stuff on one of Hewlett Packard's help sites.'

'Where?' asked Leonard, 'I've been looking, and I haven't found anything you've written.'

Aha! So he was watching me, and suspicious. I knew it. I'd taken the view with Leonard that I couldn't prevent him feeling suspicious but I had hoped I could manage his level of suspicion so I didn't lose my job. I always spoke soothingly to him, never raised my voice and told him often what I was doing.

'I'll show them to you. Anyway, as you can see, I spend a lot of time welcoming guests.'

Leonard looked thwarted but he rallied and instantly lightened up. 'So what have you two been doing on the sites then?' he asked, almost conversationally.

Christian John turned from his desk and looked politely attentive.

'We've just finished the one on beer,' I replied. 'That only took us a day, didn't it, John?'

John nodded.

'And we're starting on ripoffs—'

'You should have done that one by now!' interrupted Leonard.

'—and then we're going on to famous inhabitants.'

'Famous inhabitants! That's no good.'

'What would you like instead?'

'How about stag parties?'

'You mean strip joints and brothels?'

'Yes.'

'No.'

'What do you mean, no?'

'I mean no. I'm not helping men to exploit women.'

Christian John broke in. 'Me either.'

'It's not exploitation,' exclaimed Leonard. 'These women *like* being prostitutes.'

'No-one likes being a prostitute, Leonard. You can live with it, but you don't choose it—unless you're a rare nympho, or you're one of the ones who gets to beat men for a living and not actually have sex with them.'

'You're a feminist! You're letting your prejudices get in the way of your work.'

'I am a feminist, yes, but they're not prejudices, they're principles.'

'Only because they're prejudices you think are true. They're just prejudices. These women *choose* to be prostitutes.'

'Right, so you're telling me that they have had a full panoply of life choices, have they? They could have studied physics, or gone into nursing, or been lawyers but instead they chose to be prostitutes.'

Leonard grinned. He had a smile—particularly the one he employed when he was enjoying a stoush—that made him very attractive. 'Alright, maybe they couldn't have studied physics. But why are they doing it? They could have been cleaners.'

'Y-e-e-a-h. You're not convincing me that choosing between being a badly paid cleaner and a marginally better paid prostitute is an indication that they enjoy what they do. The only ones I'll grant you—the *only* ones,' I said, pre-empting Leonard's next remark, 'are the ones who run their own businesses out of their homes. No pimps, no streets—just chicks with kids and no supporter, who have to make a living. At least they do it on their own terms and at their own price. It's actually not much of a choice, but it's marginally better than being exploited.'

'I'm going to prove to you that they enjoy it.'

'Good luck with your trying.'

'But since Rachael is going to be so obdurate, I suppose we'll have to move on. We'll do the gay scene.'

'Yes, okay, that's actually a pretty good idea,' I said. 'The gay scene has a lot going on, and I don't think anyone else is doing it.'

'Uh.' We turned to look at Christian John. 'Uh. I won't do a gay site.'

I was astonished. 'Whyever not? It's not discriminatory.'

'It's against my religious beliefs.'

There was a slight frozen moment. Especially because Amanda, gay as a treeful of parrots and working at the PC behind us, answering queries with a devil's horns headset on her purple hair, appeared to have heard us. She politely declined to allow her quiver to be acknowledged.

'I told you he was a Christian.' Leonard said this with such satisfaction that it crossed my mind that he knew Christian John would say this. Had he asked him already?

'I can't write a gay site,' said John, quietly but firmly. 'I've said before I won't do it.'

Jesus, that Leonard is a prick.

Leonard giggled. 'What about a beer site, then—does that offend you?'

He really was annoying. John, for a young man of twenty-two, displayed remarkable composure. 'No, I can do a beer site.'

'Not against your religious beliefs then?' simpered Leonard. 'No.'

I caught John's eye as he spoke. 'How about a site on traditional Czech food?' I asked Leonard. 'Pork schnitzel, ham steak and dumplings, *svíčková* . . .' *Svíčková* was a beef dish.

Leonard turned red. 'No!' he shouted. 'We're not doing anything about killing animals.' He was spitting at me. 'Oh, you don't mind killing animals, do you? Women can't have sex for money but you'd send a pig to its death. You know pigs are as intelligent as dogs, don't you? More so! Would you eat your dog?'

'So let me get this straight,' I said to him as calmly as I could muster. 'I won't do brothels, John won't do the gay scene and you won't do animals. Is there anything left in Prague we all agree we can do?'

Leonard caught up short. There was a tense beat. Then he laughed: 'We're going to do the brothels. I'm going to prove to you that women like being prostitutes.'

I winked at John, who smiled gently back at me. And a little wearily, I thought. Poor fella. He was only twenty-two.

25

My writing was going badly. It had been my original plan to live in my delightful Prague flat, walk the cobbled streets gaining inspiration from the romantic city, hobnob with local writers (in Czech) and write a novel a year for the next ten years, gradually freeing myself from boring office work until Hollywood discovered my quirky oeuvre and paid for my retirement. What was in fact happening was that I was increasingly stressed by my work at The Three Bells, I was finding the Czech surliness difficult to cope with on a day-to-day level and my writing had dried up completely. I was writing exactly nothing.

I'd sought out other writers, only to be disappointed. Writing, contrary to popular belief, is not a solitary occupation. It only really works in groups, at least for me. I need other people to bounce off, to discuss my work with and to keep me motivated.

I'd met a poet through the Thursday night Lazy Vinohrady dinners and he seemed a nice enough guy—Australian, as it happened, and an ex-garbo. Nice enough, yes, but not inspiring. He didn't write my kind of poetry. He sent me some, quite a lot actually, and I had the embarrassing experience of having to come up with non-committal things to say about it. 'Mmm. You know, really I'm not much of a poet. I don't really get poetry.'

'But what did you think?' he pressed me.

'Well I . . . I, er . . . I liked the bit about the golem. That spoke to me.'

'I see it as my ironic take on the despair men and women feel when they try to connect and fail.'

'Mmm. Mmm. I see. Yes.'

A silence fell.

'*Ještě jedno*?' I asked. Another beer?

Then Andy put me in touch with a friend of his who knew a writer, Ed, and for a while Ed and I formed a writing group of two. At least, I wrote. Ed mainly told me about his girlfriend: how she wanted him to marry her and buy a flat together, and that he wanted to be with her but he didn't like the sort of flats she liked, or the sort of furniture. How she wanted everything new and a big new flat in the suburbs and that Ed wanted to keep his ratty old sofa and loft bed in a leaky attic flat in the Old Town. What did I think? Is this what happened to everyone? Did he have to make this compromise? It didn't seem fair.

'Depends on how much you love her, I guess.'

Ed brooded. How much did he love her? That was the question.

I didn't mind this so much because at least I got to write to a deadline, even though Ed never seemed to have read what I had written. In fact, what I was writing was rubbish but I needed someone else to send it to, to see if I could find my feet. My work, far from flourishing in the land of Kafka, was getting increasingly stony and dull.

Even my letters home were a struggle, but I was at least forced to make them readable and amusing. What I liked to refer to as my 'novel'—a pile of unrelated paragraphs—was coming along in tedious, stricken grunts. I hated every second of it. My imagination had dried up into a tiny raisin pit somewhere deep inside me, refusing to drink or move. It was a struggle.

Sometimes Ed's lack of interest helped. I was like a lonely child who'd lost the desire to be noticed and only hoped to go unmolested by the tow-haired thugs. However, at one point I put everything together and asked Ed what he thought I should do with all this material.

His email response put an end to our partnership. It was tremendously long and scathing, finishing on these words:

'What is this? It's nothing. I read a bit of it and it seems like a travelogue, and then another bit seems like you're writing a blog, and then some of it is a novel. It's a mess; it's all over the place!'

Yes, I explained to him, first drafts were often like that.

'It's not a first draft—it's a disaster.'

Ed seemed surprised when I said I thought our writing group wasn't really helping me much in my writing and disbanded it.

I went to an established Prague writing group once, and only once. I found myself surrounded by the worst kind of egomaniacal men, all of them dispossessed Americans and Brits, all competing about who was the more windswept and tortured. None of whom had written a word worth repeating but all were ready with a nasty comment to make about my own work. I gave it two hours then left, annoyed.

It had been a relief to meet the lovely Debra. She at least wrote good poetry and I had finally found someone I could trust to share my work with. We met each Wednesday night to exchange notes on our progress that week. Mine was always painful but at least it gave me something to aim for each week, even if the work itself was agonising. I had bought a book called *The Artist's Way* to try to break myself out of the slump I was in. It was aimed primarily at middle-class Americans with lots of money who found themselves trapped in soulless lawyer-like jobs and its suggestions often involved things Debra and I couldn't afford—massages and tap classes and ethnic cushions to release your inner artist. However, we bravely soldiered on, doing the exercises and typing out our weekly morsels.

Debra had carved out a life as an editor and I began to think that editing might suit me much better than a life spent constantly trying to mollify Leonard. When the Czechs finally entered the Schengen zone at the end of 2007, I had managed to cobble together an understanding of what would be required to stay legal. If I could successfully get legal, I began to see how I could escape The Three Bells before Leonard finally turned the full blast of his paranoia on me.

The Schengen zone was created by an agreement between certain EU members that they would not operate borders between their countries. When the Czechs joined, it created instant chaos because suddenly you couldn't just trot off to Dresden every three months, put both feet over the border for two seconds and step back again—a legal tourist. Now all of us had to apply for long-term visas. And you couldn't apply for this visa in Prague—we all had to go outside the country to apply for, and collect, the visa. They made you do that, so other expats told me in our endless and feverish conversations about it, to maintain the fiction that you were not already living in the country under a tourist visa—you really were a tourist, not a resident.

And that would have been perfectly reasonable were it not for the fact that in order to apply successfully for a visa you had to first prove that you lived in the Czech Republic and had a permanent address there. Having proved residency, you were then forced to make two trips out of the country—one to apply for the visa and one to collect it. Most people made three or four trips because, unaccountably, there was little concrete information available on the extremely complex visa requirements. Embassies in nearby countries were stormed by many thousands of annoyed Americans.

And it's not even as though this visa made you a Schengen citizen. In every other country you got a visa that was good for the whole zone but in the Czech Republic there was a tediously complicated set of rules that meant you could only leave the country five times and after that you had to move to a country outside the Schengen zone (Bulgaria was the closest) before they'd let you back in.

It was not even that simple, though. I was just beginning to understand the nuances of the new system. In order to get the precious long-term visa, you first had to apply for your *živno*, which meant you were registered as a particular kind of self-employed worker and could carry out your business legally. Only *then* could you apply for your long-term visa. It involved incredible amounts of paperwork, all needing to be translated and stamped and signed. I had messed about for ages in a panic, dreading even getting started on the whole ghastly business. It was the talk of the expat community. Everyone—even those employed by the big IT companies— was in a hellish lather of stamps and lines and offices and translations.

You didn't just have to go to one office, you had to find your way to at least four to prove your tax status, get your health insurance, get your criminal record certification stamped and get a proof of address. It was utterly hair-raising and appallingly bureaucratic. Furthermore, the bureaucrats weren't prepared for the several thousand expats who'd been living in their country in peaceful harmony—in a system that up to now had let them get on with building their lives and contributing to the economy—to suddenly jam their offices.

The final destination, once you had all your paperwork, was the delightfully named Foreign Police, who had become so swamped with Americans, Canadians and Australians wanting their visas registered that they had come completely undone. By the time I eventually got around to going to the Foreign Police, I had to line up at three in the morning just to be sure to get a ticket for an interview that day.

One of the things most attractive about the job with The Three Bells had always been Leonard's promise that he would help me get a *živno,* and pay for it. But a *živno* was a pain in the nuts as it was, in theory, a self-employment visa—a business visa in a way—and Dita's persistent problem had been that she didn't know what to put me down as. There was no category for 'writer'.

'Can't you just put me in another category?'

'You're a writer, though—we have to put you in the right category.' She was half Czech, Dita, and hence incapable of seeing paperwork for what it was—a means to an end. For her it actually meant something.

'So what am I going to go down as?'

'I don't know! You'll have to work it out.'

'Dita, I really think I need your help here,' I said through patiently gritted teeth. 'I can't speak Czech and that's really why you have this admin job—because you can speak Czech and you can answer these questions for me.'

'I just can't think! I'm in so much pain!'

I backed away.

Eventually she put me down as 'administrator'. The category mattered because the *živno* linked you to one type of job. You couldn't get your *živno* as a plumber and then work as a seamstress. Dita was terrified that we were saying I was an administrator when I was actually doing editing work.

'It's not the right category!' she wailed.

I ignored her, fished 3000 crowns out of petty cash. Dita was so confused, I could have put any old expense in and she'd not have noticed.

'It's okay, Leonard knows I'm taking it.' Leonard didn't know I was taking it but if I'd told Dita that she'd have made me pay for it myself and Leonard would not have given it back. I knew that the bastard was getting less trustworthy.

I left the office and caught the train to Dresden.

At last I was on the precious *živno* list.

———◆———

One evening, shortly after my Dresden trip, I was at home with Debra for our artists' evening. She had just arrived when my phone rang.

'Hello?' I asked.

There was giggling on the line. 'Rachael?'

I paused. 'Leonard?'

There was more giggling.

'I've got someone who wants to speak to you.'

'What?' I felt an emotion I was increasingly experiencing around Leonard—wary patience.

'Here's Tony.' Leonard sounded very pleased with himself. A new voice came on the phone, sounding a little more cautious than Leonard.

'Hello?'

'Hello, Tony,' I said in the crisp voice I keep for bolshy young secretaries who join my team and think they're going to twang my strings. It's a voice that suggests that a brief summary of requirements would be the best conversational form to adopt with me at this point.

There was a muffled exchange on the other end, in which I could hear Leonard in the background saying, 'No, go on.'

Tony elected not to go on and Leonard came back on the line. 'What did you say to him? He was only going to tell you about brothels. Tony owns Big Sister. Do you know it?'

I had heard of Big Sister. This was the one where sex was free—you just had to agree to be filmed. The source of 'amateur' video, I suppose. Grainy grunting.

'He's the owner. You should go some time. I want to set you up with Tony, I think he's your sort of man. He likes strong women. I told him you were a feminist, but he said he didn't mind.'

'Yeah, I'm not sure I'm interested.'

'Why?' Leonard jumped on that. 'Because he owns a brothel? He told me—they like working there. Do you think Tony's forcing them? Slave labour?'

I sighed inwardly, then put on a joking tone. 'I'm sure they love being under all those sweaty fat men. Honestly, Leonard, you don't really think women like sex with hideous, smelly strangers, do you? I mean, seriously.'

'It's probably what they'd get in a husband,' he replied, perfectly reasonably.

'True enough, old boy, and that's why I'd restructure the entire notion of nuclear family. You know there's a society in China where the family is headed by the mother, and her brothers help her to bring up the kids. The lovers come when they're told. Now that's a society of happy women.'

Leonard was in a good mood. 'You're probably too feminist for Tony. Or for any man, I should think.'

'It's a gift.'

He rang off.

'Who was that?' asked Debra.

'Leonard. I suspect this job isn't going to last too long.'

26

In March 2008 my book, *Me, Myself and Prague,* was published and with that began one of the strangest periods of my life. Briefly, and only in Prague, I became famous.

When it first came out, I had to return to Australia to promote its initial publication. My visit home took place knowing that if I left I was not, strictly speaking, legally allowed back in for three months. The trouble was that I had grown used to the idea of Czech border laxity. Although I had assiduously crossed the border every three months, some people who'd been in Prague for a long time had stopped doing even that because quite frankly the border police never even checked their passports. I once went to Hungary and got a stamp going in, but none coming out. Technically, after that I wasn't in the Czech Republic—I was still in Budapest.

People like Tanya and Marion had been living here for fifteen years like that, running fully-fledged businesses without once notifying the authorities that they weren't tourists. They paid mortgages and taxes and spoke Czech, although Marion always pretended she couldn't speak Czech when she came back from America so no-one got suspicious. This was the only precaution she'd taken in a decade and a half.

It was Andy who told me, just before I went to Australia, that as I'd now applied for my *živno* the clock had stopped and I'd be okay. I didn't check this with any official source because I wanted to believe him and because the whole subject had become so frustrating and irritating that my brain would shut down at the mere thought.

Marion told me she thought Andy was wrong and she began, very kindly, to tell me what I could do about it. 'You could check with your embassy . . . Oh, you don't have one here. Well, I guess there's one in Dresden and maybe you could get an interim visa from them. There's a website they have, but I looked it up and it doesn't seem very clear. I think that if you applied for a visa before 21 December you might be alright but if you applied afterwards you may have to get a stamp in your passport that indicates you—'

'I don't care! I just don't care. I hate these people, with their stamps and their forms and their six different bureaus depending on which type of visa you require and no information anywhere you can find it. I'm taking my chances.'

So it was all my fault that I found myself in Sri Lanka, on my last stop before coming home to Prague, reading an article sent to me by Debra that made it abundantly clear that the Czechs were not recognising 'applied for visa' to mean 'has visa and is legal'. Unbelievable! And unnerving. What was I going to do if they didn't let me in at the border?

That depended on where they sent me. If they sent me back to Sri Lanka, I planned to travel up through India for a month. If they sent me to a non-Schengen country I was going to sit out my time in Istanbul. In fact, I was rather hoping the bastards *would* kick me out. A bit of time travelling might be quite fun. I was fed up with the whole visa business.

However, just to be on the safe side I emailed Andy to check. He emailed back saying there'd been an official announcement that border control was going easy on people who were applying, owing to the length of time it was taking to get the forms processed. So it could go either way.

My sense of bravado notwithstanding, I got to the Immigration window at Prague Airport just the tiniest bit concerned. Czechs in charge of The Stamp are very important people. No-one argues with The Stamp and The Stampers take their duties very, very seriously. What if this one hadn't read the official communiqué?

I waited on one foot, trying to look innocent, while the Immigration guy flipped through my passport. Then he flipped through it again. And then one more time. Unfortunately, he kept skipping the page with the stamp in it that said I had applied for my *živno*.

I strained to keep the look of unconcern on my face.

'Do you speak Czech?' he asked me, in Czech.

'Yes, I do,' I replied, and he smiled. Okay, I thought, we're off to a good start. Perhaps there's a chance I can talk him around. We carried on in Czech.

'Where have you come from?'

'Sri Lanka and Sydney.'

More flipping through the pages. For god's sake! When was he going to spot my visa? I decided to take action and asked if I could show him something in my passport. Taking it, I opened it to the visa page. 'See?'

'You don't need a visa,' he said.

Aha! He hasn't noticed that I've not been out for three months! Woo hoo!

He picked up his stamp and I felt my relief starting to well up. He turned to the page where all the Czech entry stamps were recorded. He lifted his stamp. His hand descended.

And then it stopped. He put his stamp down. My relief froze. He peered at the other stamps.

Oh fuck, he's seen that the dates are wrong! Okay, don't panic, you just need to explain about the communiqué. Oh fuck fuck fuck!

He turned the passport around and looked at it closely. He picked up his stamp. His hand wavered.

'Look how these idiots have done these stamps,' he said to me. 'There's no room here for mine.'

And I saw that his hesitation was nothing to do with the fact that I was illegally entering his country. What concerned him was the fact that if he wasn't careful one line on the edge of his stamp might miss the page.

Luckily he was careful. These things really matter in the Czech Republic.

27

When *Me, Myself and Prague* was published in Australia, I wondered how I could get it into Czech bookshops. I started out with the big one—Palác Knih (Palace of Books) on Wenceslas Square—figuring that they might like to have it in their English-language section for all the foreigners. A trip to Palác Knih soon put an end to that idea. My hesitant approach to the woman behind the counter was met with cold incomprehension.

'Erm. I have written a book about Prague and I wanted to speak to someone about distributing it through Palác Knih.'

'I know nothing about this.'

'No, right. Right. But perhaps the manager—'

'She is not here.' *Who is this importuning worm?*

To be honest, I didn't have the courage to keep pushing. It's hard enough to lob up to someone and ask them a favour, harder still to keep asking if they're staring at you and refusing to answer your polite questions with more than a short blast. I reeled home and got under the duvet.

A couple of weeks later I tried a bookshop I loved, an antiquarian bookshop near the Old Town. As soon as I walked in, I realised I was probably on a losing game. There was no-one there and although I loved it, the selection was small and quirkily beyond the reach of commercialisation. How they made money was anyone's guess.

I tried my spiel on the young man at the counter, but he looked blank. 'You want to what?'

I braced my shoulders. 'I have written this book and I want to have a launch. I'm looking for an English-language bookstore to have it in.'

He gazed at me silently. 'No, we do not do that.'

Right. I left without a fight—not even a request to see the manager or owner.

Next stop was the small but infinitely cool Big Ben Bookshop, which was tucked behind a small square off the Old Town Square in a tiny dead-end street, Malá Štupartská. Big Ben was one of the go-to bookshops for the expat brigade, along with Shakespeare and Sons on the other side of town. Where the bigger, more commercial Palác Knih stocked the standards and the old classics, Big Ben stocked a more idiosyncratic range. It was tiny, with comfy armchairs and outdoor seating.

On the day I went there, there were two other customers in the shop. Embarrassed by my mission, I hung back until they'd been served. The second customer, a small woman with unruly dark hair, was in deep conversation with the man behind the desk. Although I stood well back, I caught her accent—Australian.

When she'd finished, I couldn't stop myself. As she turned towards me, I smiled and said, 'That's a familiar accent.'

She didn't look as though she welcomed this acknowledgement, so I prepared to move on. Not every expat wants to engage with other expats and I'm never offended by coolness in those situations. Sometimes you've left your home country precisely because you never want to hear the accent again.

However, seeing me disengaging from her, she relented. 'Do you live here?'

'Yes,' I said, 'you?'

'Partly. Half the time here and half the time in Melbourne.'

'That sounds like my ideal.'

'Yes,' she replied, 'it is pretty ideal.'

'What do you do that lets you manage that?'

'I'm a writer.'

'Oh, so am I.' Keeping it cool, like I really was a writer and not just a harried hotel worker barely able to churn out a letter home—well, dammit, I had a second book on the shelves, didn't I?

'What do you write?'

'Travel memoirs. You?'

'Fantasy fiction.'

'How many have you published?' I asked her, feeling not a little smug about my two and fully expecting her to give me the usual response: 'I've got a good draft and I'm nearly there.'

'About twenty-seven, I think.'

'What!? How have you managed to write twenty-seven books??'

She laughed. 'It's teenage fantasy fiction, so they're not very long.'

'Are you famous? I know nothing about fantasy fiction.'

'I don't know as you'd call me famous, but I have a following.'

Her name was Isobelle Carmody and no doubt any fourteen-year-old readers of this book will be swooning and wanting to touch the hand that shook hands with Isobelle Carmody. But I had no idea who she was. I googled her later and she was being unduly modest about her fame—she's very well known.

We talked about where she lived and when she travelled between the countries. She said it was difficult to make ends meet, but she managed it by doing book festivals and giving talks. I told her about my struggles with writing my third book and she was sympathetic, observing, 'When it comes down to it, you just have to write what you like and keep going.'

She wished me luck with my book and I wished her luck with hers, and she left. The shop was now empty apart from the young man behind the counter, so I approached him. It was a bit easier after knowing that Isobelle had already talked to him. I could say I was another Australian writer. Still, after the reception at the other bookshops, I can't say I was feeling full of confidence.

'I've just written this book,' I flourished a copy like a magician, hoping it would distract him from my nervous spiel. 'I was wondering . . . if you would stock it.' I hurried on. 'I was thinking that, you know, maybe, I could have a launch here? And invite everyone I knew? You'd sell lots of copies.'

The young man nodded, smiled and listened to me as I lengthily explained how good this would be for his shop. He waited for me to pause for breath and then said, 'Wait! I will get Miro.'

He disappeared into the back of the shop and I took a look through the shelves, particularly the travel memoir shelves, checking the competition and alternately gnashing my teeth (good book) or feeling superior (rubbish book).

An explosion behind me spun me around: 'YES! YES! You are the writer, yes? We have many writers here! Yes! I will help you! Together, we will launch your book! I will do this!'

This, I took it, was Miro. I'd have expressed my thanks and gratitude to him—after the comprehensive rejection by the other two bookshops, to be met with this level of enthusiasm and support overwhelmed my heart—but I couldn't get a word in edgewise.

'YES! I will do this. Your book and our bookshop will launch you! We will sell this book together!! This book will be our best seller! Yes!'

28

Miro was Croatian. He had a wife and several small children, but I wondered if he ever got to see them. His whole life was spent hustling and enthusing in order to keep his bookshop going. In the days that followed our meeting, during which we organised the delivery of books and the launch, I'd have the occasional coffee with him outside the shop, sitting in the sun. He would describe a life so frenetic I felt exhausted just listening to him. He had myriad relationships with writers and publishers and distributors, which seemed to involve him in endless journeys and meetings and deals. I wondered if it was a corrupt industry—did he have to pay bribes? He was in constant wars with the bigger bookshops who tried to tie up the publishers in exclusive deals.

Together we organised shipping through a UK distributor to his store, and I set up a launch, inviting everyone I knew.

Miro was a man of energy and action—positive, enthusiastic, always smiling and ready for a cig and a coffee. His verve lifted me and in between shifts at the hotel I organised everything, spurred on by Miro's 'YES! We will do this! Yes!'

About three weeks before the book launch, I received two letters from O2, the telecommunications company. I'd never seen anything like these letters before—they weren't bills or invoices—so it took me a bit of time with the dictionary to work out what they were. The first one turned out to be a notification telling me that I had received a telegram. It said that in order to hear the contents of the telegram I needed to call O2.

The second letter turned out to be an identical copy of the first. You might ask yourself, as I asked myself, why they wouldn't just *send me the telegram*. But I had accepted by this time that certain things happened in Czech bureaucracies that were not worth trying to work out or fret about.

I called the number and spoke to a lovely woman—in Czech after we established she had no English—who told me I had called that number because I had a telegram.

'Yes, I know. Can you send it to me?'

'No, we don't send telegrams.'

'Uh-huh.' I paused, waiting for her to continue. She was silent. 'Can you tell me what it says?'

She could and did. She read it out in Czech and I had trouble understanding what she was saying, but I caught the words 'passport' and 'visa' so I assumed it was something pretty important. She repeated the message at my request, slowly, but eventually, after failing to make me understand its contents, she said she would find someone who spoke English.

That was a relief until the English speaker got on the phone and she told me that the telegram said that I had to provide my passport, an original power of attorney in Czech and English, my visa stamp, an original CERC form (whatever that was) in Czech and English, proof of accommodation in Prague, a copy of a bank transfer and a *plná moc* (whatever *that* was). And they all had to be notarised.

'And I have to provide these to O2?'

'I am sorry?'

'Who wants these things?'

There was a long pause. Then she said, 'You must call this number.' And gave me another number.

At this point, figuring this had something to do with the books, I called Miro and said I thought someone with fluent Czech might be required and could he please call the number and find out what on earth was going on.

'YES! I will call! I will sort this out!! Together we will do this!!'

Within two minutes of hanging up from Miro my phone rang and a man with perfect English spoke to me. 'Miss Weiss, you must provide these documents. I will email them to you and then, when you have completed them, I will have someone come to pick them up.'

It was like magic. This was what the rich and powerful must experience all the time—people around them solving their problems while the poor died from the stress of constantly having to work out impenetrable crap. Suddenly a hugely complicated situation looked a lot easier and I began to perceive that Miro was a good man to have in your corner.

The nice helpful man—who was from TNT as it turned out, the people who were bringing in the books and who'd sent me the telegram via O2—emailed me the forms. I photocopied my passport, filled in all the forms, got them translated and stamped and he sent a courier to pick them up.

A week went by. I called the nice man at TNT—Jakub was his name—just to see how it was going. I was in no rush—we had a fortnight to the launch, plenty of time. But Jakub said, awfully nicely, 'Ah yes, Miss Weiss, there is a problem. We need the page in your passport with your entry stamp.'

I was getting quite good at retaining equanimity in the face of Czech administration and so I registered not the tiniest flip of the heart or annoyance at this news. No problem. I got the passport page photocopied and Jakub sent a courier to pick it up.

A couple of days later, just to be on the safe side, now with twelve days to go, I called him to check on progress.

'Ah yes, Miss Weiss, there is another problem. We need a copy of all the entry stamps in your passport.'

Why the Sam Hill he couldn't have called me to tell me this I wasn't sure. Gritting my teeth, I photocopied the entire passport and he sent another courier.

Three days went by and I heard nothing. I thought perhaps I'd better phone and find out how things were going. However, when I called Jakub's number, it was answered by a woman.

'Jakub? Jakub has left TNT.'

'I see,' I said. 'And my consignment?'

The woman put me through to another man, Radek. 'He is looking after it now.'

The good news was that Radek spoke English, although not as well as Jakub, but he was just as pleasant.

'And are my books coming out of Customs any time soon?'

'It seems my colleague did not check the paperwork well enough,' said Radek, ominously. 'We need your address in Australia on the CERC form, not your address in Prague.'

'Fine,' I said, trying not to sound pissy. It wasn't his fault, and we still had nine days to go—no need to panic. So I filled in another form, which Radek had kindly emailed, and another courier arrived at the door.

The launch was on a Saturday. On the Monday of that week, I called Radek. 'How are we going with those books?'

'There is a problem with the invoice,' said Radek. 'The invoice does not say that the currency is Australian dollars.'

Really? It doesn't say Australian dollars? It does say 'dollars', though, doesn't it? And the books have come from an Australian company with an Australian address, and from an Australian port, but let's not go berserk and assume it's in Australian currency!!

I breathed deeply through my nose. They needed a new invoice. Radek told me that he had emailed Allied in Australia.

'Did you actually speak to anyone?'

'No.'

'Goddamn it, why do I have to make this phone call? Why didn't you just call me?' I shouted, losing my temper.

He had no reply.

I realised that at this point that we may not have books for the launch and that this could go on forever. There was no guarantee that this was the last bit of paper these people would need and I was having a panic attack.

I know: I'll call Miro. He's done launches before; this can't be the first time this has happened. There must be some standard way of dealing with this. He'll know what to do.

So I called him and explained the situation.

'Oh my GOD!' cried Miro, 'This is a disaster! A disaster! If you don't have books at the launch, you are going to have to do something really spectacular. I mean, you are going to have to dance half naked. Something. Oh my god, this isn't happening. Naked, I'm telling you! You're going to have to be naked!!'

I spent the next night on the phone frantically trying to get an invoice from Allied. Then, wide awake and sweating in the early hours of Tuesday morning, I remembered that they'd sent me one a long time ago in an email. I'd ignored it, thinking I'd just pay the one that came with the box. I hunted it down through the depths of my Inbox and printed it, then, in my neatest handwriting, I put an AUD next to the dollar sign and raced down to Big Ben at 9 am to fax it off to them.

'Pole dancing!' shouted Miro.

By this time, Miro and I were both calling TNT every hour on the hour. By Wednesday morning there was still no news, but Radek did tell us that we'd need to have them out of Customs that afternoon to guarantee delivery by Saturday as Thursday was a Czech national holiday. And then he said, 'You know it is hand written, the currency. I do not know if they will accept handwriting on the invoice.'

It was at this point that I wondered if I was missing something culturally significant. Was it possible that at this point I should offer a bribe?

You hear a lot about how everyone expects a bribe here in Prague, but, quite frankly, I've never met anyone who's successfully bribed an official, apart from a policeman. I've met lots of people who say they know someone who knows someone who has, and plenty of people who will tell you that bribery is expected, but honestly, most officials I've come across have starched beehive hairdos and a look of unassailable rectitude.

But perhaps I wasn't seeing something.

'Look, Radek,' I said, trying to sound knowing, 'is there *something I can do* to expedite this problem?'

'No, no there is nothing you can do.'

Hmm. Perhaps I wasn't using the right code. 'Are you sure there's not something, you know, something that might *smooth things over*?'

'I'm sorry?' Radek sounded puzzled, as well he might.

'Well, like, well . . . Oh never mind—when are we going to know if it will be released today?'

'We will know at 2 pm. I will call you.' Well he didn't, of course. I called *him*, but by this time he wasn't taking my calls. Miro finally managed to find out that the books had not been released. We were screwed.

On Friday morning, Miro called up TNT and screamed. Radek told us that it was still possible the books might get out of Customs, and that we'd know at 2 o'clock. At 2 o'clock I called him and he told me we'd know at 4 o'clock. Miro called up and screamed some more.

At 4 o'clock on Friday afternoon, the day before the launch—miracle of miracles—Radek said the books had cleared Customs and would be sent by special delivery and that they would be at my flat by 8 o'clock at the latest. He tried to tell me that special delivery would cost extra but I told him that if I was charged any fee, the CEO of TNT Worldwide would hear about it personally and graphically.

I waited on the edge of my seat while the hours passed.

Finally, finally, at 8 o'clock that Friday night, at the last possible moment, a special TNT delivery was made to my flat—eighty bottles of face cream, especially imported from France for the Hotel Leonardo.

The Hotel Leonardo had no use for fifty copies of *Me, Myself and Prague* and so sent the TNT man who delivered them back to my flat. I received the books at 10 o'clock that night.

29

My book was launched and friends bought it. It was stocked on the shelves of Miro's bookshop and I thought nothing more of it. And then one morning, sitting at my desk and struggling over the novel that wasn't appearing, I got an email asking me if I'd like to appear on *Dobré rano*. The hosts of the show had read my book and wanted to interview me on their morning television programme that coming Friday, if I was free. A driver would pick me up and bring me to the studio. He would be at my flat at 6.30 in the morning. The sender claimed to be 'Kateřina Němcová, Producer, *Dobré ráno*'.

It had to be one of my friends being funny. Anna or Stani. Stani, probably. There was, however, something indefinably authentic about it. It's hard to say what, but I didn't utterly dismiss the email. I called Anna.

'Is this you having a lend?'

'Having a what? A lend?'

'Yes, it means making fun of me.'

'Ha ha ha. I like that. But why a lend? What have I lent you?'

'I don't know.' It was always like this with Anna. Why a raw prawn? 'Anyway, I thought this must surely be someone joking.'

'I don't know. It's clever if it is. I would have done that if I'd thought of it. There is a *Dobré ráno*. It's a morning talk show. Very popular. Read it out to me again?'

I did, finishing with 'We would like to invite you to be our special guest on this Friday's programme.'

'Hmm. Special guest. They do have special guests. Writers and actors, usually. Why don't you write back and see what happens?'

So I did.

And Kateřina replied. 'Wonderful! Our driver will pick you up at 6.30. What is your address?'

I called Anna.

'Wow!' We both paused to digest it. 'I think you're going to be on *Dobré ráno*.'

'Is it a big show?'

'Nationwide. All the housewives watch it.'

'Wow! Still . . . it might still be Stani playing with me.'

'Guess you'll know on Friday.'

On Friday I got up at five. I didn't possess a hair dryer and I wanted plenty of time for my hair to dry. There'd been one more email from Kateřina, then silence. Stani was out of town, so I didn't ask him if he was pulling my leg. It might have been a joke, or it might not, but I was getting excited. Excited enough to get up early and put on a black top that

I thought would make me look thin . . . Well, thinner, not quite as fat, not as fat as I felt, I don't know . . . that would anyway look alright. And I shaped my hair into something that would look neat, or sexy, or attractive, or anyway not the usual bird's nest.

Makeup I wasn't sure about. I have a regular makeup routine I worked out when I was eighteen and have never changed. I've only worn a full face of it a handful of times— on stage, photo shoots, dress-up parties, if I'm a bridesmaid. Hardly ever, really. But I practised it religiously when I was a teenager, getting it right, so I could do it. I did it now.

Some of my makeup had been with me, I think, since those early practising days. None of it was younger than ten years old. There was one lipstick that might have been fifteen years old. It's ludicrous, really, how long that stuff will last. It's like the legend of those McDonald's hamburgers that are found years after they've been dropped behind couches, still in pristine condition—the buns just a little crumbly at the edges, the cheese and meat exactly the same as the day they first came off the industrial hot plate.

At 6.30 I went downstairs into the early morning light to wait for the car I still wasn't sure would really turn up. Part of me expected Stani to come prancing down the street laughing. However, as I stepped out into the street, a polite middle aged man in a cloth cap came up. '*Dobré ráno?*'

'*Ano, prosím.*' Yes, please.

I was going to be on national television. It didn't seem real. He drove me through town and over a bridge.

'I've never seen this part of the city before,' I said to him. 'I've never been over this bridge.' We were heading somewhere in a part of Prague I'd never visited. Somewhere you had to drive to get to.

At the studio, he dropped me off. 'I'll wait for you. I'm driving you back.'

I felt like a movie star. He took me to the glass doors and ushered me into a wide foyer. A girl appeared: '*Paní Weiss?*'

'*Ano.*'

She broke into a long stream of Czech.

'Ah . . .'

She looked surprised and spoke even more rapid Czech.

'*Mluvíte česky?*' she asked at last. Do you speak Czech?

'*Trochu.*' A little.

Dear god in heaven, did they not realise I couldn't speak Czech? Surely Kateřina had picked that up when I kept answering her in English. When, indeed, she wrote to me in English. Would she really have written to me in English if she thought I could conduct an entire interview in Czech? I was going to have to find her, explain to someone before they got me on TV.

'*Tudy, prosím.*' This way.

This one clearly didn't have any authority so I decided just to let them push me into chairs and rooms and do what they would with me until a manager came along.

She showed me a room with a thin man in it, who was playing with what looked like sound equipment. Right, no idea why I needed to see that. Then I was shown another room with mirrors and chairs. Then she took me out of there and put me in yet another room, one with chairs and bits of equipment stacked against the walls and just enough leg space for me and the snaked cables.

The girl went away and brought me back a glass of water, handing it to me silently. *No, we can't communicate. Go report this to your boss. She needs to know.*

I sat there for five minutes before another girl came in and beckoned me back to the room with chairs and mirrors, where she sat me in a red vinyl padded chair facing the mirror. She was a lovely young girl, who smiled at me very gently before taking the cleansing wipes to my face.

I felt relief—at least this wasn't going to be a disaster. I may not understand a word the interviewer said, but at least I'd look alright. The girl took the fifteen-year-old make up off and redid me. I looked pretty much the same.

Then I was plonked back in the equipment room. The first girl came in and asked if I wanted some more water. I did. She left again. A very much younger girl came back a few minutes later with a glass. I thanked her. She left.

More minutes ticked by.

A bright thin woman in her sixties—all giant red wooden beads and good posture under her skin-tight black top—went past the room, before doubling back and standing at the door. 'Rachael?'

'Yes!'

She came in and stuck out her hand. I'm short and she came up to my shoulder. 'I'm Jana,' she twinkled up at me, her tanned face crinkling over good bones. 'I'm your interpreter.'

Well, phew!

'I wondered how this was going to work,' I said to Jana.

'It's simultaneous translation.' Her accent was Oxford smooth, with the tiniest, tiniest Slavic slide to the occasional vowel. Somewhere in your atavistic mind you'd register her as foreign, but it would take a while for the evidence to reach the forefront of your mind. A contralto with a cigs-and-red-wine rasp. 'You won't even see me. I sit in a little box with headphones on and, while you're talking, I translate.'

'At exactly the same time?'

'At exactly the same time. Don't worry, I've done this loads of times. I used to do it for the president's wife when they travelled.'

'Klaus?' He was a notorious idiot, Václav Klaus, and his wife a deranged bitch, at least that was the goss. The goss was also that a young boy travelled with Klaus wherever he went and his wife's bedroom had remained unvisited since before the wedding. That's the sort of goss a macho country will spread about someone they really hate. Jana must have had a hell of a time if she'd been travelling with Klaus. (Google 'Václav Klaus' and after the Wikipedia entry you'll get forty pages of footage showing him stealing a ceremonial pen.)

'Havel,' she replied.

Jesus Christ. Václav Havel—an authentic Czech god.

'How utterly cool.'

'Yeah, it was a bit. They're lovely. That was his first wife, not the new one.'

Jana said this with the contempt that all Czechs have for the revered former president's new wife. The worthy old one, who'd been by his side through every iteration of his life—as penniless young dramatist and activist, jailed revolutionary, beloved first president and who had been loved by him and by all—had died of cancer, poor chicken, whereupon he'd immediately (with unseemly haste, the usual phrase used) married a much younger woman, an actress who he thenceforth insisted be cast in all his plays. She was considered beneath his dignity by the normally quite forgiving Czechs. A tramp.

'Olga was lovely,' reminisced Jana, sighing. 'I used to travel all over with them, translating for her at conferences. Anyway,' she said briskly, 'after that, it's all a piece of cake. You'll have an earpiece and as Marta's asking you the questions I'll be translating in your ear. Then, when you talk, I'll be translating you to the audience. You won't hear me, you'll just hear yourself. See you after?'

'Sure.' And she buzzed off in a blaze of red.

A few minutes later the first girl came back: '*Prosím.*' Come with me, please.

It was 7.25 and I'd been told I would be on at 7.30. They seemed to be cutting it a bit fine. When was I going to have the pre-interview chat? So far, no-one had asked me anything.

The girl led me to a small room with a linoleum floor. In it there were three large television cameras on wheels with tired fat men sitting behind them dressed in drooping t-shirts. The cameras were pointing in the direction of a curved bench, behind which sat three immaculate people: two serious iron-grey men and a very pretty—and very young—black-haired woman with a gorgeous hairdo in an updated sixties style.

The cameramen glanced at me, listless and uninterested. It must be a mighty dull job, just pointing the camera at talking heads and switching it on or off as required. I doubted they even did that. This is probably the lowliest job a cameraman can get. It must represent job security and very little else; they wouldn't look so drained otherwise.

The room itself was weirdly unglamorous, considering how peppy and upbeat these morning shows are—all trumpet flourishes and cutting to our correspondent in New York, where Fashion Week is just about to open. It was dark (yes, you'd have to work in a twilit room at fuck o'clock in the morning as well; no wonder these fat, weary men had circles under the eyes) and it was bare, apart from a couple of people standing around with clipboards and headsets, and the three cameramen. The desk itself was jerry-built from silver cardboard and appeared to be on the point of teetering over. The desk and the three presenters were all lit up and behind them was a blank wall. Bright but blank.

The trumpet flourish sounded through the headphones and the sixties hairdo presenter got out of her chair and moved to another one at the end of the desk. A figure emerged from the darkness around me, took my elbow, hurried me up to the chair across the desk from her and fitted headphones to my ears.

The presenter was adjusting herself, apparently oblivious to my presence. Perhaps we were just going to have a bit of a chat. She glanced up at me, expressionless, almost as though she would have looked right past me. I, however, being Australian, looked her in the eye, smiled and said, 'Krásný účes.' Great hairdo.

The transformation was magical. A great smile swept her face. At that moment the volume came up in my ear, a bit of transitional music, and then I heard the voice over say the words 'Australská autorka—Australian author. The presenter straightened her back and her eyes took on a professional glaze. Good fucking lord. It had started.

And then I was hearing Jana's voice in my ear and the presenter was looking straight at me and asking me a question, both at the same time. Just like that—without so much as a by-your-leave—I was on Czech national television, being interviewed. So it hadn't been Stani after all.

'First a box-office-smashing film,' said Jana's voice, 'now an Oscar nomination. You must be pleased?'

What the?? What now? The who, the what? Oscar? It had never dawned on me that people would think 'Rachel Weisz' when they heard 'Rachael Weiss' and make a joke about it. It's my name and so of radically different cognitive significance to me than it is to anyone else in the world, apart from my parents. In a nanosecond I realised that everyone probably thinks that when they meet me.

'Ha ha ha,' I laughed in the nick of time.

'But seriously . . . ,' said Jana's voice. I honestly don't remember hearing another word, except registering that they knew an amazing amount about me. That Kateřina had done an exceptional research job. I did remember, however, to say nice things about the Czechs whenever I could. I think I talked about their attitude to artists in general and to sculptor David Černý, and about how few countries revered their artists like the Czechs did, and how different that was to the world I came from, and how it helped me in my writing.

I said I'd come to live there because I felt something move me to write even when I did something as simple as travel on the trams. I surprised myself with that one. Where had that come from? It was true, but I'd forgotten that's how Prague had once inspired my writing. I think I said something about how you can feel their history soaked into the ground.

I find that in moments of panic, everything you know that can save you comes back to you. And so it was now. I heard voices in my head saying 'If you praise the Czechs, this can only go well.' And it did. At one point, Jana's voice asked me if I was learning the language.

Feeling suddenly, absurdly, light and confident, I said, *'Jsem učit česky a jsem mluvila pár slov, ale doufám, že k lepšímu.'* I'm learning Czech and I know a few words, but I hope to get better.

My interviewer started back in surprise. Jana kept her head and didn't translate into Czech, although I could almost hear her brain calculating furiously in the fraction of a second it took to register that the first words were in Czech, not English.

At the end of the interview, which the black-haired woman had conducted with steel-polished charm, and when the camera had switched to Jiří with the sports update, I leaned across and said, 'Thank you for a lovely interview' in Czech. Her face broke into a wide, shy smile, which was quickly smothered as she left her chair to go on to the next section of the show.

An unseen hand ushered me out of my own chair towards the door. As I passed one of the cameramen, he put out a hand to stop me. He looked a bit less miserable than he'd been when I first saw him, a bit more perk about him. 'Thank you for saying such nice things about the Czechs,' he said, in Czech.

'Je to všechno pravda.' It's all true.

Czechs, like Australians, like to hear good things about themselves. We share a degree of uncertainty about our place in the world.

'Was that alright?' I asked Jana, who was waiting for me at the door of the building with my driver.

'Perfect,' she replied. 'It makes a nice change to translate someone who can string a sentence together.' I felt we were going to get along famously. Jana and I made an arrangement to meet up for a red wine the following week and then my driver took me home.

By 9 am I was back in my flat and by far the most glamorous thing that ever had, ever would, or ever will happen to me was over. I'd been on Czech national television, on the show watched around the country by everyone without a job, being interviewed about the book I wrote about the country I lived in. For a day, maybe even two, the frantic voice on my shoulder badgering me to be better, go further, be smarter, get thinner, write more and meet more people shut itself up. Then I resolved that for the next book I wrote I'd study hard so I could conduct the whole interview in fluent Czech.

30

My book became the best seller at Big Ben Bookshop.

'What's your definition of "best seller"?' I asked Miro, not really believing him. He was the kind of man who'd tell you something nice just to make you feel good.

'Let me put it to you like this: your book sells ten times more than my next best seller.'

Wow. Even I was impressed. A writer from Lonely Planet took me out to lunch and put the book into his list of recommended reads.

I met Debra for lunch one day at a vegan restaurant. She'd researched the tiny handful of places in Prague she could go to for a meal and this was one of the few. I always let her choose where we ate. She had been there earlier that day, having morning tea with a friend.

'I boasted to her I was going to meet you,' said Debra.

'Boasted?'

'Yeah. You're famous. Didn't you know that? It adds to my cachet just knowing you. She asked what you were like.'

It makes me laugh to write this even now. She asked what I was like. Utterly bizarre.

'What did you say?'

'Oh, you know, that you were just like ordinary people.'

'You didn't!'

'I did. It's like you're not real.'

And then one day Anna and I were outside shul, waiting for it to open. I was telling her about hiking. A woman came up to us.

'Excuse me, are you Rachael Weiss?'

I didn't recognise her at all, not even a mental quiver. 'Uh, I'm sorry I don't . . .'

'Oh, that's okay you don't know me. Did you write *Me, Myself and Prague*?'

'Uh, I . . . what? Yes, but how did you . . . ?'

'I was passing by and I heard an Australian voice talking about hiking and I thought "How many Jewish Australians into hiking can there be in Prague?" I read your book on the way over here. Anyway, just wanted to say hi and that I loved it.'

I hardly knew what to say. Anna was staring at me.

'Thanks, that means a lot.'

And she was off with a wave.

Then, on my way to synagogue on the Friday after I appeared on TV, another complete stranger came up to me and said, 'Didn't I see you on *Dobré ráno*? Are you the Australian?' I floated on to shul in a peculiar, and temporary, space—famous. It felt amazing.

Stani was there putting out chairs: 'Hey, my mother said she saw you on *Dobré ráno*! She rang me. I can't believe it! She was so excited. She's ringing all her friends and saying "My son knows that author!" You've made her day.'

After the service it happened again. One of the Friday night regulars, an elderly Czech man, said to me, 'Hey, I saw you on *Dobré ráno*! It was you, right? Only, I didn't think it was you at first because you looked so beautiful. No, really. So beautiful, and I was thinking "Oh no that can't possibly be her!" It was the makeup. Why don't you wear makeup more often?'

His wife stood next to him, nodding. 'Why did you wear your glasses? You look so much better without them. Why?'

No doubt they were trying to be helpful, but I began to see how being famous might become a strain quite quickly. They seemed to think that I was theirs to comment on as they pleased. Or perhaps it was just that they were Czechs and so, like my father, considered criticism their own special gift.

I received some occasional fan email, which was nice. They were always sweet, except for the only actual letter on paper I received. It was from a Czech, an old guy living in Australia, who corrected all my grammatical errors and disputed some of my historical facts. Yes, I enjoyed fame, but I was quite glad it was only going to be a short burst.

31

One day, Dita didn't show up at work. The stress of being employed by Leonard had finally done her in and she had been carted off to hospital. The doctors told her she had to take six months off work. So Leonard fired her, or rather, because he'd not given her a contract, he let her go with no recourse to legal protection.

'She had an attitude problem,' he said, dismissing her hospitalisation from his mind. I began to be quite concerned about my visa. I had my *živno*, and I was quietly investigating editing work. The *živno* meant I was partway to my visa, but I had been relying on Dita to get me all the way there.

When Dita left, Leonard had to hire a new manager. The job was poison, of course, but someone had to be desperate enough to do it. He got an application from a thirty-year-old woman and asked me how he could find out if she was planning to get pregnant without alerting her to the fact. 'If I ask her directly, she'll just lie. Do you think I can stick electrodes on her head and wire her up to a lie detector?'

'What does it matter if she gets pregnant?'

'Because then there are all these ridiculous laws that say I have to pay her to stay at home.'

'I see why you've chosen to work outside the US, UK and Australia.'

'Well, yes, and it's a pain if she starts and then stops.'

'Weren't you worried I'd get pregnant?'

'Oh, you can get pregnant—you're the web writer and you're not important. I can replace you.'

He had just hired a web designer who he told me was 'really old, *really* old'.

'How old?'

'Forty at least.'

'I see. I'm old and unimportant.'

'No, no,' he replied unconvincingly. I made him admit that he was forty-six.

In the end he hired her. Martine was thin, attractive, ambitious, efficient and bossy, so I figured he thought he could work her into the ground and she'd be too young to know she could do better.

Shortly after she started, excitement descended on the hotel.

'Art Garfunkel's coming to stay! cried Leonard. 'He's booked the Oak Rooms! All of them! But we're supposed to be keeping it a secret so it's just between you and me.' He was in a lather, literally a lather. His mouth was more foamy than ever and sweat pools sagged his shirt. He was spitting uncontrollably.

Martine came in and he told her excitedly, 'Art Garfunkel's coming to stay! It's a secret—so don't tell anyone.'

'You told me this last night. And Antoine. And Amanda.'

'Yes, well, we can know but no-one else. He wants to be here incognito.'

The phone rang and Martine picked it up. 'Hi Jana. Yes . . . Yes . . . Yes . . . It's true, Art Garfunkel. He's just told us. I knooooooow!'

Leonard paced the room. 'We have to throw all the other guests out. Check how full it is and rehouse them. It shouldn't be too bad, he's not coming for another six weeks. Jana can put them up at hers. I'll take a cut, for passing on the business to her.' He passed me at a flapping rate. 'It's important you don't mess this up.'

'This is nothing to do with me, I just write the websites.'

'And whatever you do, don't tell anyone. I wonder how we can put this on the website without him noticing?'

'I'm pretty sure he'd notice that.'

'Maybe we could just say, "Famous person comes to stay"! We could have a guessing competition.'

The guests were all ejected and the Oak Rooms were repainted. The hand-held showers were replaced by standardised Western showers. When Art Garfunkel finally arrived, he came attended by his son (a miniature Art with red hair) and for the first time I saw how terrible it must be to be famous. The son behaved like a man who's found himself looking into the inexplicably awed eyes of strangers all his life, wondering what he's done to merit that look. He was elaborately 'at home' with the staff, the poor poppet, while teenage-ly self-conscious and with the added burden of knowing that people were staring at his pimples. Not that he had many pimples. He was far too rich, with access to specialist doctors and expensive creams, good food and whatever else keeps the spectacularly wealthy so smooth.

He and Art were accompanied by what could only be called a retinue—a secretary, who had efficiently and sweetly been our contact up to now, and a couple of elderly retainers. Leonard pranced about spitting excitedly, fluttering around the boy and Art like a besotted aging ballerina. Antoine and I were commanded to follow with the luggage while Leonard personally escorted them to the newly refurbished Oak Rooms, which had been dusted of any previous occupants and where the new curtains had only been put up that morning.

Getting the showers installed in the bathrooms in six weeks had been touch and go. Our non-celebrity guests had been begging for normal showers ever since the hotel started.

'Tell them it's good enough for the Czechs,' Leonard snarled, whenever we let him know a guest had complained about them. The restaurant feedback sheets would often mention the exorbitant price they paid for the rooms only to be given a vegan breakfast and a crap Czech hand-held shower.

Team Garfunkel inspected their rooms and got themselves together while I waited patiently in the lobby, in case the Lord and Master required my services. Antoine was assigned to the retainers.

I was standing on one foot and then the other, practising looking like a servant but getting tired of waiting, when a quiet voice behind me said, 'Excuse me?'

I turned to see the secretary. She was about thirty, neatly dressed and with the knack of fading into the background, which I suppose is crucial when you're in service.

'Hi.'

'I'm sorry to bother you, but I was wondering if you knew where I could get dope?'

She saw the surprise on my face and said, hurriedly, 'I thought everyone here smoked it?'

'Oh, they do, we do,' I said, 'It's just that actually I've never bought it here. I'm as ignorant as you.'

'What are you ignorant about? Apart from everything!' Leonard had come hurtling down the stairs.

The secretary blushed.

'Do you know where to get dope, Leonard?' I asked.

'Oh no, I . . . please, really it's okay . . .' The poor secretary—I should have been more tactful.

'Of course I don't. Ask Antoine—he's black, he'll know.'

'No really, I . . .'

I pressed her arm soothingly. 'Sorry about that,' I said. 'But let me get you some. I'll get myself some at the same time.'

Meantime, Art Junior expressed an interest in going out to a typically Czech place.

'I know just where to go!' cried Leonard

It was freezing, early April, and there we all were, straggling down the street. Art up front with Leonard telling him incomprehensible bits of Prague inconsequentialia, the boy making laboured conversation with the retainers and me. Suddenly I noticed the female elderly retainer looking distinctly white. Of course—she had just got off a plane from America, she must be feeling exhausted. She was stoically responding to every bit of self-involved trivia coming out of the son's mouth and for a moment I looked into the life of the poor cousin, the family retainer, the folk who depended on the rich.

'Are you alright? Perhaps you should go back to the hotel,' I suggested. 'You look like jet lag is about to hit.'

She looked at me gratefully, as if few people had ever asked how she felt in her whole life.

Art's son now emerged from his teenage reverie. 'Yes, yes, you go on back and get some sleep. We can go with Rachael.'

So I had dinner with Art Garfunkel's son and his secretary. And Leonard.

Next day, I was telling Amanda and Christian John about the dope.

'. . . and Leonard said, "Antoine can get it, he's black."' Amanda and I roared. Christian John didn't laugh, but then he often found the humour in the office difficult to take.

He was always sweetly serious, even though he was often slightly disjointed by things. Amanda being gay, for instance—what did he think about that? It was *WRONG*, of course, and she was going to *HELL*, but he didn't dislike her or treat her with contempt. Far from it.

Christian John had always treated everyone with respect and as much understanding as a lad of twenty-two could muster, even when Amanda and Leonard were giving each other stick. 'I thought you were gay when I first met you,' Amanda once told Leonard (and it was true: he did look as though he was probably gay; he had that queered-by-public-school air about him). 'I thought you were straight!' Leonard had shot back.

Now Christian John moved uneasily in his chair. I couldn't guess what his thoughts were, I could only see his discomfort, valiantly held down as ever by his innate pleasantness and farm-boy good manners.

Christian John's wife—yes, he had a wife—was pregnant. They were going to have a baby. He chose this moment to tell us he was leaving.

He said to me: 'To be honest, it was the dope. That was one step too far.'

I hadn't even noticed that that had caused him more uneasiness than anything else—the talk of strip clubs, the racism, the rudeness, the brothels, the lesbians and gays (Antoine and Amanda and I frequently discussed their same-sex partners). Yes, it was the dope that finally did him in.

Although Christian John had told Leonard he was leaving to return to America now that he was having a child, bizarrely Leonard was hurt and took it personally.

'He has a nerve!' Suddenly Leonard was shouting and spitting. 'I don't need him! I don't need him and his endless criticism. Who does he think he is?'

I waited, fascinated, for the inevitable. Was he really going to say it? About John? The most level, loyal, dogged employee anyone had ever had?

'He has an attitude problem!' screamed Leonard.

Yes, yes he was. And he believed it too.

32

My propensity for falling in love with deeply unsuitable men showed no sign of abating. My little 'thing' for Leonard had long ago disappeared, but the fact that I'd ever entertained such thoughts about him should tell you how desperately I needed love. My loves were as intense and undiscriminating as a teenager's.

One of my earliest crushes was a fellow at the synagogue. I met him at a Friday night dinner, where he sat next to me and flirted delightfully and engaged me in a conversation about the meaning of God in which he defended his position as a fundamentalist—yes, he actually believed that the world was five thousand years old and that God had personally handed tablets to Moses—so charmingly that I found myself twinkling at him over my glasses. He was superbright, so that went some way to explaining it, but mad as a cut snake, and I developed an instant and total crush.

'Really? Samuel?' said Anna, somewhat taken aback when I told her about it. 'Samuel may not be such a good choice.'

Apparently, he was chronically depressed. He didn't believe in drugs and he spent a lot of time in his house—not answering the door, the phone or emails—just coping with his illness.

'I guess I can see why you like him. He's very honest. There's no game playing about him.' She paused. 'But what about the depression?'

'Everyone has their cross to bear. I get depressed too.'

Insanely, I thought that the perfect relationship would cure him. I pictured evenings spent engaged in intellectual debate, I the only woman to understand him.

'He doesn't believe in evolution,' Anna said.

She had a valid point. I ignored it. I ignored it through overheated email exchanges and thrilling meetings at Friday night dinners. I ignored it until his next episode, a mere six weeks later, when he disappeared from the face of the earth. After a month when he didn't answer texts and emails from the woman who was going to save him, I gave up and turned my attentions elsewhere.

In ordinary circumstances I don't suppose Stani and I would have been friends. He read fantasy novels, played computer games and was a boy in his early twenties. I read Jane Austen, played the piano and was a woman in my early forties. But we weren't in ordinary circumstances, at least I wasn't. I was a stranger living in a strange land. He, for some reason, wanted to hang out.

Neither of us could manage to maintain a relationship. I couldn't even get a date and while Stani got plenty they all ended suddenly and with him brooding on the perfidy of women. Mostly he ditched them, but one girlfriend chose to end the relationship to become a lesbian, another checked herself into rehab and another had a nervous collapse.

No-one I got a crush on—from mattress salesmen to real estate agents—ever felt the same way about me. I was going to expat events and coming up with nothing. Stani and I used to discuss our tragically unfulfilled love lives over moody beers. He was the only single man I had an emotional relationship with. He was the last sort of man I should have found attractive. And yet.

The fact was that I was finding him increasingly attractive. I kept telling myself that it was out of the question, for all sorts of reasons: it had no legs, would never last, and might ruin a lovely friendship. Oh yes, I kept telling myself that. To no avail. More and more I was arguing the case for, and ignoring the case against.

This was easy to do, as I could sense that the same thoughts frequently crossed his mind. It was in the air—increasingly so, as loneliness and libido bit into me—and we both knew it. We never said anything, but it was there. On one occasion, we went to see a movie with a terrifyingly explicit sex scene and in the dark our embarrassment thickened around us. Neither of us could mention it afterwards—we discussed the whole film, but not that scene. The idea grew around us, heavy in the air, and we both pretended it wasn't happening.

It had crossed my mind more than once just to say, 'Oh fuck it, let's have sex.' Just to connect with someone, on some level other than the pub/social level. Just to feel something, anything—to have my heart stirred, my skin heated, my senses frayed. I wanted, desperately, to have my heart held by another human being. But even though it crossed my mind, I always had the good sense to let the thought pass right out again.

And then one night we were sitting next to each other in a pub, drunker than usual, and one of us said, 'So, are we going to talk about it?' We both smiled and looked into each other's eyes. It seemed so right. We started to kiss. And then we couldn't stop.

Who knew a boy of twenty-three would know how to kiss that well? My skin burned and my throat softened. My body melted into the kiss, the kiss that went on for hours.

At four in the morning we left the pub. The question of going home together did not arise and a tiny voice in my head asked, *Why is that so?* We staggered around trying to find the night tram. And then Stani got bored and said, 'Just take a taxi.' In my drunken haze I heard the voice of a man with regrets (*Why is that so?*), but I pushed it to the back of my mind.

That night I lay on my bed, my head spinning, my skin sizzling, my veins and flesh bursting their banks with the glory of contact at last. I allowed my self-discipline to evaporate and my long-hibernating desire for love to engulf me. And my sense.

The tiny voice at the back of my mind kept saying *computer games, computer games—he likes computer games* but I shushed it. Yes, yes, computer games—but this wasn't forever, this was just a little fling. *Your heart will break, you know it will, you know what you're like.* Yes, yes, probably, but at some undefined time in the future. Now my heart was blazing. And I needed that. I really needed that.

Computer games, computer games. It was no good. My senses had been awakened and the king tide of my emotions was not going to be pushed back by the tiny broom of my sensible self. My poor old sensible self. It tries its best.

Next morning, I was woken by a text message from Stani. 'I think it is better if we forget that happened. I am in love with someone else.'

At first I couldn't believe what I was reading. What the fuck was he doing, kissing me when he was in love with someone else? And what the fuck was he doing telling me this by text, the coward!

I hit the green button on my mobile: 'I'll meet you at Anděl.'

'Okay,' he replied.

I stood at Anděl station in the cold April air, feeling pale and limp-haired and murderously hungover. I let the pain wash over me. I knew now that I was in danger of losing a friend as well as losing a lover.

The lover bit I'd accepted between crawling out from under the quilt and standing under the shower. That bit was gone. But I had a sixth sense that my friendship was in jeopardy now too.

Stani came towards me, expressionless. 'Where will we go?'

Christ, the last thing I needed was to be making restaurant decisions. 'I don't know. Anywhere.'

'Where do you want to go?'

Sigh. 'McDonald's?' McDonald's is hideous of course, but the Sausage & Egg McMuffin is perfect hangover food.

But then I changed my mind. 'No, I can't talk about my most intimate feelings in McDonald's.'

Stani smiled briefly. 'No.'

'Okay then, Café Louvre.' They do a hot chocolate there that I thought I'd need. We made our way there in silence, both of us grateful for it. We managed to avoid saying anything until we'd ordered.

'So.'

Stani said nothing.

'Can I ask why you kissed me if you were in love with someone else?' I said crisply. I'm a woman of forty-one. I get crisp when I'm annoyed.

'I don't know.'

We fell silent.

I needed more than this. I needed 'Sorry, you're special, I feel something for you.' I did not need 'You are a mistake, I feel something for someone else.'

Then I started to cry quietly. It was just too much for me. I saw a chasm opening up where there would be no friendship, no love, not even the possibility of a ludicrously impossible affair—just a blank future and my heart back in its box. My skin was untouched, my blood running thin.

Stani remained silent. More than anything, I wanted him to put his arms around me, or even touch me, to say *something*. But he said nothing. I guess he just wanted the whole thing to be over with.

Nothing more was said. I stopped crying eventually. Breakfast was untouched. Mine, at least. Stani got through his with no problems.

We walked in silence back to the tram stop.

I said the one thing I knew was very, very important. 'You know what worries me? These things can wreck friendships if you're not careful.'

Stani said nothing. I never saw him again.

33

After Stani, it was like a dam had burst and the loneliness I'd kept behind the dam wall came bursting forth, sweeping aside all sense in its path. I fell in love more frequently and violently than ever, and with the most unsuitable men. At least once every two months I'd crash into love with someone, my loneliness expunging any of the generally plentiful evidence against his being the man of my dreams. I was at a loss to explain it, except probably by my isolation and sense of dislocation and desperation to cling onto something—anything—warm and loving. Desperation for there to be someone apart from me in my inner life.

My lonely heart sent me spinning and I began to fancy myself in love with any man who crossed my path: the Seventh Day Adventist at synagogue who'd converted to Judaism and couldn't speak a word of English but seemed like the sweetest guy in the world ('Who needs language when the love is there?' 'You do,' replied Anna), the moody Norwegian who occasionally turned up to the Lazy Vinohradian dinners, brusquely rejecting all attempts to draw him out ('I ski. That is all. I ski.'), the young, dreadlocked teacher who took us for Summer Intensive at my Czech school (my Czech was still abysmal, but I struggled on with classes, still fantasising about the day I'd understand every word I heard around me). None of these men showed the slightest interest in me.

My singleness and my loneliness was the subject of endless conversations. Marion said I should try affirmations.

'If you say to yourself "I am loved", then you will feel loved. And when you feel love, you will attract love to you. As long as you are saying "I don't want to be alone", you'll be alone.'

It sounded dubious to me. Americans have so much *faith*. If you're an Australian you tend to think if you convince your-self you're loved *when you're not* you may as well join a cult. But I was willing to give anything a go.

'What you resist, persists,' said Marion, and that did ring true.

I am loved, I am loved, I am loved, I chanted silently each morning. *But I'm not!* Shhhhh. *I am loved I am loved I am loved.* I was folding towels in the bathroom when it all caught up with me. I sat on the toilet and cried and cried. No, I wasn't loved.

In desperation, I asked my friends to keep an eye out for likely dates for me.

Mike, the leader of the Lazy Vinohradians, kindly took me out to a bar. 'The way to meet people is to go cruising in pairs. I'll be your wingman.'

We went to a sports bar we knew off the Old Town Square. It was loads of fun coming to this bar with Mike and Mathematics Neil when the football or tennis was on, drinking a few pints and becoming deeply involved in the fortunes of Andy Murray. It was less appealing sitting at the bar and waiting to be hit on.

I looked around. 'See, what gets me is this,' I said to Mike. 'I don't actually like going to bars in general. I only come here with you. I'd always prefer a restaurant or a Scrabble game at Tanya's. So suppose I meet someone here. He's likely to want to hang out in more bars. And what am I going to say to that?'

'That is a problem, yes,' Mike agreed. 'And I'm not seeing anyone promising, are you?'

'Thank god you said that. No. Let's give up.'

Mike had just got himself a lovely new Czech girlfriend who was a flight attendant, and she set up a date for me with a pilot she knew. That did seem quite promising—pilots fly everywhere, so think of the air miles I could get!

I met Honza at Starbucks, which immediately put me off, Starbucks being a place I'd normally not set foot in.

'It's my favourite coffee here,' said Honza as we waited to order. He was an extraordinarily handsome man so for a brief moment I experienced that feeling of two opposite ideas existing at the same time in the brain—'fantastically handsome' (*woo hoo!*) and 'thinks Starbucks coffee is not just good but the best' (*blecchhh!*). I let the moment pass and ordered a tea, and we went outside to one of the tables on the Old Town Square to get to know each other in the sunshine.

'It must be so great to travel all over,' I began.

'It is the best thing about being a pilot.'

'Where have you been?'

'Where have I *not* been might be an easier question to answer!'

I laughed. 'Tell me about some of them. Have you been to Moldova? I've always wanted to go there.'

'Yes, I have flown to Moldova. I've been to every European country and most of Asia. I have been to Sydney and Melbourne. I like to collect countries. I am trying to go to every one.'

'And what is Moldova like?'

'Oh, the airport is terrible of course. It is what you would expect.'

This seemed an odd response. Had I been unclear? 'And what about Moldova itself?'

'I never left the airport.'

'Oh, I see.' Surely that was cheating? You can't say you've been to Moldova when you've only been to the airport.

'So what are some of your favourite destinations?' I tried again.

'They are all the same, aren't they? One airport is very much like another.'

'But don't you get out and look around? I mean, aren't you there for a few days?'

'Sometimes, not always, and I generally just stay in the hotel.'

'So when you say you want to visit every country in the world . . .'

'I am going to touch down in every country, yes.'

'I see.'

My dreams of travelling extensively with this man evaporated. The conversation lagged while I searched around for something else to ask him.

Another peculiar thing about Honza was that he showed absolutely no interest in me. He didn't ask me a single question about myself and seemed content to talk solely about himself. I asked him about his hobbies.

'I build handmade furniture.'

Now this seemed interesting. 'What do you build?'

'I make tables and chairs. Just for friends, but I hope to have a business making furniture when I retire.'

'So you are that good?'

'Oh yes,' he said, and I believed him.

'That's a lovely thing to do.'

'Yes, I love it. I hate being a pilot. I wish I could build furniture for a living.'

'Why can't you—if you're good at it and your friends like it?'

Honza looked taken aback at the suggestion. 'But I would need a website.'

Yes, and? Puzzled, I tried another tack. 'Do you have a workshop?'

'Yes.'

'And all the tools you need?'

'Yes.'

'So the only thing you need is a website and some marketing?'

'Yes, but it is not safe.'

'Why not?'

'I would have to borrow money from a bank.'

Honza hated being a pilot and wanted to build furniture but was afraid to do that because of the few thousand crowns he would need to borrow. So he was going to wait the fifteen

264

years to retirement and then do the thing he loved. And in the meantime he counted airports.

We parted as quickly as I decently could. Bizarrely, Honza wanted a second date. I turned him down.

———————

It was Barbara, Andy's wife, who suggested I try internet dating. It was obvious by then that I was unlikely to find a partner in Prague just through socialising. The fact was that the expat women very rarely did. The expat men who lived in Prague generally married Czech women, or wanted to marry a Czech woman—why marry an Australian with a loudly feminist outlook when you could marry a woman who'd do your washing for you? And Czech men shared that view.

If Anna was finding it hard (and she *would* do your washing for you), what chance did I have? So I joined an internet dating site, not a Czech one but an international one, where my dream man could come from any part of the world.

I'd chosen a paid site and completed a profile specifying who I was looking for. A lot of people on the site lived in America, so distance was a problem for some men who might otherwise quite have suited me. Nonetheless, I started a few email flirtations.

An artist in Florida seemed quite promising. He mentioned finding an alligator in his pool, thus nicely evoking masculinity and exotica in the peacock tail he was waving before me. I imagined myself living with an artist in the swampy south, developing an interest in orchid hunting and accompanying him to his art gallery openings. Indeed, he seemed to find me just as exotic and it went on for quite some time before eventually fading under the impossibility of the distance and the gradually surfacing evidence of his predilection for the gloomy—he seemed to suffer from the intolerable weight of the world. Because I myself struggle to keep cheery, I thought I'd best find someone who could help me in my quest for happiness, rather than someone who was going to need me to propel him.

Still, our email exchanges and occasional Skype calls did much to calm the frantic part of me that could not stand being single; they convinced me that, at the very least, I should keep on dating. *Dating*—see how Americanised I'd become? Who dates in Australia? There you meet someone, you hang about together for a bit, and you either end up together or you don't.

The next man I met on the site was a pilot, my second in a romantic context. I was in correspondence with two men at the time, one who lived in Michigan, and this pilot.

The Michigan one had an odd life. He lived with his father and worked for Skoda—in their plant in Michigan, but every year he got sent to their plant in the Czech Republic, in Brno, where he would spend six weeks. I never really got to the bottom of what he did or why Skoda sent him to this plant every year, but he loved it. He really loved Brno and wanted the firm to keep him there.

Conversations with him were mildly downbeat given the state of the US car industry—he seemed to be forever on the verge of losing his job and the room he lived in seemed to be some kind of basement. We did meet up when he went to Brno, and we maintained an affectionate friendship, but he was never really right for me.

266

The pilot flew all over the world for a private airline and so, although American, he could come and meet me in Prague for a coffee when his schedule allowed. He had a rich client he was ferrying about at the time. I learnt that the life of a pilot was not an easy one—it was almost as fraught as the life of a freelance editor; living from job to job, trying to build up a client base through reputation, fighting for scraps of work and hoping some rich company would come along and pay you a salary with a pension. He told me it was not easy to get a job as an airline pilot because anyone who had those positions never let go of them. He was a cheery soul but after one glance I knew he wasn't for me. There was no chemistry whatsoever.

These failures were disheartening, especially given that these were the highlights among a host of interactions that generally ended after the first email exchange, or indeed after the first read of the profile. I had very little interest in anyone in Prague, except for a Czech chap who told me his wife refused to have sex with him and asked whether I would be interested in an affair. I thought about it and thought, 'Why not? At least I'd get to have sex.' And then I slept with him. It was tedious as all get out. I'd like to say I rejected him at that point on moral grounds, but I'd be lying. We slept together twice more—I was hoping it would get better and it never did—and only *then* did I resolve not to sleep with him again.

One day we were talking about the morality of cheating. He was saying we couldn't tell anyone, in case his wife found out.

'Absolutely. If there's one thing that can't happen it's that your wife is hurt in any way.'

'And you can't say anything now anyway, since you're just as guilty,' he said.

I laughed. 'Oh yeah? How do you figure that?'

He looked startled. 'Well, you're just as involved as I am. You're sleeping with me. You're just as responsible!' His shock was palpable.

'No I'm not. I didn't make a promise to be faithful to your wife. You did. The only one doing any cheating here is you.'

He went white. 'If I'd known you felt like that . . .'

'What—you'd never have slept with me? My mouth is shut because I have no wish to hurt your wife's feelings. But the guilt is entirely yours.'

And that was the end of that. I must say that I was astonished at his naked grab for complicity, the coward. If you're going to cheat on your wife, at least have the good grace to call it like it is. The cheek of trying to say I was responsible for his actions! Like most Czech men, the idea that a woman might not be responsible for men's behaviour hadn't been presented to him before. It was very, very satisfying to spell it out.

The sex was rubbish anyway. No wonder his poor wife was refusing to sleep with him. That week, for his horoscope (Aries) I wrote: 'A moral truth will confront you this week. Don't be afraid to face reality. You are responsible for your actions, no-one else.'

34

For all the difficulties I faced in Prague, during the summer months they largely dissolved away in the sheer pleasures of living in the city. Prague is an easy city to get around. It is not a horrific nightmare of freeways and skyscrapers and wind tunnels; your gaze can rest on the charming castles and medieval roofs from the city's parks and beer gardens, where people gather in shorts and sandals, drinking the fabulous beer, chatting, playing games and smoking the odd joint. You can get anywhere at any time on the network of trams that cover the entire city and ding to a stop every few minutes. Living as I did in Žižkov, on the 9, 22 and 23 trams, I could be at home in my pyjamas and half an hour later I could be in a beer garden across town looking glam and chatting in the sun with Andy and any number of Andy's numberless friends.

At the beginning of every summer the Prague Fringe Festival was held. It is a week of short plays and performances from around the world, played in four or five theatres around the Old Town and in Kampa Park, which is on an island on the river in the middle of the city. It became a Prague ritual to see as many performances as we could and then go to the bars where the actors hung out to meet them. Marion, Tanya, Zsuzsa and I were regulars, as were Andy and Barbara and Debra. It was a magical week—drinking, socialising, seeing performances, the sunshine warming us from the long winter, the days easy and bright, the light fading only at nine in the evening.

It was Andy, Barbara and Debra who were with me on the shortest night of the year. One of the exciting things about being in Europe is the way the days swing from six hours long in the dead of winter to eighteen hours long at the height of summer. The winter and summer solstices occur on 21 December and 21 June respectively. I don't know why it should be so exciting, but it is. Almost as exciting as snow, which drew me to the window, fascinated, every—and I mean *every*—time it fell from the sky, no matter how lightly or briefly.

The summer solstice fell on a Saturday that year and I persuaded Andy, Barbara and Debra that it would be fun to stay out all night and greet the dawn on the Charles Bridge on this momentous day.

'What's so momentous about it?' asked Barbara, not sounding as enthusiastic as I thought she might.

'It's the shortest day of the year!'

She didn't seem to think that that alone was enough to make the day exciting. 'So what—there are fewer hours of dark? And more of light?'

'Yeah!'

'I tell you what,' said Andy, 'how about we go see a band and see how long we get through the night.'

Andy was a man who always went the whole night, and he usually had to rely on his stoner journalist mates to keep him company. He probably thought I wouldn't make it. I agreed to his idea, and secretly planned to keep them all drinking until dawn broke.

We started the night on Střelecký ostrov, the biggest island on the river, which during summer was a permanent festival of outdoor cinema and music. The summer film programme was stocked with cinema classics, but the music was a bit more cutting edge. Andy described the band we were going to see, Peppa Voltarelli, as 'rocked-up Calabrian folkie'.

I am sure they were both rocked-up and folkie, but I got there late. I'd taken a group out for a hike that day and it had become long-ish, about five hours, partly because we had a casualty—one poor guy did his hip in about halfway through. This was made more stressful by my getting us lost (twice) and so adding another hour to the trip, with the poor fella hobbling along trying not to kill me. However, it was entirely his own fault—for god's sake, who turns up to a hike in tennis shoes?

During the hike I'd been telling Irish Pam about the summer solstice and how excited I was, and how we were going to stay out all night and see the dawn and did she want to come?

'What's so exciting about the shortest night of the year?' she asked.

'It's the shortest night of the year!' Why was I the only one thrilled about this?

'Isn't it a leap year?'

Was it a leap year? 'Yes,' I said, calculating. 'So?'

'Well if it's a leap year, then the summer solstice was on 20 June.'

'Last night? Last night was the shortest night of the year?'

'Yup.'

Bugger. I decided not to mention this to Andy, Debra and Barbara. It was only not the shortest night by about a minute. Who was going to notice? I couldn't have stayed up all Friday anyway, because of the hike. So I went home, had a bath and a little lie down, then went to Střelecký ostrov.

I heard the second last and the last folk-rock songs as I was making my way up the river to the island. Then, after the concert ended there was a bit of milling about and drinking of beer—Andy's many friends joining us, not joining us, hooking up with wives and husbands, deciding whether to eat. No-one was in the least bit interested in the summer solstice.

While people were deciding whether to carry on with the evening, Andy and I went and got some street food—a fried lump of cheese on a hamburger bun for Andy and a fatty sausage on bread for me. When we returned to the island, those who were going to kick on had voted for Bokovka, a non-smoking wine bar, where we had several bottles of Argentinian red, the name of which has been wiped from my memory.

I still hadn't managed to persuade anyone that staying out all night would be fun, but a rumour had spread that Peppa Voltarelli were playing an unadvertised gig at a bar called Duende at around midnight. Using that as bait, I managed to get a group of people that far. And there, as often happened in Prague, some really cool and interesting people turned up and were fun and witty and, before you knew it it was two in the morning. Peppa Voltarelli were there, but they decided to drink instead of play.

So now I just had to get people to stay up until dawn. Once you've gone past the 2.30 am mark, it's hard to argue against staying up until 4, which, I assured them, was dawn. Or maybe 4.10. I couldn't remember.

'Well, which?' Debra wanted to know.

'4.10.' Was it 4.10? 'I'm sure it's 4.10. I remember now, I looked it up.'

Someone had lit a joint. So what with that, the Argentinian red, the beer, the five-hour hike and the fact that I'd been up since 6 o'clock that morning, I was hallucinating. Had I really checked the sunrise time? That didn't sound like me at all. What sounded more like me was coming out on the wrong night and not bothering to take the thirty seconds or so it would have taken to check the time on the internet.

'What time does Duende close?' asked Barbara at one point, hoping she wouldn't be made to go to the Charles Bridge.

'When we're finished' was the cool, but not completely accurate, answer. Duende started putting chairs on tables around 3.45 am so we walked to the bridge, three people and me. By this time I had admitted that it was not actually the summer solstice.

'So let me get this straight,' said Andy. 'We're celebrating the equal-second-longest day of the year, is that right?'

'Oh come on. Only by one minute. No wait, it's two minutes shorter than the longest day.'

But since none of them had ever been on the Charles Bridge at dawn, they came along—razzing me all the way, of course.

So, there we were on the bridge—and it was *beautiful*. The pre-dawn soft light washed over the city and the colours gradually sharpened—the iron-green spires came to life first, then the white and red walls under the Castle, with black stripes marking out the sides of the buildings. The water glowed blue from the lights.

'When's dawn again?' asked Debra.

'Will you stop whining? Dawn's at 4.10. Or maybe 4.'

At 4.30 Barbara said, 'I don't think it's dawn yet.'

'It's dawn. See how light everything is?'

'There's no light. If there was light it would reflect off the hills. And it isn't.'

'It must be.'

'It isn't.'

Barbara and Andy went to get us more street food. I stayed gazing at the city, imagining I would come out here with my crayons every dawn and draw it, in blocks of colour only. See, I told you I was hallucinating.

I managed to get everyone to stay until 4.50 am. But when I insisted we should walk half an hour to get to our tram stop, so we could stay out in the glorious, equal-third-longest-day-of-the-year dawn, everyone baulked. They wanted to get the shorter metro ride and go home to bed. I, grittily determined to be purist and romantic, made Debra walk with me all the way to the nearest tram stop.

A weary Debra left me at the stop and shuffled off to the metro station. I was sufficiently stoned to gaze in wonder and delight at the dawn-kissed buildings, and to pride myself on how superior I was in sensitivity to my friends, who had no sense of the soul of Prague. They could only think of their beds at a time when nature was giving us something as special as a summer solstice.

Then I started to wonder where the bloody hell the tram was.

No, no—stay with the glory of the newborn day, I admonished myself, and gazed once again at the fresh face of the day.

I stayed in my glowing space until the tram made its clanking early morning appearance. I got on, feeling like a woman who'd really lived, sat down and almost instantly felt something was not right. I moved my butt gingerly and heard a squelching sound. I'd sat in a seat soaked in pee.

I stood for the rest of the journey, terrified of the disease I was going to get. When I got home, my jeans and knickers and everything that might have even remotely come into contact with the pee went into the wash with extra disinfectant.

I spent Sunday in bed drinking champagne and reading. It seemed like a fitting end to a splendid evening. That day, Barbara sent me an email. Dawn had been at 4.53. We'd missed it by three minutes.

35

The end of my job at The Three Bells came one morning in May. I presented Leonard with the invoice from the embassy for my visa.

'I never said I'd get you a visa!'

'That's exactly what you said. That is why I started working for you.'

'You started working for me because no-one else would hire you. You don't do any of the work I tell you to anyway.'

At moments like these, implacability enters my soul. I followed Leonard into the kitchen and trapped him, sweating and spitting, cornered against the new/old cupboard.

'You told me you'd take care of my visa. You lied to me.'

Leonard sweated more. 'I don't pay for anyone's visas. Why would I pay for yours?'

'You lied to me,' I said, just stating a fact. 'You lied to me.'

That week I 'worked from home', writing my book. On Friday afternoon I went into the office, deleted all my files, and said calmly to Martine, 'Here is the invoice from the embassy. Leonard said I should just get it from petty cash.'

It was 6000 crowns. Martine nodded and counted out the cash.

'Thank you. And now I am resigning.'

Martine met my eye. 'I won't tell him.'

'Good luck, kid.'

And then I left. I didn't know what I was going to do, but I was free. And it felt good.

———•———

By this time, Debra and my writing group had been joined by Suzy, an American painter. We called ourselves the Prague Artists Group and we met every Wednesday night at my place over vegan nut snacks and coffee. Suzy lived around the corner from me with her Czech boyfriend in his grandmother's flat. The grandmother was in a nursing home and his parents had retired to the country. As if the Czech passion for hand-held showers weren't enough, the bath was in the kitchen.

'I hated being an American whining princess,' said Suzy, 'but I made Marek put in a wall-mounted shower and shower curtain before I'd move in.'

When she had gone back to America to visit, she returned to a world where all her friends were married to successful husbands, having babies and redecorating their homes. They were politely stunned when Suzy told them that she had a bath in her kitchen. We were all disconnecting from the status we'd had in our Western lives. I was no longer a chief administrator but an ex-bullied hotel dogsbody; Debra was not a PhD student but an editor just scraping by; Suzy didn't have a newly promoted husband and a redecorated living room, she had a bath in her kitchen. When I went to visit Suzy, I saw in her spare room a dark-wood cabinet with sliding glass doors filled with china knick-knacks that were exact replicas of the knick-knacks in my own grandmother's cabinets that stood in my father's flat in the Prague suburbs.

'Ya,' said Suzy, '*All* old Czechs have these.'

Debra, Suzy and I worked our way each week through a chapter of *The Artist's Way,* releasing our Inner Goddesses, or whatever.

'Name five careers you'd like to have had,' I read out.

'Hitman,' said Suzy. Yes! I hadn't put that one down but now she had said it, I realised I'd often hankered after being a hitman.

Debra hadn't done this exercise. 'It just didn't speak to me.' She was apologetic and seemed to feel she'd let the side down.

'Not at all, old girl,' I told her. 'This is only meant to be an exercise. Not all of them will work. Me, I wanted to be a concert pianist, a long-haul truck driver—I like silence and being on my own—a gardener, a forensic pathologist and a marine biologist. All of which require me being on my own. That's the only thing I could find that they said about me.'

None of us felt like a window into our souls had been opened up, except for the hitman one, which was brilliant. We talked about why it was so appealing (because of the instant justice, and the anger release, and we thought that killing might be fun) and then that morphed into a conversation about why we'd need to have a vigilante job (because we

278

were so frequently angry and unable to express it), and then on to why this was so (because of the frustrations of living in the Czech Republic). We ended up on the topic that took up the rest of the session—how unhappy we were in Prague.

At the end of the session I read out the book's instructions. Our homework was to read the chapter and do the exercises, which were something like changing your cushions, or throwing out old clothes, or starting a hobby you'd always wanted to do, I can't remember now.

By the following week I'd done them but neither Debra nor Suzy had. Suzy had done a painting instead, and they still hadn't spoken to Debra. We had a brief discussion about it and then quickly returned to the topic of how difficult life was in Prague and how we were all sick of it.

Now that I look back on it, I think the problem was we'd all done what the book was suggesting—the three of us had left our comfortable grooves and thrown ourselves into lives that came from the imagination, rather than any sense that retirement and mortgages need to be considered. And there we were—not happy and not creating.

The group was great for sorting out work problems. Over time, all of us were at the mercy of the unscrupulous and we turned out to be great at analysing each other's problems and coming up with ways of subverting the power of those bosses. It made our lives considerably easier.

I wrote an excruciating bit of an awkward novel, but Debra never wrote another poem. Suzy painted more and more, but I doubt it was a result of the Prague Artists Group.

36

I had become a stalwart of the synagogue community. Although the choir had folded I still went every Friday and sometimes stood up to sing. Come the middle of July, when both Peter and Anna were on holidays, they asked me if I would like to run services.

I explained that I hadn't the faintest idea how to do most of the prayers. There are some prayers in the service that are half-sung/half-spoken. All children learn these prayers for their bar/bat mitzvahs, when they are twelve or thirteen. I, however, was never bat miztvahed and never learned them. I hear people in the synagogue all the time, saying them with the same familiarity I have with the Lord's Prayer and the Australian national anthem—the only two songs of worship I ever learnt at school—and it's a matter of some embarrassment to me that I don't know these basic Jewish prayers.

'Not to worry,' said Anna, 'you only have to say the first line, then you can mumble. It's easy.'

So, believing her, I went to her place one Wednesday and she took me through the prayer book. I scribbled pencilled notes in the margin: Ask everyone to stand. Tell them to sit. Face the Ark. Say this phrase, mumble here, give them time to read the prayer here. (Gosh, is that why there was always a sudden unexplained silence at this bit of the service? While I was staring vacantly into space, wondering what was going on, people were reading a prayer in Hebrew. Go figure.)

Some bits of the service I knew well but others were just a forest of pencil notes by the time I'd finished. Anna told me that all shuls have different tunes and, if people didn't recognise what I was half-singing/half-saying, they'd just think we did things differently. Some bits of the service are said the world over, every Friday, specifically the Amidah (silent prayer—no need to worry about that one, since I didn't have to do anything other than tell everyone to stand and face the Ark) and the Shema (again, no problem). The Shema is two sentences long and I've sung it a thousand times. Those ones I wasn't worried about. The rest, less comfortable.

Come that Friday I was nervous as a nineteenth-century bride on her wedding night. Okay, maybe not that nervous but still pretty tense. I'd prepared a sermon on looking on the bright side. For someone as prone to depression as I am, I do a heck of a lot of looking on the bright side. Maybe that's what's getting me down. Maybe I should look on the dark side for a change.

I planned to tell a Chinese story called 'Good Luck, Bad Luck, Who Knows?', about a farmer whose horse runs off. All his neighbours say 'What terrible luck', but he says, 'Good luck, bad luck, who knows?' Then the horse comes back with a whole herd of horses and the neighbours all say, 'What wonderful luck', and the farmer says, 'Good luck, bad luck, who knows?' Then the farmer's son breaks his leg taming one of the wild horses and the neighbours say, 'What terrible luck', and the farmer replies, 'Good luck, bad luck, who knows?' And so it goes on.

The point of the story was that things that look like bad luck are often good luck. Of course, it goes the other way around too, but you have to give an upbeat message when you're in a religious setting. I was sorely tempted to say, 'So, just when you think things are going well, God can strike you down. So watch your back, people.' But that would have been giving my sense of the surreal too great a rein. They might never have asked me to run the services again. Wait! Why didn't I think of that before?

I began the service and although my voice was a bit flat and dull I managed to get us going with a cheery Sabbath welcoming song. Pages one, two and three were pretty straightforward, with few pencil marks and many tunes so familiar to me I could do them in my sleep. Pages four and five were a little more hair-raising—telling people to sit, stand, say a prayer, blah blah blah.

But then I flipped over to page six and my heart thumped. The page was grey with pencil marks. I could barely see the text for my notes. Sweat beads exploded out of my forehead. Keeping my face calm and my eyes down so they couldn't see the panic, I searched for the first note. Like an idiot, I seemed to have written notes everywhere and sent arrows shooting across the page to the relevant section. Frantically, I searched for the first one.

Ah, there it is. Okay, everyone sits. Now sing this bit—how does it go? *Yikes, I can't remember.* I babbled out some crude approximation of the prayer. *Gosh, that was terrible. Surely people will twig I've got no idea what I'm doing.* Okay—now what? *Silent—well phew. Curses—more singing. Dammit, what is the tune here?* Never mind, mumblemumblemumble. And so on through a sweaty page, trying to stay calm.

'Page seven,' I said, turning the page. As I did I noticed a certain something. A certain frisson. Something was coming to me through the atmosphere, penetrating even the dense concentration on my notes. I looked up. Five faces of friends were in the front row, all looking at me with varying degrees of consternation.

'Uh,' said one.

'What?' I couldn't see the problem.

'Uh . . . the Shema?'

Yes, in my furious focusing on my notes, I had completely forgotten an absolutely central part of the service. It appeared at the top of page six unannotated because it was so bleeding obvious. So horrified was I that an oath was ripped from my lips.

'Jesus Christ! Oops. I mean . . . the Shema. Yes. Of course. We'll do that now.'

It wasn't all downhill from there, but I was so shaken that I started to fear I'd forget the most basic things. Would I remember the tunes? (Yes, as it happened, but mainly because my friends in the front row were bellowing them out for me.) I delivered my sermon about how unlucky things often turn out to be lucky (right, so it was actually good luck that I forgot the Shema, then yelled 'Jesus Christ!' in shul) and we limped home to the finishing line, a sorry day for the punters.

Later, a girl came up to me to tell me how touched she'd been by the sermon and how much it had meant to her. I said, 'Hmm, shame we couldn't get the service right,' and she said no, it had been great. She was from a very informal shul and she had been worried that a European one would be hideously formal. An informal service was the very thing she needed to make her feel at home.

So there you go. One happy congregant. I was actually quite chuffed. Maybe that Chinese farmer was right—who knows if it's good luck or bad luck? Oh please! I didn't like Pollyanna the first time around.

37

With my time at The Three Bells over, and my *živno* tucked under my belt, I started to build my editing business by targeting the biggest companies in Prague. With editing, as with English teaching, you could either do low-paid jobs for cowboys and be badly treated, or you could work in quality jobs and pave your way into the higher paid ones.

I took my cue from the teachers I knew. Some of them worked for Charles University and their jobs, although not riveting and only just above the bottom of the university food chain, were at least relatively stable. They worked set terms and set hours, they had set pay and conditions. They were treated with contempt by the more senior academics but, hey, this was the higher-education sector—a finely graded hierarchy where your position within it was relatively safe, as long as you knew and kept your place. No PhD, no pleasantries.

I knew one woman who specialised in teaching English to the children of the orthodox Jewish community, she herself being a strict practitioner. Her market edge lay in her being able to understand and support the orthodox values. It was a clever move—she'd been a marketing director in New York, and she knew the importance of putting a high price on yourself.

Other teachers, however, worked for cheap outfits that sold cut-price lessons to immigrants from the eastern European countries who had Russian but no English. Or they struggled with private lessons, suffering from arbitrary cancellations, students dropping out altogether and from a constant need for more students as existing ones got bored or fed up and left. Theirs was a hand-to-mouth existence, where even the loss of one student could mean the difference between a life you could live and one in which bills might not be payable.

I had no doubt about which market I was going to pitch to. I might be living in Prague but there was no way I was going to live on Czech wages. No. Way. The strategy I chose—of working as a freelancer—was risky, in that it would take a long time for business to build and I might starve along the way. But I could see, even before I made my first cold call, that it was a risk worth taking. If you lived on Czech wages, you had to work any*where*, any*time*. If I dictated my own terms I could stipulate my own hours, have fewer clients and still work on my novel.

I also knew from my years working in Australian universities that it was important to pitch yourself as high-quality goods. I'd once made the mistake of taking a low-level job just to get into a company, only to discover that my upward path entailed crawling slowly up each rung of the ladder, one at a time. Since my nominal job was colour-coding files while my actual work was helping my eight-rungs-higher illiterate boss write her letters and reports, I could see I'd made a strategic error. I never made that mistake again. From then on I decided to talk my way into companies at a high level and demand a good salary up front. I knew the value of titles; the loftier the title, the more you got paid and the less people scowled at you outright. I wanted a life where no-one scowled at me.

Using this strategy I eventually built up enough of a client base to cover the bills. I became quite fond of freelance editing as I could do it in my pyjamas at any time of the day or night. The jobs were sometimes mind-bogglingly tedious, and I couldn't afford life's luxuries, but my high-class clientele treated me well and I never had to put up with a deranged boss demanding I cheat and lie for him. And sometimes I got really quite interesting clients.

One day an advertising agency I'd cold-called contacted me, asking if I'd come in for a chat—not an interview, a chat. They'd just landed a huge new account and their copywriter was leaving to write a novel.

They had offices near Petřín Park overlooking Prague and a sweeping great foyer with a blond wood reception desk. Outside the front door, creative types in ripped jeans and ponytails smoked feverishly in intense Gauloise-clouded clusters or slightly apart, brooding.

A smoothly elegant receptionist, young and with full consciousness of her importance, bade me sit, made a discreet call then directed me to the office of the Creative Director. I had no idea my appointment was with His Eminence.

The Creative Director was an impeccably dressed man of about forty, English and wonderfully urbane. We began by not even discussing the job at all. I told him about my Prague book, to impress him, and he told me about his life before he became the Creative Director. He had travelled for some years, mainly in India and China, backpacking and making his way around Asia. We discussed the Czechs and their food, and what we missed about the West. After a while, matters turned to the job.

'Gregor is leaving and we are wondering what to do to replace him. He feels stifled. He doesn't even want to have a part-time job. He feels he needs to give all his energies to his novel.'

I nodded sagely.

'We were thinking of replacing him full time. Is that something you might be interested in?'

I was firm about it. 'Not really. I have my own work to do and I am building up an editing business.' *And I'm trying to write my own novel,* but I was fully alive to the person I'd become if I had no deadlines in my life, just the task of writing a work of literary genius.

'Hm-hm.' He thought for a bit. 'We would be asking you to do spelling and typo checks, and perhaps help us to craft some words every now and then. We have very creative people here, but they are Czech and the campaign is international and in English.'

He talked some more about the work and intimated that it could get more complex and interesting if we liked each other. It was all sounding quite doable and even moderately interesting until we got to the topic of the client.

'This is a very important client for us. It's a really major campaign and will set up the company for years to come. We are keen to get this right.' There was a pause. The Creative Director looked at the floor. Then he looked at me through his rectangular glasses, keenly. I waited. He moved his chin and then said, a little diffidently and after another pause, 'Would you have any objection to working on an alcohol account?'

There was a long, staggered silence while I tried to compute this question.

'You mean . . . a moral objection?'

'Yes,' he replied. Then feeling perhaps an explanation was necessary, 'Well, some people might.'

I wanted to say, 'Just let me get this straight. We're in the Czech Republic and you're asking a writer if she's got a moral objection to booze? Do you have any conception what I'd do for money? I don't think you can have.'

But I didn't. I said, urbanely, 'No, no, that's fine. I can write about alcohol.'

The advertising agency turned out to be my most lucrative and enjoyable client, in a strangely Kafka-esque way. They had landed the European worldwide account for Jack Daniels and Finlandia Vodka. I spent my days editing endless proposals and materials for both brands.

Finlandia was particularly spooky—lots of clean, blond, sparkling images, happy, slender people with fresh skin and long bright vistas of untouched Scandinavian wilderness. Some part of me kept thinking, *Vodka is a drink, right? I mean it's not a health food, is it?* At least Jack Daniels had the grace to be masculine and tough, although with a lot of guff about pure, natural . . . Hmm, now that I'm writing this, I can see they were just as bad.

Yes, I suppose in some tiny distant part of myself there was a slight moral objection to all this, but I honestly didn't care that much. The company was pleasant, they paid well and they respected me. Mainly they respected me because apparently advertising was peopled with idiots. I worked on copy that could have been written more clearly by my cat Thelma.

On one occasion I gave them some copy and the idiots forgot to integrate it—they put their own work before the client. The Creative Director blew into a thousand pieces and the pony-tailed drongos tried to blame me. More idiocy. I carefully took him through the differences between 'Before' and 'After' copyediting. After that, everyone, including the accounts department, asked after my wellbeing during email exchanges.

A second piece of luck came from a consultancy company. This was more straightforward. They called me in for an interview, then gave me a trial piece. Apparently the director they showed it to liked it and so I was hired. I only ever worked for that one director, always via email, and he was the source of one piece roughly every two weeks, usually an agonisingly badly written presentation to a client involving about a hundred slides. Their previous editor had been telling him it took an hour per slide. He certainly needed his hand held but I was able to undercut the competition by half and still have time to spare.

He was an absolute sweetheart, this director. Possibly the most boring man who ever lived, judging by the work he engaged in. He always needed a 24-hour turnaround but he was always supremely grateful and we had a wonderful working relationship, despite never meeting even once.

38

Hiking was a constant in my Prague life. Every Saturday, without fail, I organised a hike, advertising it on the expats.cz social site and picking a trail at random. I kept it up until the bitter cold of November (the first November, Mathematics Neil and I had to eat lunch while walking, because stopping meant freezing over) and started again the instant I could in March. Life in Prague was gradually wearing me down, what with my failure to become a prolific writer and the lack of fresh vegetables and cheery faces and the life of work seeming to be mostly a choice between being bullied or bored. But every Saturday, as I laced on my boots, my heart swelled.

I had an enormous collection of walking maps and had walked every trail within an hour's train ride from Prague, and many further afield. I can't say that I'd made any new friends on these hikes. The new people who came along simply didn't grow into friends, but Irish Pam and Mathematics Neil were regulars. It was a lovely punctuation to each week.

One Saturday, Pam and I were due to hike with a new guy, Igor, and I was at Hlavní Nádraží, the main Prague train station. The train was leaving at 8.26. At five past eight, Pam was still not there and I'd not heard from Igor. I called Pam.

'Oh my god, is it Saturday?' I sensed that Pam's *craic* had been more fun than usual. 'Sorry, doll, I'm going to give it a miss today. Maybe see you later?'

Just when I was thinking I'd be hiking alone, my phone rang. It was Igor.

'Rrrrachael?' He was shouting down the phone and I could hear lots of traffic noise in the background. 'Ai em et station! Ai can't see you! Vere are you?!'

'I'm at ticket line number two. I'm in hiking gear—you can't miss me. I'll wait for you here.'

'Ai don't know vere ai em!' He sounded panicked.

I slowed down my English for him. 'Just come to ticket line TWO. Ticket. Line. Two. I'm here.'

After fifteen minutes, worried I'd miss the train, I called Igor.

'Igor, where are you?'

'Ai don't know! Ai em et exit!'

I sighed inwardly. 'Okay, look, I'm going to buy a ticket and get on the Řevnice train. Buy a ticket and meet me if you can.'

'Ai don't know vere ai em!'

I collected my ticket and raced for the train, making it with just thirty seconds to spare. Panting in my seat, I called Igor again. 'Come to Platform One. PLATFORM ONE, Igor. Run!'

'Vat?'

The train doors shut.

The trail that day was from a small village called Řevnice, thirty kilometres south of Prague. It was always a beautiful train ride south. The track followed the river, sparkling and wide in the sunlight, with green hills rising from the meadows on its banks. We passed through tiny rundown stations, with the cladding falling off the station buildings in a picturesque way that stirred my poetic soul but was no doubt depressing to live with. Twenty minutes into the journey, Igor texted me. Miraculously, he'd made the train. I texted back telling him to meet me at the other end.

Řevnice station was in moderately better shape than most. Its station house was painted but its platform was pretty bare, with no flowers or seating. I got off the train and looked around for a man in hiking gear. He should have been easy to spot, yet I could see no-one. The few alighting passengers drained away down the stairs to the exit until only one man was left hovering at the top of the steps looking lost and anxious.

Was this really Igor? He was tall with a bowl of straight black hair over a pale face. His shoulders were rounded and a pot belly pressed against his t-shirt. He gave the impression of doughy softness. I raised my hand. He raised his. It was Igor. My heart sank.

I always hoped, just quietly and barely admitting it even to myself, that the new men turning up on these hikes would be, you know, *my* new man. Not only was Igor not going to be my new man, he was going to be yet another useless hiker. He was wearing black jeans and white tennis shoes—not in itself too terrible, although not the most practical clothes for a hike that's been advertised as being twenty kilometres long. No, the clothes weren't the clincher. It was his bag, an enormous sports bag, the sort you might take on a weekend trip away—a giant capacious oblong that stuck out a foot in front of him and a foot behind and so deep that it reached from his neck down to his hip. He had this ridiculous thing slung over his shoulder. Who goes on a day-long hike equipped with cabin baggage? I sighed, less inwardly this time.

I was going to spend the entire day with this man and I had no choice but to make the best of it so when I reached him I smiled and shook his hand and bade him welcome.

'Ai em lookink forward to zis hike,' he said.

'Yes, it should be a good one. You know it'll take about five hours?'

Pause. Igor looked flabbergasted.

'Have you been hiking before, Igor?'

'Not so much.'

Uh-huh. 'Well, it's easy once you get the hang of finding the trails,' I said patiently. 'I'll show you how.'

It's generally better if other people on the hike can help with the business of hiking—looking for the trail markers, following the map, deciding where to stop for lunch and the rest of it. I'd woken up feeling a bit sick—not too sick, just a bit headachy and off. I needed people who would take a bit of the load off my shoulders. This I was not going to get with Igor.

I say this to give you a sense of my frame of mind. When hearing the story of Igor, people often ask, But why didn't you leave *then*, when you saw the bag and you were feeling sick? Why not indeed? Mainly, at first, because I was being a good hiker, straightening my shoulders and looking on the bright side. Standing next to him at the station, I noticed he had the smell of a man who's been on the piss all night and had not bothered to shower—a dank, seedy smell that I was familiar with from the early morning trams. Even then, rather than quit the day, I just made a mental note to walk on Igor's leeward side.

I led him out of the station and located the first trail marker, which was right across the road. I showed Igor which markers were for us and which for the cyclists. I showed him which were for the local Czech paths, and which were for the longer European paths. I pointed out our own marker and explained what the arrow meant, and told him that we'd both need to look out for the signs because they could be hard to find. He seemed to be faintly annoyed that I was giving him all this information.

'Yis, yis. Marker,' he said, frowning, 'But vich vay?'

'This way,' I replied, continuing to point at the arrow.

'Yis, yis.'

So we headed off down the dusty road of the tiny village towards the forest, I on the upwind side and Igor filling me in on The Igor Story.

'Yem software ingineer. Ai come from Kyrgyzstan. You know vere is Kyrgyzstan?'

'Uh . . .'

'Is near China. Yem not Russian. Yem Chinese.'

'Uh-huh.'

'Kyrgyzstan not Russia. Many people zink it is.' I was one of them, but there you go.

'No. Is in Russia, but is more laik China.'

Actually, this I found quite interesting. Here was someone from the former USSR staking a claim to a different culture. I'm moderately interested in that strange part of the world where Russia meets China and I would have taken up this fruitful discussion with Igor except for one thing: as we'd been walking along, Igor had been leaning into me more and more, ignoring all my attempts to walk in a straight line. At this moment in his story he managed to push me right off the path.

Oh well, I thought, suppressing my annoyance, *some people list to the left*. So I moved around to his other side. Whereupon Igor started listing to the right, pressing me the other way.

Igor was babbling on about China and Kyrgyzstan, seemingly unaware of the dance we were doing. I moved back to the left and he moved with me. I did my yoga neck exercises to release the muscle tension. *He's concentrating on what he's saying. It'll be okay when we're on the trail.* Igor kept up his dissertation without pause on what made Kyrgyzstan oriental rather than occidental, simultaneously veering into me no matter where I placed myself.

I moved off the path altogether and he followed me into the road that ran alongside it, seemingly determined to shove me into the opposite fence. He was yammering away, his enormous bag hitched on his shoulder adding ballast to his insistent steering. I pressed my fingers to the bridge of my nose to ease my headache.

We came to our turn-off into the forest—a leafy, cool haven the pain in my head welcomed. The forest canopy closed overhead, letting in lovely filtered rays of sun, the temperature dropped a soothing few degrees and the path widened hugely so that I was able to weave more slowly around the tacking, chatting Igor. My personal space regained, my attention could wander to the prettiness of the undergrowth and the feel of the breeze on my face. I uttered the occasional 'mmm' to keep him thinking I was listening as my mind drifted and I began to think this might be quite enjoyable. A man who can entertain himself requires no input from me and I could give over my thoughts to whatever I wanted. I soaked up the meditative atmosphere of the forest, the spa-like feel of the air on my skin, the sound of the woodpeckers.

Five minutes in we came across a party of villagers heading home. They had with them a little dog. We walked past and when they were out of earshot Igor turned to me.

'Nice dog.' He paused. 'Vould be good cooked.'

I started. 'What? Uh, right.' I had heard that joke before but somehow it didn't seem so funny coming from the pale, sweaty Igor.

'Yem just kiddink,' said Igor, seeing I wasn't doubled over laughing. 'In Kyrgyzstan vee eat dog. But not here.'

And then he carried on for quite some time about eating dogs, where they were and were not eaten, why the fact that the Chinese ate dogs made him feel especially sure that he was Chinese and not Russian, how the Russians did not eat dogs and why that made them inferior. And on and on and on.

We'd been walking for about ten minutes and were deep into the forest, not another soul within cooee, when Igor fell silent. *Thank god*, was all I could think. I hoped that if I greeted silence with silence he might pick up the hint and we could have a quiet day. But then Igor piped up again.

'Of course, ai don't eat dog here in Czech. Ai eat pork.'

297

Oh Christ, not more on the dog meat. 'Uh-huh.'

'You know vy ai laik pork meat?'

'Um . . .'

'Because it is closest to human meat . . .'

I stumbled.

'. . . and ai vould laik to eat human meat.'

'Ah, I, ah . . .' *What the FUCK? What did he just say??*

But Igor was off on some insane rant about how he'd like to live in a forest with sausage trees—sausages hanging from the branches so he could just pluck them off, how wonderful it would be to have meat falling from the sky, how he would dance through the forest like a little child eating sausage, sausage, sausage.

'Would not zis be a heaven? Blood sausage, pork sausage, even hot sausage! Yes! Hot sausage right zair on ze trees!' Igor swung his bag gleefully as he wound himself higher and higher on the glories of sausage trees.

I wanted to say to him, 'You know, Igor, the usual topics of conversation among strangers on these hikes run along the lines of what you do for a living and how long you've been in Prague. And, as tedious as that can be, it's not as fucking tedious as listening to the deranged meat-based blatherings of an unwashed Kyrgyzstani software engineer.' But it was *so* deranged that instinct was telling me to treat the man carefully.

I did at this point contemplate cutting the hike short and wondered if Igor was quite right in the head. But then I told myself not to be silly. It was surely just a cultural thing. My god, I was forever getting startled looks from Czechs when I accidentally used the informal mode of address to an elder or mixed up my word endings. Alright, so he'd clearly been on the piss the night before. And he didn't wash. And he was obsessed with sausage. Was that so different to most Czechs? The human meat comment was bizarre but maybe he just had a strange sense of humour.

Let's not make hysterical assumptions, I told myself briskly. *He'll get tired of this soon, and we'll move onto normal things.*

'Ai laik to kill things.'

My heart stopped.

'Ai vould laik to kill a human being.'

At this moment my mind became strangely clear in a suddenly paralysed body. I weighed up my options. We were twenty minutes into a deep forest with not a soul around—we were alone. If he was a murderer, and a cannibal, what should I do? I tried to tell myself that the chances of this were slim but the trouble was that if I made that assumption and I was wrong, the consequences would be very, very bad.

Should I run? It was a long way back to the village, and he was bigger and stronger than me. If he was intent on killing me then seeing me panic would convince him to bring his plans forward, knowing his window of opportunity had just got narrower. He would surely catch me if I ran.

No, my only option, I decided, was to try to stay calm, maintain the psychological upper hand, keep him in my sight, and watch for any sudden movements. I eyed the bag. What did he have in there? I stepped behind him on the path.

'Ai laik to eat human meat.'

My eyes swept the ground frantically for a weapon.

'Ai laik to kill a human and eat him. But ven ai eat him, ai am cryink, cryink, cryink all ze time because ai remember how much ai loff him and how it hurts me to kill him. So ai am eatink him, but ai am cryink at ze same time. Cryink all ze time.'

Jesus Fucking Christ. I was going to die! My heart pounding, panic pouring through me, I spotted a stick—it was thick and straight and had a devilish point at one end. I picked it up and pointed it at Igor's back.

'In Kyrgyzstan we laik to kill.'

My head was screaming. This had to stop. I had to assert myself.

'Igor.'

'Yis?' He turned around.

'That's enough now,' I said in the best approximation of an authoritative and calm voice I could muster, looking him straight in the eye. 'That's enough about killing and eating humans. We need to talk about something else.'

Was that enough? I had tried to sound like a stern parent to a child. Did I have the upper hand?

'Yis, yis,' said Igor, 'Yem just kiddink.' He shifted his bag from one shoulder to the other and something made a clinking sound. A chain saw? A hack knife? *Get a grip, girl, he's just socially dysfunctional.* I stayed behind him with the stick pointed at his kidneys.

We walked along in silence for a while. My tension levels were so high I could feel acid in my veins. I tried to talk myself down. *Stay calm, don't panic. He's a lunatic, but you'll be okay. The next village is an hour-and-a-half away and then you can get rid of him and go home.*

Slowly, under the influence of this stern mind-to-heart talk, my pulse rate started to subside. I kept my stick at the ready but there was no more from Igor about feasting on human flesh.

But then he started some tangled tale about Chinese girls in Taiwan, which got my blood pounding again. *Christ, was he really telling me about hookers?*

'I laik bitches,' he continued. My heart lurched. *Oh great. Now not only was I going to die, my death was going to have some ghastly sexual component.* But instead the story died and we had blessed silence for a bit.

I was just telling myself that I'd got all worked up over nothing and was wondering if I really would need to go home on the first train I could find when Igor piped up again.

'In Kyrgyzstan ve laik to shoot zings. Ve shoot zem, zen ve use ze knife. You know, ve use ze knife to cut zem up. Vould be fun to shoot human, ai zink.'

Oh for crying out loud! More?? But I felt that if I voiced my concern I might provoke confrontation and that might lead to death. Mine. So I walked behind him, simmering, my nerves screaming, while he carried on and on about knifing things, interspersing his monologue on the joys of murder and cannibalism with an itinerary of all the places he'd lived. They all seemed to be remote—Kyrgyzstan, a small town in China, a village in Siberia, somewhere in Africa—and he hadn't stayed in any of them very long. *Why not?* I wondered. *Was he running from previous butcheries, staying under the radar of the law?* Who knows? It seemed as likely as any other explanation.

And just when I thought things were as bad as they could get, the situation took a turn for the worst. Markers are often hard to find on these trails. Mostly they're obvious but you usually lose one or two. This trail, it turned out, was spectacularly badly marked. I'd taken a few wrong turnings but now, an hour into our walk, I lost the trail completely. My only option was to take a detour down a narrow, overgrown goat track to see if I could find the right path again. Igor was no longer in front but squeezing up behind me. I was terrified.

What if we were lost? What if I couldn't get us to the next village? What if, now that I couldn't see him, he'd take his chance and butcher me with a buzz saw? My stress levels were redlining. The grass was tall and densely packed and we were wading through it. I kept finding ticks on my skin and brushing them off. Raspberry brambles clogged the path up to head height, snagging my clothes and tearing at my arms.

Igor walked behind me really, really close. So close I could feel his breath on my neck.

'Igor, don't walk so close, you'll get hit by the raspberry branches.'

'Yis, yis, is alright.'

No it fucking isn't, you bastard, I thought viciously, letting a bramble whack back onto him. It made no difference—he stuck to me like a leech.

After fifteen minutes of bush-bashing that passed as if they were fifteen hours, I found the right path. As soon as we were on the new track I swung back behind Igor, my stick aimed at his spine. I felt like a World War II soldier bringing my prisoner in. The forest was deep and isolated. We passed no-one. We heard no-one. We were alone. *Please, God, let me get to the next village. Please, God, don't let me die with only this fat fucker around to see my last moments.*

After two hours—two hours!—we emerged from the forest and hit a logging trail and five minutes later, loggers. They

were blank-faced and suspicious and one of them said something snide that made all the others laugh as we passed—but
how I loved those loggers! Through the trees I began to see
chaty, the cottages Czechs keep for weekend getaways. It was
the weekend, surely some of them would be in use. At least
now, if I screamed someone might hear me. I began to feel a
fraction, just a fraction, safer.

Igor chose that moment to open the subject of murder
again.

Grinding my teeth but staying polite, I said, 'Igor. You
must stop talking about killing things.'

'Yis, yis, yem just kiddink. But ai vill stop teasink you.'

'It's not the teasing I mind, Igor.' Now that we were
nearer civilisation and people I felt stronger. I called on the
last reserves of psychic strength I had and pretended I was
a schoolmarm—one of the really tough ones—chastising
a small child. I decided to meet him head on. 'It's not the
teasing I mind. It's that I'm afraid you're going to kill me.'

That seemed to sober him up somewhat. He stopped
yammering and we continued in silence, me still behind him
with my stick-weapon at the ready. And then, as the outskirts
of the village appeared before us, a strange thing happened.
Igor stopped talking about murder and bitches and instead
told me about his daily life as a programmer, quite as though
he were a normal human being.

We walked through the village towards the station. I was
determined that our walk was now coming to an abrupt end,
even though we'd only been going for two hours. I dropped
my stick and said, 'Igor, I'm catching the train back home.'

'Yis, yis, ai sink ai hev hed enough too.'

303

While we sat on the platform waiting, me not saying a word, just bathing in the relief of being alive and no longer in danger and allowing my unspeakable rage to work itself out, Igor picked up his bag and pulled something out of it—a jar filled with yellow liquid.

'Bourbon. Vant some?'

'No thanks, Igor.' And silently I thanked God he hadn't pulled that out in the forest. The thought of a drunk Kyrgyzstani killer was worse than a sober one.

Igor took a swig. 'Rachael,' he cried, wiping his mouth, 'tonight let's see music!'

'No.'

There was a short silence. Then in a sad voice he said, 'It's just that ai em so tired of being alone.'

And at once I felt sorry for him. Poor guy, he really was lonely. But it was no surprise if his normal conversation was like the ones we had had today. He might have been a deranged cannibal but he was a deeply lonely deranged cannibal, and even deranged cannibals deserve companionship.

Not mine, however. I made sure to get out at a different stop from Igor and I never posted a hike again.

39

But then I met a man—again on the net—who really did seem promising. His name was Joe and he was a sergeant in the US air force. Yup, Joe. The boys in the Lazy Vinohrady group immediately dubbed him GI Joe, inevitably I suppose.

I realise that a sergeant in the US air force is not what you'd think of if you were dreaming up the perfect man for me, but a few things made me like this guy. First off, he was five years younger than I was and I respect a man who'll go out with an older woman. There are too many men of forty-five looking for '25–35'-year-old women. Who do they think they are? Joe, like me, had put down an age range ten years younger and ten years older. Actually what he'd said was 'Old enough to drink and not as old as my mother.' Cute.

So we began to correspond, and he was funny and smart and interesting and he took his job seriously and I liked him.

But a couple of things made me slightly concerned. He didn't believe in fidelity for one. I do, but I am prepared to explore other ways of being. I don't necessarily think that I'm right—plenty of people I knew in Prague had open relationships and it seemed to work for them. In fact, most people I knew seemed to be a bit French about fidelity. So I was prepared to revisit my attitude. Certainly, even as we were flirting and getting to know one another, Joe was quite open about sleeping with other women. I found it painful and difficult, and was quite open about that. He became less open about it and I was grateful.

Neither of us was sure if we were right for the other. The fidelity question was the big one but there was also the matter of utter difference. Joe was from smalltown USA and thought Stephen King was the last word in literary genius. He had been in the armed forces practically from school, lived a regimented life and was, let's face it, a guy who killed people for a living. He personally didn't kill people but he did believe in the necessity of war—the glory of war, even. He was a patriot and a soldier.

I was a fey, decadent writer, a feminist, pootling about in Prague, making a vague living writing and doing odd jobs. I suppose I had discipline of a kind, but not of the up-at-5 am-working-to-save-the-world-until-7 pm kind that Joe had. I had more of an up-at-10 am-after-lying-in-bed-giving-myself-a-good-kicking-and-battling-with-writer's-block kind. Joe was hard-bodied and virile, a practical man. I sat around with my artist friends dissecting our inner lives and fretting.

Joe was stationed in Germany at Ramstein Air Base, a short five-hour drive from Prague. We planned a weekend when he would come out to visit me but a week before he was due to arrive I changed my mind. 'I'm sorry, but I just don't think this will work,' I told him.

We'd been back and forth over this, so he wasn't surprised, but he did say, 'How about I come over anyway. Who knows? We might be friends, and I need friends.'

It was a sweet thing to say, and one of the things I deeply liked about him—there was no macho bullshit about him and he was honourable. He didn't pout or try to make me feel bad, he just accepted that things had changed. And he admitted to needing friends. I needed friends too.

The weekend Joe was coming, I was unaccountably nervous. He'd said he'd be there at ten in the morning. On the dot of 10 am the front doorbell rang.

The buzzer didn't work (they never did in those old apartment blocks) so I went down the four flights of stairs to open the main doors. There, standing in the frame, was a tall, handsome man with blue eyes and a blond buzz cut, chewing gum.

'Hi,' he said.

If I'd tried to paint an American serviceman I couldn't have come up with a more perfect model than Joe. Even in civvies he looked like he was in uniform—neatly pressed jeans and t-shirt, clean shoes, not a hair or muscle out of place, teeth perfectly even and white. He was gorgeous.

Well, that first weekend I took him on my tour of Prague, the one I always take visiting friends on. I showed him the sights, of course: the Charles Bridge, the Judith Tower, St Vitus' Cathedral, the palace, the Old Town Square. Then I took him to see my favourite buildings.

The Fred and Ginger building is a modern marvel at the end of Jiráskův Bridge, best seen when crossing over the bridge to get the full effect. It's a Frank Gehry design and it's called the Dancing Building, or Fred and Ginger, because it looks like two elegant dancers. Then there was the insurance building on Národní třída, opposite the National Theatre, with its decorations picked out in brightly coloured tiles and gold leaf, so high you have to know they're up there or you'll miss them.

I took him to see a building I found spooky but never knew why.

'It's because the proportions are all wrong,' said Joe, contemplating the façade. 'See how the columns are wide for a tall building, but too short? And its dark material looks like it's looming over you, like a thug about to beat you up.'

He was right. That was exactly why it was spooky. We walked all day and all night. And in the end we did end up sleeping together—I guess that was always going to happen.

At the end of the weekend Joe said, 'It was lovely to meet you. I don't think this is going to work though.'

I said, 'Oh, I was just changing my mind.' And I started to cry.

Why was I so upset? I didn't know myself. Joe held me in his arms and he cried too. We lay in my bed, still and quiet, holding each other and our sadness.

Joe went back to Ramstein the next day and I thought that would be the end of that. It had been a two-day interlude of love and comfort. For a weekend I'd had the pleasure, for the first time in a long time, of walking hand in hand with someone I could think belonged to me. I had someone to do something with on a Saturday night without having to make a date, and I'd been cuddled to sleep.

Even though we agreed we were not going to continue on with a relationship, Joe and I kept writing. He called me when he got home to make sure I was alright. I was. Was he alright? He was. And somehow, despite our avowals to each other that this was never going to work, that we weren't right for each other, we kept on writing and talking as though we were in a relationship. Every day we wrote. We kept each other up to date on the minutiae of our lives and gave each other support. Joe was getting a divorce—his third in his young life—and I kept his spirits up. I was struggling to write, struggling to make something of my new life—Joe was encouraging and cheering. No, we weren't the same, not at all, but we gave each other the love and care we both desperately needed and that, it turned out, was a relationship.

40

My work strategy seemed to be paying off. I wasn't making a huge amount of money from editing—just enough to keep my bills paid and I still needed to find other work to keep me going—but it was easy and it gave me a modicum of self-respect.

Bits and pieces drifted in. I edited a book by a completely insane man who was passionate about raw food—he thought the world was doomed unless we all abandoned cooking. Editing his work was a strange experience because he was so angry and strident and maddened by the thought that no-one was listening to him. It was like inhabiting a room with a lunatic at my shoulder who was frothing at the mouth and yelling at me. It was weirdly stressful.

I got the job because his Czech to English translator was Czech. You can really only translate well if you're a native speaker. Even the lingua-genius Anna betrayed herself as a non-native speaker sometimes in things as minor as party invitations. There's a certain rhythm—complex rules about which words go where, depending on the context—that you really only know if you've been speaking a language from birth. So I was cleaning up the translator's work, which was often incomprehensible and very often completely bizarre.

On one occasion the translator called me, sounding quite upset.

'I find this a difficult assignment,' she said.

'I'm not surprised,' I replied. 'He's insane.'

'But do you not think that there is something in what he says?'

'No.'

'Not even some of it?'

I could hear that the poor girl was suffering. If someone bellows something at you long enough you can start to believe it. I felt hearty good sense was what she needed.

'No, none of it. It's utter rubbish.'

'It sounds so logical. Perhaps cooked food *is* bad for you. I try to eat well but it is difficult. I go out, I have friends. It is not easy.'

'The fact is that cooked food is what got us out of the trees. Did you know that? When we learned to cook food, we freed our digestive tracts up from a lot of work and were able to devote that energy to our brains. That's how we evolved to where we are now. Not only is cooked food beneficial, it's been around since before the Stone Age, so it's hard to see how it could be poisoning us.'

'Is that true?'

'Yup. He sounds logical but he is in fact both out of his mind and bitterly angry. I find it difficult reading his stuff. It must be awful having to translate it.'

She seemed to feel better after that.

In addition to my big advertising and consultancy clients and my small, one-off clients, I managed to add one of the Big Four accountancy firms to my list. It promised to be really interesting work; I had to ghost-write some pieces on 'thought leadership' for them. 'Thought leadership' is the bullshit phrase corporations use to describe articles they plant in industry mags to convince everyone they're ahead of the curve—they're neither thought nor leadership, as evidenced by the fact that they were outsourcing this task to me. I had a lot of fun with it, but it went nowhere in the firm—the guy pushing that particular barrow seemed to lose his political influence and was shunted into the basement, along with his thought leadership.

After that, my main contact at the firm managed to get some of their marketing department editing work outsourced to me. Then one day she called me and asked whether I had any ideas about a new logo they were trialling.

'We're developing a new brand and the consultants have come up with this image. I've got a meeting about it—we need some text to go with it, a key message sort of thing. We're going to brainstorm some ideas. Can you come up with something?'

Now, I knew nothing about marketing, nothing about branding and precious little about the Big Four accountancy firms and what their marketing pitches might consist of. However, if a client asks you to do work, you do not say

'Sorry, I know nothing about that,' you say, 'Sure, send it over and I'll shoot something back to you this afternoon.'

So my contact sent over six or seven pictures the consultants had been playing with. They were all of hot air balloons in a blue sky. I laid them out in front of me and asked myself, 'What does this say to me?'

Bear in mind that this was in the context of the global financial crisis, which in 2008 was still in early enough days that we were only hesitantly saying 'GFC', unsure if this three-letter acronym would stick. The Big Fours and Big Eights and other multiples were losing clients and money and were desperate to get everyone thinking brave again, brave enough to trust a bunch of glassy-eyed bastards with their pension funds. At least one of the Bigs had teetered over the edge and was lying in splinters on the canyon floor. Free clients were there for the taking.

Instantly, the obvious came to mind. I wrote them down quickly:

Blue sky thinking
New horizons
Bird's eye view
Trusted old firm, going new places
Eagle's eye view
Able to see the whole picture
Uplifting, optimistic
On a journey
Rising

That seemed to be enough. I left it for an hour, went back to it and thought . . . no, that would do it. That afternoon I sent the list off with a few paragraphs, putting the phrases into a narrative along with a set of catchphrases she could present. 'This company is a trusted old company, but optimistic, looking to the future, able to see the whole picture. It takes the eagle's eye view of the landscape, giving clients the best possible conditions under which to make investment decisions . . .' and so on.

It turned out surprisingly well. My contact presented the ideas as her own, of course—that's what I was paid for and I bore no grudge whatsoever. My pay-off was that I got to write all that in my pyjamas, three feet from my bed and a nice nap when I needed it and free from any political infighting. She could take the kudos with my pleasure; I'd take the cheque.

She was dead pleased with me as her contribution had looked very good. (I was fairly astonished at how little effort it had taken.) She told me I would get a call from Marketing with the results of the brainstorm; she had suggested to them that I be hired to write the brief for the image consultant based on their notes.

Next day a young man called. He told me about the brainstorming session and gave me some background.

'This is a very important step for the firm. These are difficult times and we see the launch of the re-brand as key to our success in the marketplace. The image consultants sent us a few images and we have spent some time deciding which are the most suited to the company and the market. We have some ideas—a few phrases which we think tell the best story to our clients and potential clients. We'd like you to take these paragraphs and tidy them up and expand on them a little, so we have a summary and then a fuller description of the branding position. I have included a list of words you might use in the fuller description. I will email you the paper.'

I expressed my willingness to do all I could to help them and we rang off. I opened my inbox and there was the missive. I opened the attachment.

'This company is a trusted old company, but optimistic, looking to the future, able to see the whole picture. It takes the eagle's eye view of the landscape, giving clients the best possible conditions under which to make investment decisions . . .' It was followed by a list.

Blue sky thinking
New horizons
Bird's eye view
Trusted old firm, going new places
Eagle's eye view
Able to see the whole picture
Uplifting, optimistic
On a journey
Rising

Yes, it was exactly my own work. Not even slightly changed. Of course, he had no idea I was the originator—how could he?—but I was flabbergasted to think how little work and skill had gone into the brainstorming session where, apparently, the entire marketing department had been gathered to ponder the supposedly key question of positioning the firm in a difficult market in order to keep the bleeding firm alive! It was times like this I wondered how the world kept going.

However, they paid me well. I wrote the brief to their clients and enjoyed the idea that the entire campaign was dreamed up in fifteen minutes by someone in their pyjamas with not the faintest clue about branding.

41

As fun as all that was, editing barely covered food and bills. I was increasingly desperate to find more work, but nothing like the web-writing job ever appeared again in the classifieds. Getting that job in the first few months of my time in Prague, as awful as it had eventually become, had been sheer dumb luck. Suzy and Debra and I found work a constant source of anxiety. Debra managed to hold her head above water doing her legal editing, which she loathed but couldn't give away. Suzy had a job as a nanny for a brief spell, until her charges' father made a pass at her and she got the sack. Shortly after she joined our Artist's Group, she got herself a job with a company that ran events for corporates. This seemed marginally better, although the pay was low and intermittent. How to earn more cash was a frequent conversation at our Wednesday night meetings.

And yet all through 2008, while I was struggling to survive, with no reliable income and with my creativity ground to a halt, my fame grew steadily—a strange and sometimes very enjoyable thread in my life.

A fellow called Steve wrote me a fan letter—a fan letter!— after reading my book. He wondered if I was still in Prague. I wrote back and told him I was and, as it happened, lived right around the corner from him. We emailed back and forth and then he asked me to dinner.

We arranged to meet in a restaurant that Saturday night but on the Friday Steve suggested we meet at his place instead and have dinner there. I hesitated, but agreed.

Joe thought I was crazy. 'You don't know what people are like! It's dangerous. You'll be in his apartment—you don't know what he's got in mind.'

'Prague is different. He's an expat, we all make friends like this.'

'He's a man. Men are the same everywhere. Promise me you'll call me before you go, and keep your phone on you.'

'I promise. Will you stop worrying?'

Before I went around to Steve's place, I called Joe. God knows what he thought he was going to be able to do from Germany.

'Keep your phone on. I'm going to text you during the evening. Anything happens, call me.'

I admit that I was the tiniest bit nervous when I rang the bell. Was Joe right? Was I insane? Was this going to be the last night of my life?

The door opened. An enormously fat man in a pink shirt and comfy cotton trousers greeted me. 'Well hi! We meet at last!' he lisped enthusiastically.

All concerns fell away from me—he was as camp as a row of tents, a very exotic, outgoing man who made friends the Prague expat way—jumping in with both feet first.

Steve had the most amazing apartment. He was one of the early arrivers, having come to Prague in 1991 with a sense of adventure and an eye for beautiful things. His apartment was huge. The area we lived in was more rundown than most, but his place was enormous—rooms and rooms connected by panelled archways or ornate wooden doors. Stuffed into these rooms was the collection of a man with taste who'd lived for almost twenty years in a place where the local populace, freed and unaware, were throwing away their great-great-grandmothers' heavy old Viennese bureaux and investing in light-blond IKEA sofa beds. Crystal chandeliers, elaborate and sparkling, hung from every ceiling. Steve was a high-end tour guide who led groups all over the world, so he had Turkish rugs and Spanish lace, ostrich feathers, art deco lamps, porcelain figurines, Chinese vases and plates. The place was a wonderland, a treasure trove.

Steve told me that he had been the survivor of a plane crash twenty years earlier. He showed me the newspaper clippings with pictures of a skinny Steve who they were calling a hero—he'd been the one to go for help. It was a strange experience to meet a bona fide hero. Steve was clearly proud of his role but seemed, to my eyes, to also be a bit uncertain of it.

Perhaps being labelled a hero was as odd as being famous. It was something everyone else valued, but inside the experience you'd probably feel very normal and wonder what all the fuss was about. Or perhaps Steve was wondering who that man in the newspaper was; thirty-year-old Steve was a lot different to current-day Steve who was verging on the dangerously obese.

Among his treasures he boasted a superb wine collection—
he was a host who valued food and drink. I had intended to
stay for a chaste dinner and get-to-know-you session, a couple
of hours at the most, but I staggered home, almost too drunk
to walk, about eight hours later in the burgeoning dawn.

———•———

I was flogging my book as much as I could by taking it to
Australia and New Zealand trade fairs and speaking at
dinners.

At one of the trade fairs I was approached by a very tall,
very good-looking young man.

'It is such an honour to meet you,' he gushed, yes *gushed*.
I didn't quite know how to take it, since my experience of
communicating with men in Prague didn't often include
gushing. Snorting beer through their noses at the very thought
of going out with me, maybe. Gushing, not so much.

'I'm Gareth John.' He looked expectant. I looked blank.
He laughed. 'Oh, you don't watch much sport then.'

It turned out he was a famous Aussie Rules footballer,
had played for Australia and everything. Regrettably for him,
it seemed that his fame revolved around being one of the
worst injured players in the history of the game; he'd had his
larynx crushed in a ruck and had almost died. No-one knew
it was that serious at first, because after they couldn't find
the stretcher he had walked off the ground unaided, blood
pouring from his mouth.

Gareth was unstoppably charming and energetic. Where
everyone else could barely keep a visa after fifteen years and

a lifetime's investment in Prague, Gareth had managed to get dual citizenship by sheer dint of his magnetic personality. He'd simply made all the women in the Foreign Police fall in love with him and magically his papers came through.

Gareth was the most lovely man. He dressed impeccably ('Look at the detailing on this shirt. I get them handmade in Italy.') and he had more friends than you could count. His long-term girlfriend was Slovakian, a patient woman called Tatiana. Even though he hadn't married Tatiana, and it was perfectly obvious that Gareth had the tiniest crush on me (!), Tatiana bore me no ill will. I guessed that it must have happened all the time with a man of Gareth's charms.

He had written a book about his time as a footballer and wanted to get it published, so I handed him on to a friend of mine in the business in Australia. He had the ability, rare in anyone, to churn out 100,000 words over a couple of weeks, just by sitting down to do it. Unfortunately, the publisher declined but instead of turning to drink and self-pity he dropped the book idea and turned his mind to a different business venture, starting a cosmetics company with Tatiana (which is still going, by the way—it's called Aquaverse). His chronically positive, happy outlook was like sitting in the sun after a cold Prague winter. He was a walking vitamin D pill. He and I became friends and one day, early on in that friendship, he took me out to lunch.

Lunch with Gareth was not the kind of meal I was used to. Living as I did, I generally ate with the Czechs—cheap pork schnitzels, sauerkraut and brown bread in a pub. Gareth never ate such food; he could afford not to. He took me to a very zushy restaurant I'd longed to go to called Brasileiro, where they cooked Argentinean and Uruguayan beef in strange and delicious ways and then came to the table and sliced bits off for you. We'd agreed to have lunch and then go see a screening of *The Producers*, one of my favourite films, that was showing at the Kino Světozor, an arthouse cinema in town. He made the booking for 11.00 because *The Producers* was showing at 1.30.

My idea was that we'd have a salad, maybe a minute steak, a coffee and then be on our way. But Gareth lived life on a much larger palette. He had ordered the most fabulous bottle of red wine before I had a chance to say, 'You know, I don't really drink in the middle of the day.' It was a French red—a French, chocolate-y, rich, cigar-box red—and it was one of the most unbelievably delicious things I'd ever tasted.

Gareth hailed a waiter and discussed the menu with him at length. 'The food here is amazing,' he said. 'I come here all the time. Would you like me to recommend?'

'That would be wonderful.' And indeed it was. Being lunched by Gareth was like going on a date with the richest man in the world. I felt as though I was surrounded by Persian carpets and liveried servants ready to appear any moment. The waiters melted in the face of his charm and affability. He pressed wine and slivers of the finest beef onto me. At 1 o'clock Gareth looked at his watch.

'*Producers*, or another bottle?'

'Uh . . .'

'You're right. Waiter, another bottle.'

I wasn't so sure that was a wise idea. I'm a light drinker at the best of times, and two pints of beer is usually enough to have me talking merrily all night. But the beef kept coming, each slice more amazing than the last, and the second wine was as incredible as the first. Then we got into one of those happy, drunken conversations that range all over the universe. At the tail end of the meal, when he ordered *slivovice* (plum brandy) instead of coffee, a warning bell went off in my head. *This will put you over the edge. Wine is one thing. Wine and slivovice . . . you're gone.*

And indeed I was. At 5 o'clock, six hours after we had started lunch, we staggered out into the street. I had agreed to meet Andy at Lucerna, a bar across town, and although I had been there dozens of times and knew exactly where it was my internal map had gone haywire and I was having trouble seeing.

Gareth bent down from his 6 foot, 7 inch height, kissed my cheek and waved me a cheery goodbye, apparently not affected by the booze at all. 'That was great, let's do it again,' he said, and strolled off down the street.

I tried to focus on nearby buildings. *Where the heck was I??*

I sent Andy a frantic message. 'Where is Lucerna? Where am I?'

He called me. 'Where are you?'

'I have no idea. I see a tram, a church . . .' I hung up.

The phone rang again. 'Hi, this is Ben from Czech Events.'

'Ohmigod, I'm so drunk!' I can't think what possessed me to say that but in the shock of the moment all I could do was blurt out what was uppermost in, indeed completely filling, my mind.

Luckily, Ben laughed. 'Really? It's only 5 o'clock.'

'I know, I know, I've been at the longest lunch ever. I have no idea where I am.'

When I'd thrown in my job at The Three Bells, it had been Suzy who'd suggested I try Czech Events, where she was newly employed. They ran team-building events for companies—the sort of naff things companies started doing in the 80s, like paintballing and orienteering. Suzy got into it because she'd been a kayak instructor and an officer in the American armed forces.

'It's outdoors and it's fun,' she'd said. 'Although they're not always good about paying on time, they do eventually pay.'

The company was apparently looking for team leaders for its events. Again, not something I'd ever done, but I had put in an application referring to my leadership skills and company experience. It was all completely tenuous, total rubbish really, so I had no expectation that they'd reply. I was certainly not expecting this phone call now.

Ben went on to tell me that Czech Events had received my application and wanted me to come into the office for an interview. The conversation seemed to go on for some time and I'm not entirely sure what I said, or what he said, but I did manage to focus in on the important matter of giving him my email details.

After several wrong turns I finally made it to Lucerna and Andy, doing my best to stay awake and sound normal. I ordered a coffee, my brain working furiously. *Keep focused. Listen carefully to what he's saying. Okay, now say something coherent back. That's the way, one word after another. Good, good, I don't think he suspects a thing.*

Andy told me later I did quite well, but he did have to steer me through crowds. He really was a sweety.

We went to dinner with a couple of Andy's friends after that, I still utterly legless. All I could manage was two cokes. Finally, sometime around two in the morning, a hangover just settling in, I got home and collapsed into bed.

The next day, concerned I may not have been entirely coherent with Ben, I sent an email to the receptionist at Czech Events, telling her that Ben had contacted me and that he may not have my email address and could she forward it to him so he could tell me about the interview.

I was on the phone to Anna when I got the email reply. I clicked on it and what I read made my world stop. My lungs and heart ceased functioning. My brain froze. Anna was still talking but her voice was just a stream of sound.

The email said, 'I've forwarded your email to Brian, who called you.'

Brian. Not Ben. Not a ludicrously drunken conversation with Ben, a man I'd assumed was the office boy. No, I'd had a ludicrously drunken conversation with Brian, who I knew from Suzy was the owner of the company.

42

To my amazement, Brian seemed to have taken it in good part as the next day I got a call from Athena from Czech Events inviting me to come in for an interview. For the occasion I put on my suit and met her in the coffee shop she had nominated. It seemed odd to interview someone in a coffee shop, but also rather lovely.

Athena lived up to her name. She was an American woman who favoured big rings and scarves and who wore a look on her face that suggested she was just waiting for her opportunity to tell you that she didn't need drugs, she was high on life—it was a look of spiritual superciliousness. I greeted her warmly and asked her how she was, on the grounds that it's often best to get people talking about themselves.

Athena was in a wonderful state, a blissful state. She had just come back from LA, where she had a life therapy consultancy. Jennifer Aniston was one of her clients—she specialised in actors—and she had been able to help her. She didn't say how. It was so satisfying to help those in need, she told me. She was an 'enabler', bringing the best out in people.

Athena carried on like this for some time and after about half an hour I wondered if I should steer the conversation back to the matter in hand—my interview. But I became suddenly fascinated. How long, I wondered, would Athena keep talking about herself if I let her? It was a situation I'd been in in an interview before—the interviewer becomes so interested in themselves that they forget it's actually about me. I'd never experienced it beyond about fifteen minutes though. Athena had already broken the record and looked set fair to smash it for years to come. I settled back and encouraged her to tell me all about it. A 'sounds like fun!' here, and a 'really?' there was all she needed.

After an hour—yes, an hour—I saw a shadow cross her eyes as she suddenly remembered why we were there. She sat up a little straighter and said, 'But we're not here to talk about me.'

'Of course! The interview. What would you like to know?'

'I've seen your CV and from what I've seen today you'll be very suited.'

I began my spiel. 'I've had a lot of experience working in companies at high levels, dealing with external and internal stakeholders. I've also led teams and run many team events. I can take you through some of those if you'd like.'

'No, no, that's fine. I think we have all we need.'

And that was that. There was just one little matter.

'Your hair,' she said.

'My hair?'

Athena was looking at my flamingo-pink dyed hair. 'We have clients who might not understand your fashion choice.'

Huh.

I had dyed my hair more out of boredom than anything else but it had caused me some difficulty and annoyance. I had gone to the hairdresser over the road from where I lived and we'd discussed for some time the vibrancy of the shade I required. She—being middle-aged with hair dyed the same fake-mahogany red that all middle-aged Czech women used, and I mean *exactly* the same colour for all of them—at first thought it was a language mistake. However, when I kept pointing to the neon palette and saying '*růžový, růžový*' (pink, pink) she finally got the message. She would have to order it in. Fine. It would be expensive. Fine.

It wasn't actually that expensive and the result was very pleasing indeed. The cut she gave me was terrible but it was short so it didn't matter so much—it was the colour I wanted. Bright, blazing, baboon's-bot pink. Incredibly satisfying. But that night, half of it came out on my pillow, ruining the bedclothes.

I went back to the hairdresser in a blaze as bright as my hair. Why the *FUCK* had she given me semi-permanent?

She protested indignantly. What was *she* indignant about? We battled through the Czech until finally I realised she was saying that a colour that bright can only be semi-permanent, there was no such thing as a permanent bright colour. I sighed. *Really?* I'd had bright hair in my twenties, a good fifteen years ago. Neon white, Roman purple, fire-engine red, Indonesian sunset orange. None of these colours had come out on the bed sheets. It was indeed possible to achieve, just not in the Czech Republic. *Oy*.

I did not argue but I did change hairdressers, to one recommended by Suzy. This hairdresser was American and she bought in some American dyes to do my hair, bless her. She'd moved to Prague from her family's farm in North Dakota after the Czech Velvet Revolution in 1989 and had never left. She was stuck in Prague now, in her sixties, unable to go back to America—what would she do? Start again in an American salon? Life in her old country had moved on without her. I thought she was about the bravest person I knew. She was marooned in another life—cheerful and dogged, but with no way back.

My hair had been a struggle to get, it had helped me acquire one more friend in the shape of my new American hairdresser, and I was very, very pleased with it. I considered arguing the toss with Athena, and then decided against it. What did it really matter? I could always dye it again. I agreed to tone down the hair.

When I turned up to the office the next week, the only reference to my drunken conversation was made by Brian, who grinned and said, 'Sober then?' He was an absurdly young man, looking to be in his early twenties. His partner in the business was American and older, and considerably oilier. I was to learn that Brian was a man whose dial was permanently set to 'enthusiastic'.

The company, like many companies at that time, was hobbling along from one job to another. It was in a permanent state of cash shortage and desperate for the next big break.

Like most of its casual employees they were paying me cash, which was ace. It made the company vulnerable to people leaving for proper jobs but they knew that the expats were less likely to be able to find one of those.

The work at Czech Events was mostly conducting half-day tours of Prague that were a kind of treasure hunt. Each of us would take out a team of corporates—about six to ten in each team. The teams competed against each other to see who could solve the most puzzles. Clues were scattered all over Prague. They had a map and they had to find the puzzles, solve them, and be the first team back to base. Points were awarded for how many puzzles they solved, and how long it took them to complete the hunt. Our job was to make sure no-one got lost, help them with the answers if they got stumped and be there if anyone got hurt. We also had to keep their spirits up and make them feel they were being cared for and led by a professional. Ahem. It was a fairly vague remit and the work was very light.

When Suzy had started with them the company was in healthier shape and she had received a couple of days training. By the time I got there the GFC was biting and they didn't have time for such niceties; they just hired presentable people and hoped for the best. Luckily for them, I found this sort of thing a doddle. I chatted chirpily to the teams and it all went down very well with the punters. It was quite a lot of fun, as a matter of fact.

At the end of one particular gig Brian called me aside. 'I don't have enough on me to pay you right now,' he said. Brian was Canadian, and a baby. No Canadian baby gets away with that crap.

I looked at him with concern. Because I was in the same ballpark age as his mother, he squirmed. 'But,' I said, puzzled, 'I thought we always got paid at the end of a gig.'

'Yes, er well, yes.' Brian tried a boyish smile. I continued to look puzzled and he added, 'Um, but I just ran out.'

'Oh, I see.' I let the concerned pause swell. 'I'll drop by tomorrow, shall I? You'll be in the office?' I looked at Brian as if I was about to send him to his room to think carefully about his actions.

'Yes, yes! Tomorrow.'

During one of our artists meetings, Suzy had told me and Debra that she'd had to wait a week or more for her wages several times. Debra and I had tutted; it wasn't on, cheating your staff, although it happened all the time. Suzy was patient with that sort of thing, but I wasn't. I now had a slight feeling of unease—was I about to be cheated? While I knew that Brian was uncomfortable with it, I also knew that Brian's partner would rob me at the drop of a hat so the thing to do was, if he was going to cheat someone, make him decide to cheat someone else.

Brian was in the office with the cash the next day, grateful to resume being an honourable man. He never missed one of my payments again.

The work, however, was intermittent. I did feel sorry for Czech Events. They were desperately scrabbling around trying to get big enough jobs to keep the company going.

The older partner, the oily one, had a Czech wife who was as hard as nails. She had probably fallen for his patter and superficial glamour—easy to do when you are trained to think all Americans are rich—and there he was, the CEO of his own company. The scales had eventually fallen from her eyes, but not fast enough. By the time I joined the company, she was pregnant and no doubt disillusioned about the size of any divorce settlement she would get. Her eyes were constantly narrowed and she was on his neck to make the business work. He really was an unbelievable prat, and an obvious conman as well.

Poor old Brian, he was like a puppy dog bounding around his partner's feet. He had put all his savings into the business but it kept going down and within a few weeks after I started, they were forced to move from their basement offices and began operating out of Brian's flat. Most of their woes didn't touch me, but Suzy had a harder time.

She was a full-time employee, and frequently not paid. She was often left to run events when casual staff, unpaid from the last gig, didn't turn up, or when Brian or Oily (his name was Gary, but I never managed to think of him as anything other than Oily) didn't either, having much more important things to do than look after their customers. Oily was more often than not tied to the house with the baby after his wife had dropped the idea of being a full-time mother and yoga practitioner and went back to work.

More and more, Brian seemed to disappear, and we had the sense that his life was imploding around him. His wife, a college sweetheart he'd been tremendously proud of, had left him shortly after I started. What with that and the problems with the business his whole life was becoming unhinged. Astonishingly, he managed to maintain his bounding enthusiasm for the company, sure it would turn a corner at any moment.

Suzy's life was made increasingly stressful by her job. She was ex-military, and military types tend to take their responsibilities seriously. 'It's time to leave,' Debra and I told her. But she battled on valiantly. They gave her any work going, presumably because she was the only one who didn't make a fuss about being paid weeks in arrears and could be trusted to run the company line. Also, she was the soul of pleasantness with them, and even seemed to have some sympathy for their plight.

I was kept on, even though the work was dwindling rapidly. They didn't like me, which wasn't surprising since I openly refused to subscribe to the tissue of lies they had propping up the façade of their business. I'm sure they'd have loved to fire me, but they needed me as casual labour because I could reliably do the job and I didn't need to be given a lot of shifts—just enough to supplement my editing.

The other person they kept on was Athena. Athena didn't help with the events in any way and it wasn't clear what she was doing there, apart from being enthusiastic and 'marketing'. She did believe, along with Brian, that the business was going to recover. She also believed in a mishmash of bizarre other-worldly phenomena: witchcraft, horoscopes, black magic. If she got a 'vision', she was likely to send us all an email warning us that 'the next few weeks are likely to be rocky, so back up your computers every hour, don't make travel plans and watch out for people from your past crossing your dreams and emails'. She'd have done well in my old horoscope job.

For all her loopiness, she retained incredible faith in Oily and Brian. They stopped paying her and instead gave her shares in their utterly worthless business. She actually took them.

---·---

The corporate jobs dried up terrifyingly fast and the company was left scrambling for any work it could find, no matter how menial. It got so bad that we actually celebrated when Brian managed to score Czech Events a children's Christmas party gig. 'Of course, it's not much money,' he warned us. 'You'll only be paid 100 crowns an hour, because it doesn't take the skill of the corporate team work.' That was the equivalent of around five Australian dollars, but I didn't argue. Frankly, I needed the money, and even 500 crowns was going to come in handy.

The party was in a small hotel, in a room with double doors leading to a walled courtyard. I got there an hour before it started, Brian having told me, 'I'll run you through what we do and we can practise some of the games.' Part of the reason they kept me on was because I was a quick study; I was sure that an hour was more than enough for me to learn the Czech Events children's party routine and deliver it smoothly.

I got there to find Brian looking flustered. Not unusually, his other casual hadn't turned up, so it was just him and me. He also couldn't get hold of the cake lady—he didn't even know if she'd been told she had a job on. In a panic he called the ever-faithful Suzy to track down the cake.

I said to him soothingly, 'No problem, we can handle it,' and that seemed to calm him a little. 'Now, why don't we run through the order of events and practise some games?'

'Right, yes, so what games do you know?' he asked.

'What?'

'What games—what children's party games do you know?'

I looked at Brian blankly. 'None. I don't have children. Don't you have standard games you play at these events?'

'Oh, oh, yes, of course we do,' said Brian hurriedly, and I wondered if indeed he'd ever run a children's party before or if he was just making this all up as he went along.

'Um, how about this one?' Brian showed me a game where everyone stood in a circle and held hands, and then did some complicated movement and twisted up in a giant tangle together, and then magically, if they untwisted a certain way, they ended up in the same circle but all facing out. I had some doubts as to whether a) I'd remember how to get out of the tangle, and b) small children would find this phenomenon sufficiently amazing. But I said enthusiastically, 'Oh that's a great one!', to keep the poor fella's pecker up.

He then showed me another one, in which the kids all lined up and rolled a ball back and forth. I can't really remember any of the others but at least one of them involved the children running around a lot and for a long time. I took careful note of that one, thinking I'd use it a couple of times and chew up some energy and party space.

At the end of our 'training' Brian handed me a plastic bag. 'Here's your costume.'

My what now? Opening the bag, I took out a pointy red felt hat.

'The button's on the inside.'

The what now? The pointy red felt hat had blinking lights all around the rim. The button turned them on. I was a Christmas fairy.

I had no time to protest. The host kid's mother arrived, looking flustered at the apparent lack of preparation—like the fact that there were no cake or decorations. Brian had to turn on his smooth charm, reassuring her that everything was going to plan.

She looked at me askance, no doubt thinking that I didn't look like the sort of person who'd made a lifetime career of dressing up as a Christmas fairy. Did I really know what I was doing? I smiled weakly and tried to seem fey and girlish as I whipped out the tinsel and lights and strung them up anywhere I could find a space. The cake arrived with Suzy, who sized up the situation immediately and started helping me Blu-Tack the party decorations.

'Should I stay?' she whispered.

'No.' I told her I wasn't going to be complicit in her naked exploitation and I'd cope just fine. Suzy hesitated briefly then left.

The host kid was a tough little girl with ice-blue eyes, whose parents came from the overindulgence school of thought. She had the silken blonde hair and designer clothes of a child who was pampered and groomed from morning to night. Her level of entitlement was impressive, even for a nine-year-old product of neurotic parents, wealth and nannies. Her eyes swept the room and were not pleased.

'He-he-he! So you're the party girl, eh?' I offered, jovially. She gave me a frozen stare.

'That's a pretty dress.' She turned on her heel.

I sighed and went in search of Brian. The other kids had arrived in a bloc, their parents gratefully disbursing them into the party room while they went next door for a drink.

'We only have to keep them entertained for three hours,' said Brian.

'What do you want to start with?'

'Let's run them around for a bit.'

'Good idea.'

So Brian and I herded the kids into a group and Brian started the act. I have to say that he was very good. The puppy-dog charm that made him such a good salesman and such a rubbish businessman went down very well with the kids. He made an appropriate fuss of the little thug whose special day it was, got them all excited and ready to play and then he raced them around, expending as much of their energy as he could.

'Gee them up in the first hour, keep them running in the second, then start calming them in the third,' he said to me.

At one point I found myself in a fairy circle, the hand of a small child in each of mine, kicking my left leg in, my left leg out, the lights on my fairy hat blinking madly, and thinking, *I can't believe it's come to this. I've got a degree!*

It really was the last straw. That and the dwindling work. It was only a matter of time, and not a very long time at that, before Brian and Oily would be out of business. I didn't want to be there when it happened. And never again was I going to wear a red felt Christmas fairy hat with blinking lights.

43

All this time, Joe and I had been in constant communication. When Christmas came around I went to visit him in Ramstein. Neither of us wanted to be alone.

My relationship with Joe had gone a long way to soothing my chronic loneliness. We emailed each other every day, sharing the events of our lives, big and small. Sometimes we phoned and occasionally we'd visit each other. Usually at the end of these visits we'd decide that we really weren't suited and we should be sensible and move on, but the next day the emails and phone calls would start again.

I never really knew how it came about that Joe and I stayed and stayed and stayed together despite regularly realising we weren't an ideal couple. We could not have had more different tastes, on every conceivable level. Joe hated my clothes, I found his choice of books dull. We were on different sides of the political table. He wasn't Republican but he did passionately believe in the military, whereas I passionately believed in military whistleblowers—we were unable to continue the conversation we started about Bradley Manning. He liked *Star Trek* and *Battlestar Galactica*; I liked the mid-career Woody Allens.

Despite these differences, we felt a great and growing love for each other. I think we were two very lonely people, dislocated in our different ways, who badly needed care and companionship. We spent Christmas decorating the tree, drinking punch, and walking through the snowy fields and forests of Germany.

Joe didn't live on base. He lived in Stockborn, a tiny, one-street farming village nearby. His was the last house on the street. From his kitchen you could see the neighbouring fields and farms. There were no shops of any kind in Stockborn, just the fifty or so houses lining the main street. If you wanted to get bread, you walked twenty minutes to Sambach, and if you wanted more than that, you walked twenty minutes more to Otterbach.

Joe's Americanness was extraordinary. Or rather his middle-Americanness. He was from Idaho and he was by no means a sheltered man. Unlike most of the servicemen, he had chosen to live in a little village so he could be near Germans and eat German food and be somewhere not America. And yet, when I took him for his first tour around Prague, he gazed up at the many statues of half-clothed women, spellbound.

'Wow. She's nipping out. And so is she!' he exclaimed.

'What?'

'That statue up there—she's nipping out.'

'Nipping out?' I had no idea what he was talking about.

'You can see her nipples.'

I could barely comprehend his amazement. 'Sure. Does that seem strange to you?'

'I've never seen it before. You wouldn't have that in America.'

It seemed utterly incredible. I had no idea Americans were so conservative. We broke up frequently and yet Joe and I travelled together all over Europe—to Belgium and Amsterdam, Italy twice, France. We were excellent travel companions.

All through this time Joe slept around and I never got used to it, although I gave it my best shot. A couple of times I went to live with him for a month, when I was editing and could work from his place. I would sit in a study that he had decorated especially for me and had adorned with wild flowers he'd picked himself, and look out onto the field behind his house where the farmer from next door was teaching her collies to herd sheep. I went with Joe to the air force base to shop in the American mall they'd built there, buying Easy Cheese (liquid cheese that squirts out of a tube), Cool Whip (whipped cream in a tube) and cookie dough (another tube).

We ate at the base's Mexican restaurant where an utterly charming waitress showed us to a table, brought us water and searched the kitchen to fulfil Joe's request for olive oil. She smiled all the time and said, 'If there's anything else I can help you with, just let me know.'

I found it unsettling to be around such friendly, willing service.

'They work on tips,' said Joe.

'Well, yeah, but still. It's the smiling and the pleasantness I can't get used to. I'm used to waiters snarling at me and flinging bread down resentfully.'

After his tour of duty in Germany, Joe was going to go back to Idaho. Could I live in America? The service would be amazing, but if Ramstein was anything to go by the food would be dreadful—there was only so much whipped and tubed food even I could take. I was afraid that while the people would probably be friendly, they would also be incredibly conservative. Suzy told me that when she went back to America her friends looked askance at her clothes. If she wasn't in jeans and a button-down shirt, they considered her to be dressed outrageously, ostentatiously, 'like a European'—and this was just jeans and a creative blouse.

I had a wardrobe of Doris Day dresses and parasols, Morticia skirts and 1920s chorus-girl striped shirts, all of which stayed at home when I went to visit Joe. Could I really survive in America? Over the two years we were together we toyed with the idea of going to America together to live. But we never really considered it seriously. I decided to put off worrying about it until his tour was up.

44

It was Marion who found me my next job. Maria and Marek were a couple of artists she knew. They owned a gallery in the Old Town and were looking for a shop assistant. The money was rubbish, but the work was steady and easy—sitting in the shop and talking to customers. They specifically needed an English speaker for the tourists.

One of the pleasures of this job was walking there through the cobbled streets and seeing my workplace appear around a shallow bend in a tiny road behind Kampa Park, its thick white walls and mullioned windows hugging the cobbles. The gallery was a little lower than the street and the bottom of its windows just brushed the pavement. It was housed in an old palace that had been sensitively converted into very expensive flats. You entered through massive studded wooden doors into a flagged hallway that must have once shepherded carriages into the inner courtyard. The gallery was on either side of this hallway.

The 'art' Maria and Marek produced was mostly glass with some steel. They also owned a gift shop in the Old Town Square and they did very nicely out of the tourist trade. They assured me, many times, that they were very great artists. They had gone to art school and now owned a glass factory.

When tourists came, there was a routine to be followed. The shop assistants would show them around the gallery, pointing out the exceptional works of art and explaining the history of Czech glass art (they took the idea from the Venetians and did it more cheaply—now the Chinese were doing the same to the Czechs). Sometimes the tourists didn't just drop in but were part of a bigger tour that included a glass-making class. In that case, after the tour, we would take them into the back part of the gallery and show them a video of glass being made.

This began with a montage of Marek making steel art and depicted molten steel being poured into enormous moulds. The workers heaved wooden buckets into a sandpit out of which had been carved the bits that would make, in this case, a chair for a giant. After that there was footage of Marek creating the design and then shots of people in the factory blowing the glass. The whole thing lasted for about twenty-five minutes and was fascinating at first. But by the tenth viewing it was utterly excruciating.

After that, the tourists had a glass-plate-making class. During this, Marek gave them a plate of glass and some paints and everyone stood around a table and painted something. 'See!' Marek would cry, 'Everyone is an artist!'

I, along with all new employees, was forced to do this art class, as Marek wanted us all to be knowledgeable and enthusiastic about creating art. On one of his visits to Prague, Joe came to one of the classes and produced a fine plate, carefully lined up at the corners and symmetrical with all the colours matching. Mine was a hideous hotch-potch of clashing colours and experimental splashes. I think Joe may still have both plates.

The issue of cash payment was negotiated in an awkward conversation at the beginning of my employment. By now I wasn't expecting that anyone would employ me officially or pay for any health insurance. Given those conditions, 100 crowns per hour was a pathetically small rate, around 45 dollars per eight-hour shift. Maria had the good grace to look embarrassed as she offered me this sum, and said, hurriedly and defensively, 'This is a very good rate. Czechs all work for this rate.'

I toyed with her briefly by asking her about health insurance and she squirmed. 'We do not do that. You must do that yourself.' She couldn't say 'No Czech gets that' because healthcare is the normal compensation for the crap wages in Prague.

I took a firm line with Maria and Marek, telling them rather grandly that I was a writer and an editor—I was doing this job because I needed to get out of the house and see people. They were crashing snobs, so treating them with amused hauteur worked very well.

Marek said, 'You can write our brochure!'

I laughed patronisingly and told them that they couldn't afford me—I was high-end and expensive. But then, relenting,

I said I'd be happy to help them with their brochure for free, goodwill among friends. As I had expected, they treated me with kid gloves after that, never actually asking me to do anything, just proffering their brochures to me for my 'input'—'when you get the chance!'

When Czech Events finally folded owing Suzy three months' wages, I got her a job with Maria and Marek. Unfortunately, due to Suzy's work ethic and willingness to please, her experience was very different to mine. Maria and Marek were in reality a couple of bullies, which is why they responded so positively to me bullying them. They walked all over Suzy, insisting she work ludicrous hours, demanding she deal with the Czech tradesmen (she was fluent in the language, unlike dilettante me), accusing her of theft when a broom went missing. When I blithely smashed some godawful and very expensive goblet while I was cackhandedly dusting, Maria simply said, 'Oh well, accidents happen.' Unlike Suzy, I never got the hang of the credit card machine or of sending things overseas.

By employing us in this manner they were breaking any number of laws and so we were commanded, should the police pop in, to say we were just minding the till until the owners, our dear friends, returned from their brief errand.

The upside was that the work was very easy. Maria and Marek had grandly promised us that we would make '10 per cent of sales'. At the end of our first month, I totted up the sales and added 10 per cent of the ones I'd made onto the money they owed me.

'What is this?' said Maria, going red in the face.

'10 per cent of sales,' I replied, puzzled but knowing, presciently, that the deal was about to be broken.

'You do not get 10 per cent of sales generated through the tours, only the passing trade!' she shouted.

'You put no work into that!' cried Marek, when I objected. 'That is all our work—ours!'

I didn't press the point, as I really didn't need the extra money—this job was just to supplement my editing—but I noted the cheat. There was no passing trade on the street so unless Maria and Marek brought in tourist groups, no-one disturbed my day. Some days an entire eight hours would pass with no-one setting foot in the place except me. On those days I dusted the glass, attempted (and failed) to write more of my novel, emailed friends and practised my yoga breathing.

Those days passed like the days of an Anita Brookner heroine: time slowed to a ponderous liquid that was occasionally dimpled by a falling speck from the universe—a phone call from a tour operator looking for Maria, a lone tourist who'd wandered off the Golden Mile.

One afternoon I was chatting online when a man walked in. I snapped down the programme and glided out of my chair.

'May I tell you about the glass?' I asked in my quiet Anita Brookner voice, my skirt smooth and my skin spotless and relaxed from a life lived underground in still air.

The man was about fifty and well dressed—neat and moderately expensive, not flashy but with the pared nails of a man accustomed to the concept of manicures. 'I would be delighted,' he said courteously.

The glass art was particularly ugly. Maria and Marek went in for heavy bowls dabbed with thick blobs of glass, so they looked like something you might find on the Starship

Enterprise. Gold flecks and tiny semi-precious stones rippled through the glass. I thought it was not so much art as tack but I launched myself into the spiel.

'This is the finest of the goblets we have on display. This is real gold, shot through the glass, and you can see the tapering here that is typical of the artist's style. Marek has been at the forefront of Czech art for the last thirty years . . .' And so it went on. Who knew if he really had been, but I was required to say it. The glass I was holding was the one I was to smash some weeks later.

The man kept a politely interested look on his face. When I was done he said, 'And what do you really think of it?'

'Ah . . . I, ah . . .' Well, what could I say?

He twinkled at me. 'Me too.'

We fell into conversation. There in the silent, still vault, surrounded by utter rubbish, he told me that he was travelling alone. He'd come to Prague fifteen years earlier with his wife, newly married, but she had left him suddenly two years ago, just as he'd retired to make room for her career, and they were now divorced. This trip was a renewal, a re-experiencing of a place to make it his own again. He was reacquainting himself with poetry and novels, poetry mostly. It was poetry that had moved him as a young student.

'Who do you read?' I asked.

'I'm particularly fond of Robert Frost.'

'Oh, me too! " . . . And miles to go before I sleep." It's one of my favourite poems.'

And right there, in the middle of the afternoon, on the stone flagging of an ancient palace, this nice man recited *Stopping by a Wood on a Snowy Evening* very, very well. So well that as he spoke the last lines tears were falling down my cheeks.

We stood in silence for a moment.

'I don't really know how to say this, but would you care to have dinner with me this evening?'

I said that I would.

Now, I knew what was going through this man's mind. His name was Edward, by the way, and he was an American academic—a psychologist. When I said we conversed, actually what happened was that I listened to him sympathetically as he told me his life story. I told him a little about myself—just the romantic bits: living alone in Prague, writing. I didn't want to get into any of the tawdry details: being lonely and poor, badgered by visa problems, bereft of any creative writing urge. I could tell what was happening for him. He was a romantic, a man who'd changed his life for a woman he loved. Here he was, back in the town of his dreams, meeting a writer in a gallery and making her cry with his poetry. If this wasn't the start of his new life, what was?

It wasn't, but he didn't know that. I did though. When I saw him that night, it was only as we talked over cocktails in a bar that he realised this was going nowhere. It was a strange interlude in my Prague life.

In the middle of the palace that housed the art gallery was a courtyard with archways on which could be seen original fourteenth-century murals. The luxury flats above had been constructed within the original rooms, keeping the shape and character of the old palace alive. It was a glorious inner courtyard, desperately romantic. Tourist groups, Americans in particular, loved being taken into the inner sanctum and getting a sense of old Prague. They had mixed reactions to the glass art but were generally happy to have an 'experience' presented to them.

Suzy and I would give our smooth pitch—'great artist . . . Czech tradition . . . real gold flakes'—and then shepherd the tourists in for the by-now interminable video and an art class. After that it was champagne all around and more time in the courtyard. Amid sighing over the murals and imagining themselves living in one of the flats, they would inspect the glass and possibly make a purchase. It was staggering what vast sums people seemed willing to part with for a thick and ugly vase.

Increasingly, however, the tedium of our existence and the horribleness of Maria and Marek began to wear us down. The patrons, lubricated and flattered, showed a depressing tendency to treat us like maids.

At one of these functions, with a cold autumn coming on and coats getting heavy, Suzy and I were given the task of taking the coats and hanging them up. There was quite a large crowd and all of them wanted to divest themselves at once, having all arrived from a tour boat together. I grabbed them as fast as I could—with a polite 'May I?'—as they were simply dropped into my hands without a word or a backward glance. I flung them over to Suzy who was frantically hanging them up in a lather of speed. At one point, my arms filled with leather and fur up to to my chin, I looked over at Suzy and said, 'I have a degree, you know!' and Suzy said, 'Why don't you just stab me in the heart.'

We quit the next day.

45

In September 2008, I decided to spend some of my precious pennies and hire an accountant to do the Czech taxes I owed.

In Australia you can leave your taxes for years at a time then do them in one headache-inducing, teeth-grinding session. Three years was my average. I used to feel guilty about it until Cynthia told me she once left hers for nine. The Tax Office had always owed me, not the other way around, so it had never really mattered.

But the Czechs were different. This was a former communist country, still in obsessive love with forms and stamps and authority. If you failed to keep up with your paperwork they put you in jail, or fined you enormous sums. They sent around the rozzers and made you fill in even more paperwork. It was unpleasant, so I hired Mr Zeman, an accountant recommended to me by Mike's Czech girlfriend, to make sure everything went smoothly.

Mr Zeman told me that I had the wrong kind of visa but that his office could sort the whole thing out for me. 'You are registered as an administrator,' he said, 'but you are working as a writer. We must make a change.' This would considerably reduce my tax burden, he assured me. Not to mention give me the correct visa.

I told him about Dita registering me as an administrator on the *živnostenský* list because there wasn't a category for writer.

'But you are a writer and you should be registered as one,' exclaimed Mr Zeman. That seemed fair enough, and I was heartened by the prospect of a lower tax rate. His company was called Debakl Accountants. I should have read the signs.

My one-year visa was due to run out in May 2009 but, completely uncharacteristically, I presented myself at the Foreign Police in April—not three years after my visa ran out, with a thousand crumpled forms in a plastic bag, but one month *before*, with all my paperwork in spectacular order in a neat folder. Right up until the moment I got to the desk it seemed as though nothing could go wrong. I had, after all, paid a Czech accountant to tell me what to do.

The lady at the counter took my incredibly neat folder from me and removed the contents. She inspected every piece of paper, nodding at each one (was it secret approval or just me desperately searching for the smallest sign of humanity and kindness in the salt mine of the Foreign Police?) all stamped and correctly completed in Czech. The last document she picked up was my passport.

All hunky-dory there too, I felt sure. I had a valid visa and the expiry date was the following month. The counter official shuffled through my papers for my application, looked back at my passport and looked at the visa application again. I watched her do this, only faintly disquieted. Nothing could be wrong, I knew it. Then she said, 'This is not right. You are here as an administrator. Where are your administrator's papers from the Živnostenský Office?'

Ah, was that all it was? This was easy. I knew I had professionals—*accounting* professionals—on my side. I assured her that I *had* been registered as an administrator but that that had been incorrect and my accountant had taken care of it. She said something long and foreboding in Czech. So I called Mr Zeman and had him talk to her.

They talked for so long that the credit on my phone ran out. The lady at the desk handed the phone back and started to talk to me in Czech. By 2009 my Czech had improved a little. It was passable in ordinary conversations about food and what I did on my holidays and I could even name a few trees, but a complication in visa issues left it stumbling and whenever my blood pressure rose it disappeared completely. What she was saying, I had no idea.

Mr Zeman called back. He really was a dear fellow, and just the tiniest bit stricken about this turn of events. 'She says that you were registered on the *živostenský* list as an administrator and that you must reapply as an administrator.'

'Did you tell her that you had changed that?' I asked, a touch querulously.

'She said we could not change it.'

'But we *did* change it. Surely that was legal?'

'She said you cannot be here without one.'

'Didn't the . . . the . . . the . . .' I try not to remember the Czech names of the various offices I have to report to—I let their names drift past me in a miasma of stamps and extracts and signatures. 'Didn't the whatever-it-was office say I should not have a *živnostenský* list, but that I should be registered as a writer? I thought that's what you told me.'

'Yes, that is what they said.'

'Well, can we get them to write a letter saying I'm legal?'

He paused. 'Yes, I suppose I could do that.'

Okay then. Problem solved. Sometimes you just have to push the Czechs into thinking outside the narrow railway gauge of the system.

I left my papers with the lady at the Foreign Police, taking away with me a list of all the further papers she required. When I saw all those papers of mine lined up on her desk, I could have wept. There were two years of health insurance receipts; a stamped extract from the Social Security Office; a completed visa application form, signed and stamped; a stamped extract from the Finance Office attesting to my lack of outstanding debt; an official bank transcript; a notarisation from the Australian Police confirming there was no warrant for my arrest; two passport photos; a completed form from the president of my co-op apartment attesting to my right to live and work in my flat; *another* form from the co-op confirming ownership of my flat, stamped with the co-op stamp and signed by not one but *two* members of the co-op board, as required; an extract from the Land Titles Office proving that the block of flats existed, was a co-op and that I was a part of the co-op; and a statement from the Tax Office, stamped, yes bloody stamped. All of these documents were the result of waiting patiently for hours in offices spread all over Prague and stammering Czech at surly officials, patiently, patiently—the visa application form alone had taken me four hours in a queue at the Foreign Police at three in the morning, grateful I was doing it in summer and not the bitter depths of winter.

Still, I knew I was legal. I knew that for sure. All it would take now would be a letter from the Finance Office, or the *živno* office, or whatever friggin' office my accountant was going to get the letter from. And, once I had that letter, all would be well. It just had to be.

46

'The Finance Office will not write such a letter.'

'But . . . but . . .' I couldn't think, I honestly could not think what to say. 'But why not?' Why on earth wouldn't one office write to another one, assuring them that I had fulfilled my obligations to them? Why not?

'I do not know. It is crazy,' said Mr Zeman.

And with that, he seemed to have shot his bolt. He had nothing more to say. In Australia it would be unheard of. My brain had difficulty computing what was happening. I was legal in one office (the one to which I had paid money, of course) and illegal in another one or, at least, not so much illegal as no longer registered. In some limbo that surely, surely, could be resolved. Must be resolved.

'But, Mr Zeman, did you tell the Foreign Police that I do not need an administrator's *živno* because I make a living as a writer?'

'Yes, I told them.'

'Well, what did they say?'

'They said they did not know about that. I am very sorry.'

A sense of helplessness began to seep around me. An intangible fog not less but more deadly for its ungraspable quality. My accountant seemed to have simply stopped. The Finance Office would not write a letter, ergo his brain ceased functioning. An official had said no. Mr Zeman was now immobile.

Confronted with his blank helplessness, my own mind found itself frozen with helplessness too. I had nothing to say.

'I can refer you to a company that helps people to get their visas,' suggested Mr Zeman.

Yes, I thought, irritated, *I bet you can. I paid you 9000 crowns, which is a FUCK of a lot of money, to sort out my taxes, which were, after all, pretty straightforward. And now you've messed it up so much that I'm going to have to pay someone else god-knows-how-much to sort it out. Thank you so much.*

'Um, oh gee, yes. Well, yes, I guess—give them my phone number,' I snivelled. If I'd been in Australia, I'd have said, 'Not only am I not paying your bill, but *you* will pay for this to be fixed.' But when you're a foreigner, you're gulpingly vulnerable to officialdom. You are polite to everyone and do not make waves or a fuss. You do not demand your rights because, brutally, you have no rights. No enforceable ones anyway.

In Australia, I could speak the language and I could say things like, 'I must consult with my lawyer', which was code for 'I am going to get nasty'. Here, I was not going to get nasty and everyone knew it. I was stuck, like every other expat. Stuck paying bills and being polite and hoping that I would at last stumble on someone who knew the rules and could guide me through them.

For a few days I didn't do anything. I made a call to an American visa fixer I knew and he never called back. It seemed incredible to me that I could have produced all the right paperwork and paid highly qualified Czech people to tell me what to do and that I could still be faced with a wall of people who simply refused to move. The Foreign Police would not accept my application as a writer. The Finance Office would not tell the Foreign Police that I was, indeed, operating legally. And my accountant would not do what any Australian white-collar professional would to do in these circumstances—jump and scream until the bureaucrats unfroze. I felt like I was in one of Oliver Sacks' documentaries about people who are living statues.

After two days, I received a phone call.

'Hello, Mrs Weiss, this is Hana from the So-Ry Agency. Mr Zeman said you might need help with a visa issue.'

I'm afraid I was a bit short with Hana. Mr Zeman had been an expensive exercise and I was suspicious of anyone he recommended me to, even though I had agreed to him doing it. This was a blood-sucker mate, no doubt, coming in to help him feed off my carcass. I asked her how much it would cost.

'Well, it is often best if you come in and we talk about what it is you need . . .'

'Yes, well, I have paid a lot of money to get me into this position, so you'll understand if I'm focusing on that question. How much do you charge for a basic visa?'

Hana was taken aback, I could tell. 'We would normally charge around 5000 crowns for a visa.'

I breathed through my nose. That was around 280 Australian dollars. 'Right. I see. Well, I will have to weigh up my options. That seems like quite a lot to me.'

She was surprisingly pleasant. 'Please call me if you would like to proceed.'

I was holding out hopes that the American visa fixer would get back to me but he never did. I desperately wanted someone from a country I could trust to help me. The Czechs, I thought bitterly, were too quick to dip their hands into your pocket. They stole too easily. Their motto was 'If you don't steal it, someone else will.' It came from communist times, but still.

Yes, I needed an American or an Australian or a Brit, not a frickin' Czech. But the only Westerner I knew who took care of visas wasn't returning my calls. I made one more call to his mobile and when it still went unreturned I brooded on the impossibility of the Czechs for a couple of days. Then I pulled myself together and called Hana.

47

The So-Ry Agency. Yes, I really should have seen the signs.

The first time I met Hana I was greeted by a cheery young woman in a no-frills reception area. There was a whiteboard showing who was in and out of the office and where they were, plus some cheap phones and reassuringly uncluttered IKEA desks that held neatly arranged pens. That's what you want to see in a visa fixer's office—regimentation and signs that deadlines are kept. Hana had short brown hair and friendly brown eyes shining out of a round face. Instantly I was sorry I'd been rude to her.

She seemed not to have taken the slightest offence and hailed me in the most un-Czech-like manner: smiling widely, shaking my hand and offering me water. She was young, no more than thirty or so. Her English had an accent that suggested she'd practised it a lot abroad, which would explain her unusual demeanour.

She took me into the conference room—an airy, open space with a few plants and a cheap IKEA table. When I'd visited Mr Zeman's office, his two receptionists had scowled at me and shown me to a glassed-in conference room with a polished oak table and expensive art on the walls. I trust the ones with vinyl chairs—they don't have huge overheads and the focus is on the work, not on ripping you off.

Once watered and seated, Hana said, 'Now, so tell me what your situation is.'

I explained how the hotel, unable to find a *živnostenský* category for 'writer', had chosen 'administrator' and how Mr Zeman, to correct this, had changed me over to . . . And here I stumbled, because it had never been very clear to me exactly what Mr Zeman had done. I told Hana that I was registered legally with the Tax Office and the Finance Office, but that my status with the Foreign Police was unclear.

Hana looked grave. 'Yes,' she said, shaking her head. 'Mr Zeman should not have done that. You are here under an administrator's visa with a *živnostenský* licence and it cannot be changed. He did not check this with the Foreign Police. That was very bad.'

I felt strangely relieved. I mean, I already knew it was very bad but Hana had actually told me *why* it was bad. This seemed to suggest that she knew what she was doing. I needed this right now—someone who knew what they were doing.

'Mr Zeman explained to me that the Finance Office will not write a letter confirming that your tax status has changed.'

'That's right.'

'Hmm.' Hana thought for a moment. 'You must start the process again.'

'What?!' This seemed incredible. I'd been here for *three years*.

'The question is, what visa should we get you?'

'But if the Finance Office has me registered as a writer, can't I get a visa for that? I mean, *they* think I'm legal.'

'It is not so easy.'

No, it wouldn't be, would it.

'You see, there is no *živnostenský* list for a writer and so we must think of another way. One option is to simply reapply as an administrator with the Finance Office and Tax Office.'

'O-kay.' I didn't really want to have to do that because a) I was not an administrator and b) according to Mr Zeman this would mean I had to pay more tax, which seemed manifestly unfair. But if I had to . . . 'How much would that cost?'

'About 30,000 crowns.'

'Thirty thousand crowns!' That was almost eighteen hundred Australian dollars. I was horrified, and Hana saw it. 'I haven't got 30,000 crowns,' I wailed. Thirty thousand crowns just to stay in this fucking god-forsaken, communist-throwback, scowling hell-hole! Even 5000 crowns was going to be a trial for me, unless my editing work suddenly picked up.

'Well, then we will just have to find another way.' Hana seemed to understand what it meant to be in a foreign country with no money. 'Do you have perhaps a contract?'

I thought for a minute. 'Yes, I do. As a writer. It's for a book about Prague.'

'But is that with an Australian company?'

'Yes.'

Hana looked doubtful. 'Bring it in and we will see if it will be enough, but I fear it will need to be with a Czech company. Also, it should be a current contract. Do you perhaps have a contract with a magazine? One that stipulates you must write about Europe, or the Czechs, perhaps?'

No, I didn't have one of those. 'But my book is specifically about the Czechs.'

'It may be enough.'

May be enough!? What the fuck is the matter with these people?

Hana took copies of the documents I had brought with me. I kept every bit of paper obsessively, even if I didn't know what it was—in fact, especially if I didn't know what it was. I kept lists: of documents that the Foreign Police had given me, of documents that they said were missing; of documents given, stamped and handed over. Hana nodded over all of them, and took copies.

'Do you think you can sort this out?'

'Oh yes,' she replied cheerfully, 'this is not so bad. I once helped a man who got himself in a terrible tangle. He had only a few days before the police were going to deport him and to make it worse, New Year's Day fell right in the middle of it. The Foreign Police have a tradition of changing one or two rules every year, just to make life even more difficult for everyone, and he did not have all his documents like you. But I managed to help him. We have time. This will all be sorted.'

I felt immensely relieved. Yes. This would all be sorted. I had nothing to worry about.

When I got home I searched frantically for my book

contract. I knew I had a copy of it but I'd filed it so cunningly that I could no longer find it.

Godammit! Where the fuck is it? I knew I had it, I just knew it, but it was hiding somewhere. I emailed my agent and asked if she could email me a copy.

Three days later I got it. After only a brief hesitation I changed the dates to make it current, printed off the signature page and sent it to Hana. There. Problem sorted.

A few days after that, Hana called me. She had been to the Foreign Police. 'It is not enough. You will need a current contract with a Czech publisher, in Czech.'

God. Dammit.

I sat and brooded on the Czechs for a few days before I remembered Mr Hrabal. Mr Hrabal had once owned a sex magazine for swingers. I knew this because when my brother had come to live in Prague on much the same pilgrimage as my own, Mr Hrabal had hired him as a roving sex reporter and given him a contract so he could get his visa in what was then Czechoslovakia. I called Mr Hrabal in Sydney.

'Darlink! Of course I can hire you. But I hev to tell you zet the *Spotlight Magazine* no longer exists. But ve still hev the stamps! I vill send you the header.'

Mr Hrabal sent me the header and I wrote myself a letter, commanding myself to go to Prague and write about the sex and swinging scene in central Europe, focusing specifically on Prague. There.

Hana was delighted. 'I have never seen anything like this! This is perfect! My colleagues will not believe it. A sex reporter! We've never had a sex reporter before.'

Okay. So, now I had a contract. All would be well, surely.

48

When I next visited Hana some weeks later she was concerned. 'My boss does not think this letter is a good idea. The Foreign Police has agents in Australia. These things can be checked.'

I didn't want Mr Hrabal to have to lie for me, although I suspected he would enjoy it, bless him.

Soon after, a letter arrived from the Foreign Police by registered mail. I took it to Hana.

'We must act fast,' she said—never words you want to hear.

Debra had once told me that the Foreign Police only sent you the unimportant stuff in English. The more important the document, the less likely it was to be translated.

'What does it say?' I asked Hana.

'It says that you must leave the country in ten days.'

'What?! But we are still applying!'

'Yes. Once we have started your new application, I will apply to have this process stopped.'

The new application was proving a problem. Neither the Foreign Police nor Hana had any idea what sort of sole trader status I needed in order to get a visa as a writer, and the Sole Trader's Office refused to advise us, or to write a letter confirming that my accountant had changed my status, even though he had.

'They've never had anyone apply as a writer before,' said Hana. Frankly, this seemed incredible; Prague is littered with haggard Kafkas. You can't set foot in a café without tripping over a bearded latte-sipper tapping out the story of his travels through mystical India.

'You're kidding me.'

'They think one did once but no-one can remember how they did it.'

This made me wonder who that one foreign writer officially living in Prague was. (Was it Isobelle Carmody? I hadn't seen Isobelle since that day at Big Ben Bookshop.)

Hana, diligent and dogged, discovered that the Foreign Police's requirement for a Czech publishing contract, written in Czech, is the test for any Czech writers needing to prove they are writers. She demanded they come up with a different requirement for me as a non-Czech. Unfortunately, the person responsible for making such a determination was on holiday.

Meanwhile, she hunted around for other ways to let me stay. She told me to ignore the deportation order.

'They won't do anything while we are still in the process of your new application.'

I tried to believe her but the anxiety began to build as my deportation date came and went and the weeks went past without any resolution. It seems that once you had fallen outside the ambit of regulations, you were screwed. There were more offices involved here than you'd have thought possible. The Tax Office and the Social Security Office, both regular receivers of funds from me, refused to write letters saying I was a paying resident. The Office of Immigration, the Sole Trader's Office, the Finance Office and the Foreign Police—none had any regulations stipulating what bit of paper I needed to prove I was a writer.

We'd be told that we could go ahead with one application, only for that person to go on holiday and her replacement to tell us that we had received 'bad advice' and that it was not possible. No apology, no extension of time, no actual correct advice, just a blank Slavic stare and a shrug of the shoulders. It was like sliding helplessly between giant grey plastic balls—I felt squished and suffocated, unable to move.

We tried a few more avenues, always to be blocked—not by the regulations, but by the lack of any regulations.

'Even if she could prove it,' said the Foreign Police to Hana one day, 'why does she want to write in the Czech Republic?'

Why indeed? Increasingly, I didn't. But my life was in Prague, with my friends, my work and my lovely little two-room apartment in, ironically, the artists' quarter of Prague.

49

When the axe fell, in September 2009, the Foreign Police were surprisingly nice about it. By that time—because I'd been back so many times and my problem was so intransigent, tortuous and bureaucratically unjust, even by Czech standards—I had earned myself a nickname: 'The Writer', *Spisovatelka*. By the time it came to its inevitable—and it was inevitable—conclusion, everyone knew my case. Even so, they said I needed to go through the process of meeting the supervisor to beg for an extension to the twenty-four hours' notice they usually gave you to quit the country. I couldn't face it alone so Hana, bless her, agreed to come along with me to put my case in Czech.

By this time, my veins were running acid and the language had deserted me. For the last six months I'd jumped every time I heard sirens.

The week before my final interview with the supervisor, wailing police sirens stopped outside my apartment building and I watched from my fourth-floor window, frozen and appalled, as police, their blue light whirling against the trees, banged on the main door. I waited anxiously for the cuffs and the frogmarch to Ruzyně Airport.

As I waited, I reviewed the unexpected trajectory of my life, which had begun so promisingly in sunny Australia where my educated, middle-class parents had forced me to go to university so I'd have the leg up I needed. How had it come to this? An innocent writer in a foreign country, living by her wits, cheated regularly by unscrupulous employers who knew she couldn't do a thing about it, was about to be arrested. I was forty-two, for god's sake. Shouldn't I be in the suburbs with high-school children, a Range Rover and a husband doing a steady trade in conveyancing? I waited for my date with destiny.

After ten minutes (they should have found me by now—I knew I didn't have a sign outside my door, but still) I realised the blue lights and cuffs were for the Roma family who were renting the bottom apartment and keeping the rest of the Czech flat owners in a state of delighted harrumphing. But my shattered nerves barely registered the escape and I wondered if arrest might not actually be a relief.

—•—

The supervisor was perfunctory with Hana, making us wait until she'd dealt with all her other business. Hana waited with humility, her hands folded on her knees, her eyes not catching anyone else's, while I perched nervously beside her. Finally the supervisor beckoned Hana into her office.

Hana emerged a few minutes later with an order that I had a month to get the hell out. It was the most I could have expected. In my passport my visa had been cancelled, with two great red slashes proclaiming my nameless crime. How many people can say they've got a deportation order in their passport? I'm rather proud of it now.

At that time, however, it represented vulnerability. I had a month to leave the Schengen zone, but the question was where was I going to go?

One option was to go home to Australia. I could spend three months there, renew my *živno*, or start again with another *živno*, or get another three-month visa and come back. The trouble was that my home was now in the Czech Republic.

Going back to Australia would be expensive—I could barely afford the airfare and besides, how easy would it be to just drop out of my life for three months? Yes, editing was, technically, the sort of job I could do remotely, but people still needed to be able to get me on the phone. I had clients I still needed to take care of. I could, I suppose, have worked for them from Australia but the truth was I didn't have the energy for Australia. Servicing clients in Australia would mean three months of midnight phone calls while struggling by day with the officials at the Czech Embassy. I was running out of the kind of energy all that scrabbling takes.

London was an option I was toying with when another possibility presented itself: I could go to Bulgaria and stay in a flat that Marion and Tanya owned there. Bulgaria was cheap and easy to fly to, cheap to live in and I'd dealt with the embassy at Sofia before. If I had to get a short-term visa,

I might as well go some place where I didn't have to start the explanations all over again. The flat currently had no electricity but it had running water. It had no furniture either but Marion and Tanya were planning to send some of their furniture over there and were wondering how they might do that. Getting a company to send it there was going to be expensive.

'Maybe I could get a van and take it there for you,' I suggested.

'Maybe you could,' replied Marion. 'That's not a bad idea. I wonder if it would work.'

'Can it all fit into a big van?' I was licensed for a van but not for a truck and had driven vans before.

'I don't know, but I think it might. And when you got there, you could ask the unit manager to help you move it in. He's a nice guy, he'd be willing.'

Suddenly, my trip to Bulgaria seemed more interesting. I pictured myself driving across Europe, south through Slovakia, Hungary and Romania, places I'd never been to. Perhaps I'd take the long way and stop off in Moldova, a place I'd always longed to go. Perhaps I could even cut across the Ukraine . . .

It began to seem romantic and exciting. In my mind's eye I saw myself in rolled-up shirt-sleeves, one arm hanging out the window, barrelling through the densely wooded mountain regions of eastern Europe, through charmingly crumbling villages with one sleepy street and goats reluctantly moving away as I squeezed between the ancient cottages and barns, past half-collapsed castles and monasteries eaten by the forest, through long vistas of fields, crossing strange borders.

But it was the border bit that undid my dreams. I discovered that my exit visa commanded me to get the hell out of the Schengen zone immediately, without passing Go or collecting two hundred dollars. It did not allow me to leave the Schengen zone by civilised stages, such as leaving the Czech Republic and entering Slovakia, another Schengen country. At the Czech–Slovak border my passport would be stamped to say I had left the country, so if I was in Slovakia the authorities there would have had an immediate excuse to put me in jail. Or exile me for good. I tried to argue the point with Hana but it was useless from the start. There are things you simply do not argue about when it comes to visas.

My plight was underscored by Marion's friend Armand, who was in fact a furniture mover himself. Armand told Marion I was mad. He said I'd be stopped constantly by police, have my van inspected daily, be expected to hand over bribes and pay extemporaneously created taxes at all the borders; if I stopped in one of my charming villages to eat my van would be stripped bare and the furniture stolen.

I returned to Plan B.

My grandmother was born in Ruislip, a suburb of London, in 1918. She was only there for the first six months of her life before her French mother took her back to Paris. Apparently, though, that six months in 1918 entitled me to an ancestry visa in England. I went to the British Embassy in Prague, up its own side alley with the statue of Churchill guarding the entrance, and put in my application. A week later, to my utter astonishment, Her Majesty's government returned my passport stamped, legal and entitled to work for five years.

I made three calls: one to Marion, one to Armand and one to Joe. Marion said her agency could rent out my flat and Armand agreed to store my furniture and arrange for it to get to wherever I ended up next. Joe said he would come and get me and take me to Germany on my way to England.

50

I didn't wait the full month before I left. There was no need. My mind, without my really knowing it, was made up. I was done with this city.

At the end of my time in Prague I felt like a woman in the last days of a failed marriage. All my coping skills had disappeared. In the back of my mind I was aware that the Czechs couldn't really be as bad as I was painting them but just the thought that I was shortly to escape brought the stress of living with them screaming to the surface.

Now I could no longer bear any of it: the sullen ill-humour of the shopkeepers; the waiters who never see you; the expensive and badly made consumer goods; the grey, wilting vegetables; the ludicrous self-importance of the eternally communist bureaucracy with its demands for more and more and more bits of paper; the bland food; the stink of un-deodorised armpits; the stony white faces.

When a newsagent was rude to some friends who were visiting me in Prague, I had a meltdown. 'And here we have an example of truly delightful Czech grace and customer service,' I cried, sweeping my arm to indicate the newsagent, much as I had when I had indicated the Astrological Clock. 'Isn't it charming? And don't think this is something you can only see here in the Old Town. All of Prague is like this!'

I said it all out loud, not even disguising my anger. It was just too much. Was it too much to ask for a smile? Some simple courtesy?

I tried to remember the things I'd loved about Prague: the young, bongo-playing Czechs; lovely, hospitable Eva; cheery Mrs Cakes; my funny, warm, welcoming Czech friends; Friday nights at the Spanish Synagogue, singing harmonies with Anna; long summer nights in beer gardens surrounded by gentle, happy people; the beautiful, snow-clad buildings; my own sunny, cosy flat. But it was no use. I was tired of trying to make it work as an immigrant.

Joe drove from the military base in Ramstein. We packed his SUV with my clothes, some books and my laptop and I left Prague for good.

I stayed in Germany with him until I recovered my equilibrium enough to realise that a life in the US military ('You could get a job with them easily,' said Joe) followed by retirement to Idaho with the buzz-cut Joe was an absurd idea, as sweet and as stable as he was. His tour of duty was coming to an end. He was going to California, and I was going to England.

———————

One morning in January, while packing up in preparation to leave Germany, I flipped open my computer to check on the world and there was an email from Cynthia.

> From: Cynthia
> To: Rachael
> Subject: Thelma

> Thelma died at 9pm tonight. Her heart failed I think. I was holding her, here on the floor behind me. I was telling her to let go, that I loved my little pumpkin and I knew it had all got a bit too hard. She looked just lovely. So soft and pretty, our little pumpkin darling. xxx

I lay on the bed and gave myself up to grief, curled up sobbing. The light faded, night came on. I stayed with the past, remembering our life together.

My little Thelma was gone. I burst into tears and sobbed for grief and loneliness, missing my little girl, my companion of fifteen years. Gone. I would never again stroke her little ears, or talk to her over the phone, or hear her purr. My little Thelma.

51

Andy and Barbara left Prague the same time I did. They moved to Sheffield, right on the edge of the Peak District—some of England's finest hiking country. Knowing that making friends is the hardest part of starting life in a new country, I decided to move to Sheffield too.

Our expat community in Prague dispersed, as these things do, to be replaced no doubt by a new expat community. Irish Pam's company sent her to South Africa the following year and she lives there in the sunshine, doing whatever it is she does. Suzy left for America with her Czech partner and is living in Colorado making a living as a kayak instructor. I still have two of her paintings on my wall. She and her husband speak Czech at home and will raise their bilingual kids in America. Marion still owns the best real estate agency in Prague but Tanya left for America after flirting with Bulgaria.

Zsuzsa was posted to Nigeria for her next embassy stint. Mike and Mathematics Neil are still in Prague and still going to the Lazy Vinohradian dinners. Mike married his lovely Czech girlfriend and has a son, Mathematics Neil found himself a lovely Slovak girlfriend and he too got married.

Debra is still in the Czech Republic, still writing poetry and still living a hand-to-mouth existence as an editor. Not having a grandmother conveniently born in Ruislip, it's not so easy for her to live in England and experience its pleasures. She sometimes thinks of going back to Australia but it's been ten years now and, like the American hairdresser who came from North Dakota, after a while 'home' changes locations. Mrs Cakes didn't live to see 2010. Just before I left I came home one day to find her door open and police tape across the entrance. She'd died all alone.

Anna completed her conversion but didn't leave our shul—she and Peter still keep the congregation going at the Spanish Synagogue. Although the choir never took off, some of the tunes I'd learned in Sydney became part of the Friday night service and so, strangely, a small part of the Sydney service is forever in Prague. Leonard now makes his new employees meet his cats as part of the interview process—if the cats don't like them, they aren't hired.

Big Ben Bookshop has folded, sadly, but I'm still selling well at Shakespeare and Sons. The novel I tried to write, however, remains in pieces in my bottom drawer. Once I was in England, I abandoned all thoughts of romantic bohemianism in favour of standardised pay rates and a thirty-five-hour working week—I got a nice, quiet job in a university, complete with gym membership, a pension and a strong union.

I've been in that job for over a year now. Every morning I get into work at 8.15 am. I unlock my door, drop my bag under the desk and put my coat on the hook. I flip on the kettle for my daily coffee and switch on my computer. While the kettle boils I open Word to do the quiet work of the morning before emails and phone calls chew up the rest of the day. And sometimes, as I'm doing all of this, my heart swells with the pleasure of these quotidian routines and I wonder if it wasn't all worth it, just to realise how lucky I am to be living this peaceful, ordered, regular life. I'm back being a mid-level administrator—and it's wonderful.

Acknowledgements

I am tremendously grateful for the generous and insightful assistance of Richard Walsh; the Hadfield Writers Group: Linda Lee Welch, Felicity Skelton, Andrew Madden, Chris Jones, Colin Jackson and Gerard Curran; editor Ann Lennox, Czech checker Anna Pilátová, and David Poulet.

Thank you as well to all my Prague friends for giving me a wonderful time in my life.